T0162161

BLOODSTAINED

ONE HUNDRED YEARS
OF LENINIST COUNTERREVOLUTION

EDITED BY
FRIENDS OF ARON BARON

ARON BARON was born into a poor Jewish family in the Kiev province of the Ukraine in July, 1891. He was sent to Siberia following the 1905 Revolution and eventually made it to the United States in 1912. In Chicago he met his first wife, Fanya, and was active with the Russian Workers Union and the Industrial Workers of the World. They returned to the Ukraine in 1917.

Baron was an editor of the *Nabat* journal and participant in the movement of the same name. He was an active speaker and organizer. The arrests and imprisonment by the Cheka for Baron's revolutionary agitation began in 1919, and never seemed to end. In September of 1921 Fanya Baron was shot by the Cheka.

Years of exile and imprisonment followed but Baron never stopped organizing against the Bolshevik state and for the true self-emancipation of workers and peasants. He was executed with over a dozen fellow anarchists in August of 1937.

This volume is dedicated to Baron and all the anarchists murdered by Bolshevik tyranny—and those who fought to save them.

SOON THE YOUNGER
GENERATION WILL BE
CONSIGNING US TO THE
ARCHIVES, WILL THEY NOT?

NO, IT'S TOO SOON TO
PUT US IN THE ARCHIVES—
RIGHT, MY FINE, YOUNG
FRIEND?

—Aron Baron, 1925, in a letter to Mark Mrachny

Bloodstained: One Hundred Years of Leninist Counterrevolution

© 2017, copyright rests with the individual authors where not in the public domain.

This edition © 2017 AK Press (Chico, Oakland, Edinburgh, Baltimore)

ISBN: 978-1-84935-296-3
E-ISBN: 978-1-84935-297-0
Library of Congress Control Number: 2017936237

AK Press   AK Press
370 Ryan Ave. #100   33 Tower St.
Chico, CA 95973   Edinburgh EH6 7BN
USA   Scotland
www.akpress.org   www.akuk.com
akpress@akpress.org   ak@akedin.demon.co.uk

The above addresses would be delighted to provide you with the latest AK Press distribution catalog, which features books, pamphlets, zines, and stylish apparel published and/or distributed by AK Press. Alternatively, visit our websites for the complete catalog, latest news, and secure ordering.

Cover design by John Yates|stealworks.com

Printed in the USA on acid-free, recycled paper.

CONTENTS

Introduction

THE FRIENDS OF ARON BARON

History may not have ended, but it certainly has gotten strange. The social contract neoliberalism once imposed—a patchwork of economic shell games and the political rituals needed to foist them on people—has shredded with surprising speed in recent years. The result has been a rapid universalization of precarity. Unpredictability and groundlessness are ubiquitous parts of our lives, which unfold in a supposedly "post-truth" world where the basic prerequisites for understanding almost anything seem lacking—or at least seem to change with each news cycle.

This new reality was both cause and effect of Donald Trump's election as forty-fifth president of the United States. His campaign successfully harnessed the fear and desperation of our social unraveling, and he rose to power with promises to end it. He would, he said, stop the erosion of our dwindling sense of security and restore the certainty of clear borders (national and racial) and steady jobs. The trains would run on time.

Trump's success-from-the-fringe took US liberals by surprise. Anything other than the staid electoral ping-pong between managerial representatives of this or that political party had been unthinkable to them. Further along the left spectrum, there was surprise among many radicals, but perhaps less shock: they at least had the theoretical arsenal with which to explain the situation—after the fact.

The left is no less subject to historical uncertainty, nor really any more prepared to meet it or predict what's next. Lately, many radicals have been engaged in the same grasping at straws that motivated Trump voters. When the way forward is unclear, they seem to think, it's safest to go backward, into the past. They search for answers in the tried and true—even when that truth is one of massive historical failure. Thus we've seen a return to social democratic strategies, first with the tepid "socialism" of Bernie Sanders, more recently with the resuscitation of the Democratic Socialists of America. Voters in Europe figured out long ago the pointlessness of electing so-called socialists to over-see a capitalist economy. The US, as usual, has failed to learn from others' mistakes.

The hundredth anniversary of the Russian Revolution, the occasion for this book, has put an even more bizarre spin on these developments. Many see the centennial as an opportunity to rehabilitate, even celebrate, outdated forms of authoritarian state socialism. It's a tricky celebration, though, one that must either carefully ignore the human devastation that the Bolsheviks set in motion in 1917 or push it past an imaginary border beyond which, the story goes, communist possibility was hijacked by evil men, and marched off to a land of gulags and forced collectivization. Judging from their lists of recent and forthcoming titles, leftist publishers around the world will repeat these elisions and fairy tales in scores of books that praise Lenin, reframe the Bolsheviks, and attempt to rescue the Marxist jewel buried beneath a mountain of corpses.

If it was just the old guard and zealous party officials spinning these fictions, this book would be unnecessary. Their influence has steadily declined and they will eventually all die off. In these strange, unsettled times, though, a number of young people have become enamored with the ghosts of dictatorships past, sharing "Hot Young Joseph Stalin" memes on social media and sporting hammer-and-sickle baseball caps and jeweled necklaces. There's often an ironic edge to the new Bolshevik bling, like the punks of a previous generation wearing Nazi symbols. But the punks at least had a raw nihilistic honesty: they were referencing the *horror* behind their regalia to make a point. Today's new, young commu-nists are either much more oblivious to the history behind their gestures or are slyly hedging their bets by pretending there's no substance to their style, and thus no accountability. All this sug-gests a more pressing need for this book.

"Of all the revolts of the working class," writes Cornelius Castoriadas, "the Russian Revolution was the only victorious one. And of all the working class's failures it was the most thoroughgoing and the most revealing."[1] We might quibble about the word "only," but Castoriadas's point remains: there is something important to learn from the possibilities that the Russian Revolution both opened and demolished. The catastrophe in Russia obliges us, he says, to reflect "not only on the conditions for a proletarian victory, but also on the content and possible fate of such a victory, on its consolidation and development" and, most importantly, on the "seeds of failure" inherent in certain approaches to revolutionary strategy. According to Marxist-Leninists, when it comes to the Russian Revolution, those seeds were entirely external and "objective": the defeat of subsequent revolutions in Europe, foreign intervention, and a bloody civil war. The historical importance of these factors is incontestable, and largely besides the point. The real question, as Castoriadas notes, is "why the Revolution overcame its external enemies only to collapse from within."

To answer that, we need what Maurice Brinton calls, in his preface to Ida Mett's history of the Kronstadt commune, a new, genuinely *socialist* history. "What passes as socialist history," according to Brinton, "is often only a mirror image of bourgeois historiography, a percolation into the ranks of the working class movement of typically bourgeois methods of thinking." State-socialist hagiography, in all its Leninist, Trotskyist, Maoist, and Stalinist varieties, is simply a thinly veiled "great man" vision of the past, with kings and queens and presidents replaced by revolutionary "leaders of genius," brilliant strategists who supposedly led the masses to victory—or who would have if "objective factors" hadn't intervened, which, strangely, they always seem to do.

This anthology is an attempt to contribute to that new history. It is, again following Brinton, a history of the masses themselves, written, as far as possible, from their perspective, not from that of their self-declared representatives. We've collected works spanning the last century, from 1922 to 2017, that serve two purposes.

---

1. All quotations in this introduction are taken from the authors' essays in this anthology.

The first is to uncover the *living revolution* beneath the myths that the Bolsheviks and their state-socialist heirs have piled up to legitimize their otherwise indefensible actions. The living revolution is the potential inherent in any mobilized populace. It is *made*, not decreed, bestowed, or legislated into existence. And it is a powerful force. The initial stage of the Russian Revolution, stretching from February through October, was famous for its lack of bloodshed. When the masses rise up as one, there is no power that can oppose them. They create new revolutionary forms, agreed-upon practices that may or may not take institutional form. These practices, which cohered in Russia into the soviets, factory committees, and cooperatives, are the embryonic structures through which a new society might be organized.

A socialist or anarchist history must also seek to locate the seeds of failure in any revolution. These also belong to the masses. The blame for the "degeneration" of the Russian Revolution can be, and has been, spread liberally. However, making simple boogeymen of the Revolution's betrayers—Stalin being the most familiar, especially for Leninists and Trotskyists seeking their own absolution—avoids the fact that the masses could be betrayed in the first place. They fell for pretty lies and stirring speeches. They failed to resist at crucial moments or, when they did resist, they didn't go far enough. They surrendered, inch by inch, the power that *they* had taken, and they let their enemies build a very different sort of power over them. There is a reason why Lenin could say that the October coup was "easier than lifting a feather": the way had already been cleared and the state already smashed. There was nothing to lift. The masses had made the revolution and the Bolsheviks had only to step over the rubble and into the oppressors' abandoned palaces. The fact that they could do so is a warning and a lesson that the authors in this collection drive home in countless ways.

The forms of genuine revolution and the ways they were violently dismantled by Lenin and his comrades are the main themes of this book. If there is a slight emphasis on the latter it is because the anarchists, council communists, and anti-state Marxists in the pages ahead a) have an implicit faith in what Emma Goldman calls "the creative genius of the people" and b) hesitate to prescribe the details of a future society that remains to be born, under conditions and meeting challenges we cannot foresee. Real revolutions are never staged, they don't happen according to any theorist's timetable, and they rarely need help getting underway. While that fact is made clear throughout this book, there is also a crucial focus on what happens next, on the traps and pitfalls, on everything that can go wrong.

Rudolf Rocker traces the genealogy of the factors that led to the Russian Revolution's failure through the often-prophetic debates in the First International and back to the late eighteenth century. Marx and Engels, whose ideas Lenin adapted, borrowed their theory of revolution from the Jacobins and authoritarian secret societies of the French Revolution. Specifically, says Rocker, they relied upon distorted bourgeois histories of those figures. The resultant Marxist concept of the *dictatorship of the proletariat* is the "dictatorship of a given party which arrogates to itself the right to speak for that class." It is "no child of the labour movement, but a regrettable inheritance from the bourgeoisie ... linked with a lust for political power." Rocker contrasts this concept with the "organic being" and "natural form of organisation ... from the bottom upwards" that the labor movement itself forges though struggle: councils and committees networked in flexible, nonhierarchical federations.

Luigi Fabbri also sees bourgeois roots in Leninist ideology, "a frame of mind typical of bosses." Writing just after the October revolution, Fabbri cuts through the numerous misrepresentations of anarchism that even the earliest Bolshevik propaganda promulgated—and that state socialists still push—to reveal the main ideas "separating authoritarian from libertarian communists." The "fatal mistake" of Lenin and company was their belief that building a powerful state would somehow eventually lead to that same state withering away, the precondition for communism according to both Marxists and anarchists. For Fabbri, as for most contributors to this book, "The state is more than an outcome of class divisions; it is, at one and the same time, the creator of privilege, thereby bringing about new class divisions." Moreover, it "will not die away unless it is deliberately destroyed, just as capitalism will not cease to exist unless it is put to death through expropriation." Or as Iain McKay puts it in his analysis of one of Lenin's most famous books: "The Russian Revolution shows that it was not a case of the State *and* Revolution but rather the State *or* Revolution."

Leninist distortions of other revolutionary traditions hasn't changed much in the last century. Fabbri and others writing at the time of the Russian Revolution, both eye witnesses and close observers, focus our understanding of what non-Bolshevik militants were fighting for. They also give us a more clear picture of the possible forms of human liberation that the Bolsheviks methodically foreclosed. Several essays in the pages ahead give detailed accounts of the methods that the newly established state used to achieve this. Maurice Brinton and Ida Mett each focus on the massacre at Kronstadt, one of the clearest examples of how ordinary people, workers and sailors in this case, sought to push the revolution beyond the outmoded bourgeois political and economic forms Lenin imposed, only to face the guns and bayonets of Trotsky's Red Army. Barry Pateman describes the many dedicated revolutionaries who wound up in "communist" prisons, as well as the networks of solidarity that tried to get them out. Iain McKay maps the growing (rather than withering) Soviet state as it absorbed one by one the democratic, federalist institutions the masses had created in Russia, which posed a threat to the growing dictatorship. Otto Rühle describes the disastrous effects of Leninism when it was exported to Europe. Lenin's influence, says Rühle, was not merely an impediment to the revolutionary struggles of European workers, it also provided the model for fascism in Italy and Germany. "All fundamental characteristics of fascism were in his doctrine, his strategy, his social 'planning,' and his art with dealing with men ... Authority, leadership, force, exerted on one side, and organization, cadres, subordination on the other side—such was his line of reasoning."

Ultimately, though, the differences between the Bolshevik dictatorship and its many leftwing critics boils down to different ideas about how and why revolutions are made. To the Russian anarchists, certainly, Lenin's absolute divorce of theoretical, communist ends from immediate, repressive means was in itself a guarantee of revolutionary failure. The very word communism—with cognates like communal, commons, community—implies an obvious and practical set of political guidelines, a militant ethics. Yet as Nestor Makhno, who organized forces to fight both Red and White armies in the Ukraine, notes, officials at the Fourteenth Congress of the Communist Party, which was held only eight years after the Bolsheviks came to power, agreed that the word "equality" should be avoided in anything but abstract discussions of distant social relations; it had no place in the Communist present.

Emma Goldman and Alexander Berkman emigrated to Russia in 1919. While the immediate reason for their voyage had been deportation, they returned to their homeland with high hopes and a commitment to help build a new society. Within two years, those hopes had been dashed. They left in December 1921, both writing damning books about their experiences soon after (Berkman's *The Russian Tragedy* and Goldman's *My Disillusionment in Russia*). Those experiences, which ranged from the inspiration of seeing revolutionary energies unleashed on a mass scale to the horror of watching them destroyed, lend a sharp-edged clarity to the pieces we've included here, a stark contrast between competing visions of social transformation. "The Bolshevik idea," writes Berkman, was "that the Social Revolution must be directed by a special staff, vested with dictatorial powers." This not only implied a deep distrust of the masses but a willingness to use force against them, an unsurprising observation to those of us on this side of the Russian Revolution, but a shocking idea to many at the time. Berkman goes on to quote Bolshevik theorist Nikolai Bukharin: "Proletarian compulsion in all its forms ... beginning with summary execution and ending with compulsory labor, is a method of reworking the human material of the capitalist epoch into Communist humanity."

Compulsion was necessary because the Bolsheviks claimed to already know the path the revolution needed to take, even if workers and peasants seemed to be moving in a different direction.

Lenin used a Marxist playbook. His apparent flexibility, his often contradictory positions, had less to do with open-mindedness than with a single-minded focus that allowed him to say whatever was necessary to achieve his goal. He was, as Emma Goldman put it, "a nimble acrobat ... skilled in performing within the narrowest margin." After meeting him, she was convinced that "Lenin had very little concern in the Revolution and ... Communism to him was a very remote thing." Instead, the "centralized political State was Lenin's deity, to which everything else was to be sacrificed." For Goldman, the revolution depended more on the "social consciousness" and "mass psychology" of Russian workers and peasants than on any allegedly objective conditions, at least those that were written in the Marxist playbook. At first, Lenin had no choice but to endure the popular forces that were "carrying the Revolution into ever-widening channels" that weren't under Bolshevik control. "But as soon as the Communist Party felt itself sufficiently strong in the government saddle, it began to limit the scope of popular activity." It was this desire to keep all power in the hands of the Party, the supposed advance guard of the proletariat, that explains, says Goldman, "all their following policies, changes of policies, their compromises and retreats, their methods of suppression and persecution, their terrorism and extermination of all other political views."

As we've mentioned, a stock excuse for the degeneration of the Russian Revolution into one of modern history's most oppressive regimes is that the Civil War demanded strict political discipline and severe economic measures. "War communism" was supposedly the revolution's only hope. Readers will be forgiven if this reminds them of the US military's claim that it was necessary to destroy a Vietnamese village in order to save it. As Iain McKay points, out most features of war communism—one-man management of factories, centralized economic structures borrowed from capitalism, the destruction of the soviets—"all these occurred before the Civil War broke out in late May 1918."

The same is true of the Red Terror, the period of political repression and mass killings the Bolsheviks launched, ostensibly to eradicate enemies of the revolution. "Terror," here, is not a word applied by appalled historians after the fact; Lenin and Trotsky embraced the term to describe their ruthless policies at the time. Lenin died early enough to avoid having to answer for them. Trotsky, on the other hand, had to spend much of his time wriggling out of his responsibility for what the revolution became. He almost single-handedly invented an entire genre of political apologetics, firmly establishing the practice of blaming Stalin for pretty much everything. Whatever he couldn't lay at Stalin's feet, according to Paul Mattick, he blamed on historical necessity, presenting early Bolshevism as a sort of "reluctant monster, killing and torturing in mere self-defence."

The problem, says Mattick, is that there is almost nothing in Stalinism that didn't also exist in Leninism or Trotskyism. While there may be differences in the total number of victims each could claim, this had less to do with any "democratic inclinations" on Lenin's part than on his relative weakness, his "inability to destroy all non-Bolshevik organisations at once." And it was all non-Bolsheviks who were in the crosshairs, not just explicitly White reactionaries, and not excluding those who had recently fought alongside the Bolsheviks, regardless of their political orientation. "Like Stalin, Lenin catalogued all his victims under the heading 'counter-revolutionary.'" The main organ charged with carrying out Lenin's repressive orders, the Cheka (The All-Russian Emergency Commission for Combating Counter-Revolution and Sabotage), was created only weeks after the Bolsheviks came to power. "The totalitarian features of Lenin's Bolshevism were accumulating at the same rate at which its control and police power grew." In practical terms, most of the Russian population—from anarchists and Social Revolutionaries to striking workers to sailors demanding democratic election of their officers to the entire peasant class—could qualify as counterrevolutionaries. Nonetheless, as Mattick observes:

If one wants to use the term at all, the "counter-revolution" possible in the Russia of 1917 was that inherent in the Revolution itself, that is, in the opportunity it offered the Bolsheviks to restore a centrally-directed social order for the perpetuation of the capitalistic divorce of the workers from the means of production and the consequent restoration of Russia as a competing imperialist power.

On the centennial of the Russian Revolution, if there is one thing we hope you take from this book, it is the fact that all the published panegyrics to Lenin and Trotsky, all the political parties that model themselves on tyrants, all the eulogies to the "leaders of genius" at the vanguard of the Russian masses—these tributes are honoring the actual counterrevolutionaries of history, the *destroyers* of revolutions, people with the hearts of prison wardens and hangmen.

"The history of how the Russian working class was dispossessed is not, however, a matter for an esoteric discussion among political cliques," writes Brinton. "An understanding of what took place is essential for every serious socialist. It is not mere archivism." If it was, to paraphrase Marx, these dead authoritarians wouldn't still weigh like nightmares on the brains of the living. Inexplicably, Marxist-Leninist and Trotsyist parties still exist. And even when not members of such parties, many radicals have matured into political adulthood in a Marxist milieu that suffers from a split personality that no amount of dialectical reasoning can cure. Ever since the formation of the Comintern, thousands have left their countries' Communist Parties in waves, unable to tolerate this or that new betrayal. Those who remained formed extremely hard shells, but even the ones who fled had to somehow justify their relationship to a bloodstained legacy.

Unfortunately, all the soft, insulating layers of "Western Marxism" in the world cannot disguise the Leninist pea beneath the mattress. No number of "returns" to Marx—or, even better, to early Marx—can escape the inherent flaw at the core of every single instance of actually existing socialisms. Every time Marxism has been filtered through state-centered models of social change, the results have ranged from bad to horrific. This is the defect hidden within all parties, vanguards, cadre, cabals, and bureaucrats: they lead not to communism but to a new class of oppressors.

A century has been long enough. It is time for a clean break. We must remove Leninism from our revolutionary formulas and critique whatever aspects of Marxism lent themselves to the Bolshevik disaster. We must learn from the history contained in the following pages, and then make our own.

The Friends of Aron Baron

Anarchy and "Scientific" Communism

LUIGI FABBRI

I The bourgeois phraseology of "scientific" communism

A short while ago, through the publishing firm of the Communist Party of Italy, a little twelve-page pamphlet was issued by that "superlative theoretician" (as he was introduced to the public in the socialist and communist press) Nikolai Bukharin. It bore the pompous title *Anarchy and Scientific Communism*. Let us just have a look and see how much "science" there is in it.

Bukharin does not set out any true notion of anarchism, any of the points in the anarchist-communist programme as they truthfully are; nor does he take the trouble to inform himself on anarchist thinking by drawing upon the primary sources of the anarchists' historical and theoretical literature. All he does is parrot well worn *clichés*, talking without being careful to keep faith with what he has heard said, and allowing his imagination to run riot in relation to those facets of anarchism that he knows least about. It is impossible to find such a failure to comprehend the theory and tactics of anarchy since the superficial and untrustworthy hackwork of the bourgeoisie thirty or forty years ago.

When all is said and done, it is a rather banal and unimportant piece of writing. But it has been distributed in Italy through the good offices of a party most of whose members are proletarians, and it is presented to workers as a refutation of anarchism. The Italian publishers depict Bukharin's booklet as a work of "ADMIRABLE CLARITY THAT GIVES A DEFINITIVE ACCOUNT OF THE INCONSISTENCY AND ABSURDITY OF ANARCHIST DOCTRINE." So it is worth the trouble of showing how nothing can be more absurd, inconsistent or ridiculous than the "science" of know-nothing with which he tries to discredit the notion of anarchy.

On the other hand, Bukharin's pamphlet has furnished us with yet another opportunity to make propaganda for our views among the workers, who are our special target, our supreme occupation; we are certainly not trying to win over the author personally, or the publishers of his pamphlet, as this would be wasting our time.[1]

If we are to spell out the emptiness and ignorance which prevails among those who style themselves "scientific"—it's always the most ignorant who feel the need to show off their academic credentials, *bona fide* or otherwise—then the phraseology they dress up in should be sufficient.

Their terminology is like the pomp with which overbearing people surround themselves and the poses they strike, moving among folk in an arrogant fashion, saying: "Stand aside and let us through; woe betide anyone who fails to take his hat off to our excellence." And, in their boundless arrogance, they look down on all mere mortals as they speak, unaware that what they say to those they address is not only inane but also genuinely insulting—such as might be expected of some uneducated bumpkin.

Listen, for instance, to the pompous terms in which Bukharin addresses the anarchists, throwing in their faces the fact that he is condescending to debate theories of which he is ignorant.

"*We have purposely avoided arguing against anarchists as if they were delinquents, criminals, bandits, and so on.*"

That is the line of jesuits who teach one how to insult while pretending that it is not the intention.... But saying that, he only concludes further on that the anarchist groups spawn "those who expropriate for the sake of their own pockets," thieves if one likes, and that "*anarchists attract delinquents.*"

What impudence! In their hatred for rebel spirits, for all who have too much love of liberty to bow to their whims and kowtow before their impositions, whether in the labour movement today or in the revolution tomorrow, they do not shrink from taking the mud-slinging, libellous activities of officialdom and of the

---

1. It is believed that Bukharin here refers to more than just Russian anarchism and Russian anarchists. In his pamphlet he makes no distinction and speaks in a global sense. On the other hand, Russian anarchists have the same ideas and programmes as anarchists in other countries.

bourgeois press as their model in attacking the anarchists. One would think one was reading police libels! And can all this rubbish, these worst *clichés* of crude slander, be summed up under the heading "science"?

How can one conduct a debate like that? The anarchist organisation lays no claim to being composed of superior beings; naturally enough, its people have the foibles that all mortals share and consequently, like any party the anarchist organisation too has its shortcomings, its deadweight; and there will always be individuals who seek to cloak their own morbid, anti-social tendencies with its colours. But no more so than is the case with other parties. Just the opposite! In fact, the worst forms of delinquency, the spawn of selfishness and ambition, the spirit of interest and greed shun anarchism, for the simple reason that in it there is little or nothing to gain and everything to lose.

Take it from us, you "scientific," communists, that we could easily reply in kind to this sort of attack, were it not that we believe we would be demeaning ourselves and that there would be no point in so doing! It is not among the anarchists that one could most easily find *"those who"*—as Bukharin puts it—*"exploit the revolution for their own private gain,"* in Russia or outside it....

As depicted by Bukharin, anarchy would be "a product of the disintegration of capitalist society," some sort of CONTAGION, spreading chiefly among the DREGS of society, among ATOMISED INDIVIDUALS outside any class who live only for themselves, WHO DO NO WORK, ORGANICALLY UNABLE TO CREATE a new world or new values: proletarians, petite bourgeois, decadent intellectuals, impoverished peasants, and so on.

What Bukharin takes for "anarchy" would not be an ideology of the proletariat, but rather A PRODUCT OF THE IDEOLOGICAL DISSOLUTION of the working class, THE IDEOLOGY OF A HORDE OF BEGGARS. Elsewhere he calls it the "Socialism of the Mob," of an idle, vagrant proletariat.[2] In another section of his anti-anarchist pamphlet, Bukharin dubs it the "ragged mob."

---

2. See *The ABC of Communism* by Bukharin and Preobrazhensky, Editorial *Avanti!*, Milan, p. 85.

Believe me, readers, it is not a matter of exaggeration. All I have repeated up to now are word for word quotations, only shortened and condensed for considerations of space: enough, of course, to give an idea of what Bukharin sees as nothing less than THE SOCIAL BASIS OF ANARCHY.

However little they know about anarchism, workers reading us—even those least in sympathy with us—know enough to reach their own conclusions as to these extravagant simplifications. Russia is not the only place where there are anarchists, so the Italian workers need not mistake will o' the wisps for lanterns or believe fairy tales about ogres and witches. Italy's proletarians, among whom the anarchists are everywhere rather numerous, are in a position to answer for us that there is no truth in all Bukharin's fantasies.

Anarchism, while it does not claim to be the "doctrine of the proletariat"—it claims, rather, to be a human teaching—is *de facto* a teaching whose followers are almost exclusively proletarians: bourgeois, petit bourgeois, so-called intellectuals or professional people, etc., are very few and far between and wield no predominant influence. There are infinitely more of these wielding a predominant influence, in all those other parties which no doubt call themselves proletarian parties, not excluding the "communist" party. And, as a general rule, anarchist proletarians are not, in fact, an especially superior or inferior sector; they work as other workers do, belong to all trades, can be found in small as well as big industry, in factories, among the artisans, in the fields; they belong to the same labour organisations as others do, and so forth.

Naturally, there are anarchists among the lowest orders of the proletariat, too—among those whom Bukharin condescendingly labels THE RAGGED MOB—but that is by no means an exclusively anarchist phenomenon. If that were the case, if in fact all beggars, all those in rags, all the horde that suffers most under capitalist oppression, were to come into our ranks, we would not be displeased in the slightest; we should welcome them with open arms, with no unjust disdain or misplaced prejudice. But—to give

16

the lie to Bukharin's fantastic catalogue—it is a fact that anarchy does have its followers among these orders, in the same proportions as among the others, as do all the other parties, the communist party included.

And what does that leave of Bukharin's phoney scientific terminology in his attack on anarchism?

Nothing, except the so-to-speak unconscious revealing of a frame of mind that ought to put the proletariat on its guard, and alert it seriously to the risks it will be running should it have the misfortune to entrust its future to these doctrinaire champions of a dictatorial communism.

Just who is it who speaks so scornfully of the "ragged mob," the "horde of beggars," "dregs," and so on? None other than those petite bourgeois, whether old or new, coming from both the bourgeoisie and the proletariat, who rule the roost these days in organisations, parties and the labour press, leaders of all sorts who represent the ruling class of the future, yet another MINORITY group who, under some guise or other, will exploit and oppress the BROAD MASSES, and who surround themselves with the more fortunate orders of the citizen proletariat—the ones in large industry—to the exclusion and detriment of all others.

Bukharin imprudently admits as much in his little pamphlet when he makes the Revolution and communism a sort of monopoly wielded exclusively by that sector of the proletariat WELDED TOGETHER BY THE APPARATUS OF LARGESCALE PRODUCTION. "All the other strata of the poor classes," he goes on to say, "can only become agents of revolution whenever they protect the rear of the proletariat." Now, these "poor classes" outside big industry, are they not proletariat? If they are then Bakunin's prophecy that the tiny minority of industrial workers can become an exploiter and ruler over the broad masses of the poor would be proven right. Even if this is not spelled out explicitly, it can be sensed from the language that these future rulers—in Russia today they are already in a position of control—use as regards the hapless POOR CLASSES, to whom they award the passive mission of placing themselves at the rear of the minority who want to get into power. I repeat, this scornful, supercilious language reveals a frame of mind: a frame of mind typical of bosses, rulers, in dealings with their serfs and subjects. It is the same language that among us is used by careerists from the bourgeoisie and, above all, the petite bourgeoisie against the proletariat as a whole—terms like "beggar, ragamuffin, dregs, no creative ability, don't work," and so on.

Let Italian workers read Bukharin's booklet: to prove the worth of our arguments, we have no need to weave a conspiracy of silence about what our opponents write and say, nor do we need to downgrade or misrepresent their thinking. On the contrary, we have every interest in proletarians being able to compare and contrast our thinking with opposing ideas. But if they do read Bukharin's few pages of writing, we can't say what the reaction will be when they find the outrageous bourgeois terminology currently used to lash all workers and revolutionaries in Italy—including the communists, no less!—directed against anarchists.

With all this it is none other than Bukharin who has the nerve to say that the ANARCHISTS ARE AT ONE WITH THE BOURGEOISIE AND COLLABORATIONIST PARTIES AGAINST THE POWER OF THE PROLETARIAT.

Naturally enough, Bukharin takes care to back up this claim—defamation pure and simple—with arguments and facts! The facts, the whole fifty-year history of anarchism, the heroism of so many Russian anarchists killed since 1917 at the front, weapon in hand, in the defence of their country's revolution, all this goes to prove completely the opposite.

Anarchists fight all power, all dictatorship, even should it wear the proletarian colours. But they have no need to join up with the bourgeois or go in for collaboration to do so, in Russia or anywhere else. Anarchists can take pride in the fact that theirs is everywhere the only organisation that—at the cost of almost always being alone in doing so—has always since it first emerged, been implacably and intransigently opposed to any form of state collaboration or class collaboration, never wavering from their position of enmity for the bourgeoisie.

But we have not taken up our pen merely to debate and refute vacuous, libellous and outrageous turns of phrase. There is also, in Bukharin's booklet, an attempt to discuss some ideas of anarchism, or ideas with which it is credited; and it is to this (however pathetic) aspect that we shall devote the bulk of this short piece of polemic and propaganda of ours—having less to do with Bukharin and more with the arguments alluded to here and there, keeping the discussion as impersonal as possible, and taking no further notice of the irritating, anti-revolutionary terms in which our opponent couches the few arguments he is able to muster.

II The State and the Centralisation of Production

For some time now, communist writers—and Bukharin especially among them—have been wont to accuse anarchists of a certain error, which anarchists on the other hand have always denied, and which, until recent times, could be laid exclusively at the door of the social democrats of the Second International, to wit that of reducing the whole point of issue between marxism and anarchism into the question of the FINAL OBJECTIVE of the abolition or non-abolition of the state in the socialist society of the future.

At one time, democratic socialists who then, as the communists of today do, styled themselves "scientific," affirmed the need for the state in the socialist regime and in so doing claimed to be marxists. Until very recently, anarchist writers were more or less the only ones who exposed this as a misrepresentation of marxism. Now, on the other hand, an effort is under way to make them jointly responsible for that misrepresentation.

At the international socialist and workers' congress in London in 1896—where much thought was given to excluding anarchists (who, at that time, were alone in claiming the title of communists) from international congresses on the grounds that they did not accept the conquest of power as means or as end—it was none other than Errico Malatesta who mentioned that originally anarchists and socialists had shared a common goal in the abolition of the state, and that on that particular issue marxists had parted company with the theories of Marx himself.

Time without number, in the writings of anarchists, the well known anarchistic construction Karl Marx placed upon socialism in 1872, in the midst of one of his most violent polemics with Bakunin has been quoted:

> What all socialists understand by anarchy is this: once the aim of the proletarian movement, the abolition of classes, has been attained; the power of the state, which serves to keep the great majority of producers under the yoke of a numerically small exploiting minority, disappears, and the functions of government are transformed into simple administrative functions.[3]

We do not find this marxist notion of what anarchy is acceptable, for we do not believe that the state will naturally or inevitably die away automatically as a result of the abolition of classes. The state is more than an outcome of class divisions; it is, at one and the same time, the creator of privilege, thereby bringing about new class divisions. Marx was in error in thinking that once classes had been abolished the state would die a natural death, as if through lack of nourishment. The state will not die away unless it is deliberately destroyed, just as capitalism will not cease to exist unless it is put to death through expropriation. Should a state be left standing, it will create a new ruling class about itself, that is, if it chooses not to make its peace with the old one. In short, class divisions will persist and classes will never be finally abolished as long as the state remains.

But here it is not a question of seeing how much there may be in what Marx thought concerning the end of the state. It is a fact that marxism agrees with anarchism in foreseeing that communism is equivalent to the death of the state: only, according to marxism, the state must die a natural death, whereas anarchism holds that it can only die a violent one.

---

3. See Marx: "The Alliance of Socialist Democracy and the International Working Men's Association" in *Works of Marx, Engels and Lasalle* edited by *Avanti!*, Milan, vol. 2. (English translation from Marx-Engels-Lenin, *Anarchism and Anarcho-Syndicalism*, Progress Publishers, Moscow, 1972, p. 110. (Note by English editor.)

And, let us say it again, the anarchists have pointed this out— in their polemics with the social democrats—times without number from 1880 up to the present day.

Authoritarian communists, while rightly critical of the social democratic idea (which they doubtless also credit, mistakenly as it happens, to anarchists) that the basic difference between socialism and anarchism is in the final goal of eliminating the state, make in their turn a mistake that is similar and perhaps more grave.

They, and on their behalf Bukharin, maintain that the "real difference" between anarchists and state communists is this: that whereas the communist's "ideal solution ...is centralised production methodically organised in large units, THE ANARCHISTS' IDEAL CONSISTS OF ESTABLISHING TINY COMMUNES WHICH, BY THEIR VERY STRUCTURE, ARE DISQUALIFIED FROM MANAGING ANY LARGE ENTERPRISES, BUT... LINK UP THROUGH A NETWORK OF FREE CONTRACTS."[4]

It would be interesting to learn in what anarchist book, pamphlet or programme such an "ideal" is set out, or even such a hard and fast rule!

One would need to know, for instance, what structural inadequacies debar a small community from managing a large unit, and how free contracts or free exchanges and so on are necessary obstacles to that. Thus, state communists imagine that "ANARCHISTS ARE FOR SMALL SCALE DECENTRALISED PRODUCTION." Why small scale?

The belief is probably that decentralisation of functions always and everywhere means falling production and that large scale production, the existence of vast associations of producers, is impossible unless it is centrally managed from a single, central office, in accordance with a single plan of management. Now that is infantile!

Marxist communists, especially Russian ones, are beguiled by the distant mirage of big industry in the West or in America and

---

4. These and other statements, printed in quotation marks or in heavy type, are literal quotes from Bukharin's pamphlet. On the other hand, the same things are reproduced in the above-mentioned *ABC of Communism* and elsewhere in *The Programme of the Communists* published by *Avanti!* in 1920.

mistake for a system of production what is only a typically capitalist means of speculation, a means of exercising oppression all the more securely; and they do not appreciate that that sort of centralisation, far from fulfilling the real needs of production, is, on the contrary, precisely what restricts it, obstructs it and applies a brake to it in the interest of capital.

Whenever dictatorial communists talk about "necessity of production" they make no distinction between those necessities upon which hinge the procurement of a greater quantity and higher quality of products—this being all that matters from the social and communist point of view—and the necessities inherent in the bourgeois regime, the capitalists' necessity to make more profit even should it mean producing less to do so. If capitalism tends to centralise its operations, it does so not for the sake of production, but only for the sake of making and accumulating more money—something which not uncommonly leads capitalists to leave huge tracts of land untilled, or to restrict certain types of production; and even to destroy finished products! All these considerations aside, this is not the real point at issue between authoritarian communists and anarchist communists.

When it comes to the material and technical method of production, anarchists have no preconceived solutions or absolute prescriptions, and bow to what experience and conditions in a free society recommend and prescribe. What matters is that, whatever the type of production adopted, it should be adopted by the free choice of the producers themselves, and cannot possibly be imposed, any more than any form is possible of exploitation of another's labour. Given basic premises like those, the question of how production is to be organised takes a back seat. Anarchists do not *a priori* exclude any practical solution and likewise concede that there may be a number of different solutions at the same time, after having tried out the ones the workers might come up with once they know the adequate basis for increasingly bigger and better production.

Anarchists are strenuously opposed to the authoritarian, centralist spirit of government parties and all statist political thinking, which is centralist by its very nature. So they picture future social life on the basis of federalism, from the individual to the municipality, to the commune, to the region, to the nation, to the international, on the basis of solidarity and free agreement. And it is natural that this ideal should be reflected also in the organisation of production, giving preference as far as possible, to a decentralised sort of organisation; but this does not take the form of an absolute rule to be applied everywhere in every instance. A libertarian order would in itself, on the other hand, rule out the possibility of imposing such a unilateral solution.

To be sure, anarchists do reject the marxists' utopian idea of production organised in a centralised way (according to preconceived, unilateral criteria regulated by an all-seeing central office whose judgment is infallible. But the fact that they do not accept this absurd marxist solution does not mean they go to the opposite extreme, to the unilateral preconception of "small communes which engage only in small scale production" attributed to them by the pens of "scientific" communism. Quite the opposite: from 1890 onwards Kropotkin took as his point of departure "...the present condition of industries, where everything is interwoven and mutually dependent, where each aspect of production makes use of all the others"; and pointed to some of the broadest national and international organisations of production, distribution, public services and culture, as instances (duly modified) of possible anarchist communist organisations.

The authoritarians of communism, sectarians and dogmatists that they are, cannot appreciate that others are not like them; hence they charge us with their own shortcomings.

Our belief, in general terms, even when it comes to economic affairs—even though our hostility is focused mainly against its political manifestations—is that centralisation is the least useful way of running things, the least suited to the practical requirements of social living. But that does not by any means prevent us from conceding that there may be certain branches of production, certain public services, some offices of administration or exchange, and so on, where centralisation of functions is also needed. In which case no one will say a word against it. What matters for anarchists is that there should be no centralisation of power; it is worth pointing out here that there will be no imposition on everyone by force, on the pretext that it answers a practical need, of any method that has the support of only the few. A danger that will be eliminated if all government authority, and every police body, which might impose itself by force and through its monopoly of armed violence, is abolished from the outset.

To the neo-marxist error of compulsory and absolute centralisation, we do not oppose decentralisation in all things by force, for that would be to go to the opposite extreme. We prefer decentralised management; but ultimately, in practical and technical problems, we defer to free experience, in the light of which, according to the case and circumstances involved, a decision will be taken in the common interest for the expansion of production in such a way that neither under one system nor under the other can there ever arise the domination or exploitation of man by man.

There is no need to confuse the political centralisation of state power in the hands of the few with the centralisation of production. So much so that today production is not centralised in the government but is, rather, independent of it and is decentralised among the various property owners, industrialists, firms, limited companies, international companies, and so forth.

According to anarchists, the essence of the state is not (as the authoritarian communists imagine) the mechanical centralisation of production—which is a different issue, that we spoke of earlier - but, rather, centralisation of power "OR TO PUT IT ANOTHER WAY THE COERCIVE AUTHORITY" of which the state enjoys the monopoly, in that organisation of violence known as "government"; in the hierarchical despotism, juridical, police, and military despotism that imposes its laws on everyone, defends the privileges of the propertied class and creates others of its own. But it goes without saying that should economic centralisation of production be added to centralisation in the more or less dictatorial government of all military and police powers—that is to say were the state to be simultaneously gendarme and boss and were the workplace likewise a barrack—then state oppression would become unbearable—and anarchists would find their reasons for hostility toward it multiplied.

Lamentably, this is the obvious end of the road on which authoritarian communists have set out. Even they would not deny that.

As a matter of fact, what do the communists want to carry into effect? What have they begun to construct in Russia? The most centralised, oppressive and violent dictatorship, statist and military. And what's more, they simultaneously entrust or intend to entrust the management of social resources and production to this dictatorial state: which blows up state authority out of all proportion, transforming it moreover "TO THE UTTER DETREMENT OF PRODUCTION," and which results in the establishment of a new privileged class or caste in place of the old one. Above all else "TO THE DETREMENT OF PRODUCTION": that is worth emphasising; and the Russian example has shown that we were not mistaken—for if Russia finds herself in the throes of famine today it is indeed due to the infamous blockade of Western capitalism and the exceptional drought; but the "DISORGANISING" impact of dictatorial bureaucratic, political and military centralisation have contributed mightily towards it.

Authoritarian communists claim that they too wish the abolition of the state: we have known that claim since the days of Marx and Engels. But the belief or the intention is not enough: it is necessary to act consistently from the very outset. In contrast, the dictatorial communists, because of the way they run their movement and the direction they would like to impose on the revolution, set out along exactly the opposite road to the one that leads to the abolition of the state and to communism.

They are heading straight for the "strong and sovereign state" of social democratic memory, towards a more arbitrary class rule, under which the proletariat of tomorrow will find itself constrained to make a fresh revolution. Let those communists who seriously want communism reflect on this fatal mistake that is undermining the very foundations of the whole edifice of the authoritarian communist parties, instead of wasting time fantasising on the imaginary errors of anarchists—those who have every right to reply to the criticisms of these state-worshippers of communism: *"physician, heal thyself!"*

III The "Provisional" Dictatorship and the State

The truly essential point at issue, separating authoritarian from libertarian communists, is just what form the revolution should take. Some say statist; anarchistic say others.

It is fairly certain that between the capitalist regime and the socialist there will be an intervening period of struggle, during which proletariat revolutionary workers will have to work to uproot the remnants of bourgeois society, and it is fairly certain that they will have to play a leading role in this struggle, relying on the strength of their organisation. On the other hand, revolutionaries and the proletariat in general will need organisation to meet not just the demands of the struggle but also the demands of production and social life, which they cannot postpone.

But if the object of this struggle and this organisation is to free the proletariat from exploitation and state rule, then the role of guide, tutor or director cannot be entrusted to a new state, which would have an interest in pointing the revolution in a completely opposite direction.

The mistake of authoritarian communists in this connection is the belief that fighting and organising are impossible without submission to a government; and thus they regard anarchists—in view of their being hostile to any form of government, even a transitional one—as the foes of all organisation and all co-ordinated struggle. We, on the other hand, maintain that not only are revolutionary struggle and revolutionary organisation possible outside and in spite of government interference but that, indeed, that is the only really effective way to struggle and organise, for it has the active participation of all members of the collective unit, instead of their passively entrusting themselves to the authority of the supreme leaders.

Any governing body is an impediment to the real organisation of the broad masses, the majority. Where a government exists, then the only really organised people are the minority that make up the government; and, this notwithstanding, if the masses do organise, they do so against it, outside it, or at the very least, independently of it. In ossifying into a government, the revolution as such would fall apart, on account of its awarding that government the monopoly of organisation and of the means of struggle.

The outcome would be that a new government—battening on the revolution and acting throughout the more or less extended period of its "provisional" powers—would lay down the bureaucratic, military and economic foundations of a new and lasting state organisation, around which a compact network of interests and privileges would, naturally, be woven. Thus in a short space of time what one would have would not be the state abolished, but a state stronger and more energetic that its predecessor and which would come to exercise those functions proper to it—the ones Marx recognised as being such—"keeping the great majority of producers under the yoke of a numerically small exploiting minority."

This is the lesson that the history of all revolutions teaches us, from the most ancient down to the most recent; and it is confirmed—before our very eyes, one might say—by the day-to-day developments of the Russian revolution.

We need delay no longer on this issue of the "provisional" nature of dictatorial government. The harshest and most violent guise of authoritarianism would probably be temporary; but it is precisely during this violent stage of absorption and coercion that the foundations will be laid for the lasting government or state of tomorrow.

On the other hand, even the communists themselves are mightily distrustful of the "temporariness" of dictatorship. Some time ago Radek and Bordiga were telling us how it would last a generation (which is quite a long time). Now Bukharin, in his pamphlet, warns us that the dictatorship will have to last until such time as the workers have attained complete victory and such a victory will be possible "only when the proletariat has freed the whole world of the capitalist rabble and completely suffocated the bourgeoisie."[5]

If this were true, it would mean robbing the Russian people first, and every other people after them, of all hope of liberation, and put off the day of liberation to the Greek kalends, for it is well understood that however extensive and radical a revolution may be, before it manages to be victorious completely and worldwide not one but many generations must elapse.

Fortunately, such anti-revolutionary pessimism is quite erroneous. It is, what is more, an error in the pure reformist tradition, by which an attempt was made in Italy in 1919–20 to impede any revolutionary enterprise "doomed to failure unless the revolution were carried out in every other country as well." In reality, revolution is also possible in relatively restricted areas. Limitation in space implies a limitation in intensity, but the working class will still have won a measure of emancipation and liberty worthy of the efforts made, unless it makes the mistake of emasculating itself— by which we mean relying upon the good offices of a government, instead of relying solely on itself, on its own resources, its own autonomous organisation.

"THE PROLETARIAT IS ALWAY PROLETARIAT even after its victory, after it succeeds to the position of ruling class..."[6]

The proletariat is always proletariat? Oh! Then what becomes of the revolution? This is precisely the essence of the bolshevik error, of the new revolutionary jacobinism: in conceiving of the revolution, from the outset, as a merely political act, the mere stripping of the bourgeois of their governmental powers to replace them with the leaders of the communist party, while "*the proletariat remains proletariat,*" that is to say, deprived of everything and having to go on selling its labour for an hourly or daily wage if it is to make a living! If that happens, it is the expected failure of the revolution!

---

5. In Bukharin and Preobrazhensky's *ABC of Communism* they go even further: "Two or three generations of persons will have to grow up under the new conditions before the need will pass for laws and punishments and for the use of repression by the workers' state."

6. We repeat that communist objections to anarchism, which we reprint in quotations or in heavier type, are genuinely from N. Bukharin.

Sure, class differences do not vanish at the stroke of a pen whether that pen belongs to the theoreticians or to the pen-pushers who set out laws and decrees. Only action, that is to say direct (not through government) expropriation by the proletarians, directed against the privileged class, can wipe out class differences. And that is an immediate possibility, from the very outset, once the old power has been toppled; and it is a possibility for as long as no new power is set up. If, before proceeding with expropriation, the proletariat waits until a new government emerges and becomes strong, it risks never attaining success and remaining the proletariat for ever, that is to say, exploited and oppressed for ever. And the longer it waits before getting on with expropriation, the harder that expropriation will be; and if it then relies on a government to be the expropriator of the bourgeoisie, it will end up betrayed and beaten! The new government will be able to expropriate the old ruling class in whole or in part, but only so as to establish a new ruling class that will hold the greater part of the proletariat in subjection.

That will come to pass if those who make up the government and the bureaucratic, military and police minority that upholds it end up becoming the real owners of wealth when the property of everyone is made over exclusively to the state. In the first place, the failure of the revolution will be self evident. In the second, in spite of the illusions that many people create, the conditions of the proletariat will always be those of a subject class.

Capitalism would not cease to be, merely by changing from private to "state capitalism." In such a case the state would have achieved not expropriation but appropriation. A multitude of bosses would give way to a single boss, the government, which would be a more powerful boss because in addition to having unlimited wealth it would have on its side the armed force with which to bend the proletariat to its will. And the proletariat, in the factories and fields, would still be wage slaves, that is, exploited and oppressed. And conversely, the state, which is no abstraction, but rather an organism created by men, would be the organised ensemble of all the rulers and bosses of tomorrow—who would have no problem in finding some sanction for their rule in a new legality based more or less on elections or a parliament.

"But," they insist, "expropriation has to be carried out according to a given method, organised for the benefit of all; there is a need to know all about the available means of production, houses and land, and so on. Expropriation cannot be carried through by individuals or private groups that would turn it to their own selfish advantage, becoming new privileged property owners. And so there is a need for A PROLETARIAN POWER to cope with it." That would all be fine, except for the sting in the tail! These people are really odd, wanting (in theory) to achieve the abolition of the state while in practice they cannot conceive of the most elementary social function without statist overtones!

Even anarchists do not think of expropriation in terms of some sort of "help yourself" operation, left to personal judgment, in the absence of any order.[7] Even were it possible to predict as inevitable that expropriations, once disorder sets in, would take on an individualistic complexion—say, in the furthest flung places or certain areas of the countryside—anarchist communists have no intention of adopting that sort of an approach as their own. In such cases, all revolutionaries would have an interest in averting too many clashes with certain strata of the population who could later be won over more easily by propaganda and the living proof of the superiority of libertarian communist organisation. What matters, above all else, is that the day after the revolution no one should have the power or the economic wherewithal to exploit the labour of another.

But we anarchists are of the opinion that we must begin now to prepare the masses—in spiritual terms through propaganda, and in material terms by means of anarchist proletarian organisation— to get on with discharging all functions of the struggle and with social, collective living, during and after the revolution; and one of the first among those functions will be expropriation.

---

7. Bukharin is likewise critical of the antedeluvian idea of repartition of wealth, even should it be into equal shares. He is quite right, of course; but to include that in a general critique of anarchism is a real anachronism. One can find all that Bukharin says in this connection in any of the propaganda booklets or papers the anarchists have been publishing for the last forty years.

In order to steer expropriation away from the initiatives of individuals or private groups there is in fact no need for a gendarmerie, and there is in fact no need to jump out of the frying pan into the fire of state control: THERE IS NO NEED FOR GOVERNMENT.

Already, from locality to locality everywhere, and closely interlinked, the proletariat has a number of its own, free institutions, independent of the state; alliances and unions, labour rooms and co-operatives, federations, confederations, and so forth. During the revolution other collective bodies more attuned to the needs of the moment will be set up; still others of bourgeois origin, but radically altered, can be put to use, but we need not concern ourselves with them for the present except to say they are things like consortiums, independent bodies and so on. Russia herself in the earlier moments of her revolution—whenever the people still had freedom of initiative—has furnished us with the example of the creation of these new socialist and libertarian institutions in the form of her soviets and factory committees.

Anarchists have always regarded all such forms of free organisation of the proletariat and of the revolution as acceptable, despite those who nonsensically describe anarchists as being opposed to mass organisations and accuse them of steering clear of participation in organised mass activity "on principle." The truth of the matter is quite different. Anarchists see no incompatibility between the broad, collective action of the great masses and the more restricted activity of their free groups: far from it, they even strive to link the latter with the former so as to give it as far as possible the proper revolutionary sense of direction. And if anarchists do often discuss and criticise those proletarian organisations led by their opponents, they are not thereby fighting against organisation as such, but only against its taking a reformist, legalistic, authoritarian and collaborationist direction—this being something, by the way, which the authoritarian communists likewise engage in everywhere where they themselves are not the leaders of the proletarian organisation.

Some dictatorial communist writers—taking up the old social democrats' fable that the anarchists want only to destroy and not to rebuild, and that they are thus opponents of mass organisation—reach the conclusion that by taking an interest in the soviets in Russia, anarchists are being inconsistent with their ideas and that it is merely a tactic to exploit the soviets and disorganise them.

If this is not slander pure and simple, it is beyond doubt proof of the inability of these mad dogs of authoritarianism—to understand anything apart from omnipotence for the state. According to the authoritarians of communism, the soviet regime consists not of free, self-governing soviets directly managing production and public services and so on but only of the government, the self-styled soviet government, that has in reality overridden the soviets, has abolished their every freedom to act and all spontaneity in their creation, and has reduced them to passive, mechanical underlings, obedient to the dictatorial central government. A government that whenever any soviet shows signs of independence, dissolves it without further ado and sets about conjuring up another artificial one that is more to its taste.

All this goes under the name of "giving the proletarian organisations a broader power base"; and, as a result, the Russian anarchists no less, who quite logically and correctly have always opposed this real strangulation of the original soviet movement that arose freely out of the revolution (that is, they defend the soviets against dictators just as they have defended them against bourgeois aggression) the Russian anarchists turn—thanks to the miracle of marxist dialectic—into enemies of the soviets. Given their mentality, Marxists cannot understand that their so-called "soviet power" is the obliteration of the proletarian, people's soviets and that, this being the case, opponents of so-called "soviet power" can be—provided, of course that this opposition comes from within the revolutionary, proletarian camp—the best friends of the proletarian soviets.

So anarchists do not in fact have this preconceived, principled aversion to "the methodical, organised form of mass action"— usually attributed to them in clichéd argument on account of our opponents' sectarian approach—but rather oppose only the particularly authoritarian and despotic approach of the state communists, countering with the libertarian approach which is more apt to interest and mobilise the broad masses in that it leaves them scope for initiative and action and interests them in a struggle that is from the very outset a co-ordinated one, presenting them with expropriation as their chief and immediate objective.

It may be that this libertarian sense of direction will, likewise, not culminate in the abolition of the state—not because that is impossible but because there is not a sufficient number who want it, what with the still too numerous herd of humanity who feel in need of the shepherd and his stick—but in such a case it would be rendering the revolution a great service to succeed in holding on to as much freedom as possible, helping to determine that the eventual government is as weak, as decentralised, as undespotic as possible under the circumstances; that is to say, wringing the utmost utility from the revolution for the sake of the proletariat as well as the maximum well-being and freedom.

One moves towards the abolition of capitalism by expropriating the capitalists for the benefit of all, not by creating an even worse capitalism in state capitalism.

Progress towards the abolition of the state is made by fighting it as long as it survives, undermining it more and more, stripping it so far as is possible of authority and prestige, weakening it and removing from it as many social functions as the working people have equipped themselves to perform on their own through their revolutionary or class organisation—and not, as authoritarian communists claim, by building on the ruins of the bourgeois state another even stronger state with more functions and added power.

By taking this last course, it is the authoritarian communists, no less; who place obstacles before organisation and mass activity and set out along the road diametrically opposed to that which will lead to communism and abolition of the state. It is they who are the ridiculous ones, as ridiculous as anyone who, wishing to travel east, sets out in the direction of the setting sun.

IV Anarchy and Communism

There is a bad habit that we must react against. It is the habit that authoritarian communists have had for some time now, that of setting communism against anarchy, as if the two notions were necessarily contradictory; the habit of using these two words COMMUNISM and ANARCHY as if they were mutually incompatible and had opposite meanings.

In Italy, where for something over forty years these words have been used together to form a single term in which one word complements the other, to form the most accurate description of the anarchist programme, this effort to disregard such an important historical tradition and, what is more, turn the meanings of the words upside down, is absurd and can only serve to create confusion in the realm of ideas and endless misunderstandings in the realm of propaganda.

There is no harm in recalling that it was, oddly enough, at a congress of the Italian Sections of the first workers' International, meeting clandestinely near Florence in 1876, that, on a motion put forward by Errico Malatesta, it was affirmed that communism was the economic arrangement that could best make a society without government a possibility; and that anarchy (that is, the absence of all government), being the free and voluntary organisation of social relationships, was the best way to implement communism. One is effectively the guarantee for the other and vice versa. Hence the concrete formulation of ANARCHIST COMMUNISM as an ideal and as a movement of struggle.

We have indicated elsewhere[8] how in 1877 the *Arbeiter Zeitung* of Berne published the statutes of a "German speaking Anarchist Communist Party"; and how in 1880 the Congress of the Internationalist Federation of the Jura at Chaux-de-Fonds gave its approval to a memorandum from Carlo Cafiero on "Anarchy and Communism," in the same sense as before. In Italy at the time anarchists were more commonly known as socialists; but when they wanted to be specific they called themselves, as they have done ever

---

8. See Luigi Fabbri: *Dictatorship and Revolution* (in Italian) p. 140.

since, even to this day, ANARCHIST COMMUNISTS.

Later Pietro Gori used to say that socialism (communism) would constitute the economic basis of a society transformed by a revolution such as we envisaged, while anarchy would be its political culmination.

As specifications of the anarchist programme, these ideas have, as the saying used to go, acquired rights of citizenship in political language from the time when the First International was in its death throes in Italy (1880–2). As a definition or formulation of anarchism, the term ANARCHIST COMMUNISM was incorporated into their political vocabulary even by other socialist writers who, when it came to their own programme for the organisation of society from the economic point of view, did not talk about communism, but rather about collectivism, and in effect, styled themselves COLLECTIVISTS.

That was the position up to 1918; that is to say until the Russian bolsheviks, to set themselves apart from the patriotic or reformist social democrats, made up their minds to change their name, resurrecting that of "communist," which fitted the historical tradition of Marx and Engels' famous *Manifesto* of 1847, and which up to 1880 was employed by German socialists in a purely authoritarian, social democratic sense. Little by little, nearly all the socialists owning allegiance to Moscow's Third International have ended up styling themselves COMMUNISTS, disregarding the perversion of the word's meaning, the different usage of the word over the span of forty years in popular and proletarian parlance, and the changes in the stances of the parties after 1880—thereby creating a real anachronism.

But that's the authoritarian communists and not us; there would not even have been any need for us to debate the matter had they taken the bother, when they changed what they called themselves, to set out clearly what change in ideas was rerlected in this change in name. Sure, the socialists-now-become-communists have modified their platform as compared with the one laid down for Italy at the Genoa Congress of the Workers' Party in 1892, and through the Socialist International at its London Congress in 1896. But the change in programme revolves wholly and exclusively about methods of struggle (espousal of violence, dismissal of parliamentarianism, dictatorship instead of democracy, and so on); and it does not refer to the ideal of social reconstruction, the only thing to which the terms communism and collectivism can refer.

When it comes to their programme for social reconstruction, to the economic order of the future society, the socialists-communists have changed not at all; they just have not bothered. As a matter of fact, the term communism covers their old authoritarian, collectivist programme which still lingers on—having in the background, the far distant background, a vision of the disappearance of the state that is put before the masses on solemn occasions to distract their attention from a new domination, one that the communist dictators would like to yoke them to in the not so distant future.

All this is a source of misapprehension and confusion among the workers, who are told one thing in words that leads them to believe quite another.

From ancient times, the term COMMUNISM has meant, not a method of struggle, much less a special method of reasoning, but a system for the complete radical reorganisation of society on the basis of common ownership of wealth, common enjoyment of the fruits of the common labour by the members of human society, without any of them being able to appropriate social capital to themselves for their exclusive advantage to the exclusion or detriment of others. It is an ideal of the economic reorganisation of society, common to a number of schools of socialism (anarchy included); and the marxists were by no means the first to formulate that ideal.

Marx and Engels did write a programme for the German Communist Party in 1847, it is true, setting out its theoretical and tactical guidelines; but the Communist Party already existed before that. They drew their notion of communism from others and were by no means its creators.

In that superb hothouse of ideas, the First International, the concept of communism was increasingly clarified; and it took on its special importance in confrontation with collectivism, which around 1880 was, by common agreement, incorporated into the political and social vocabulary of anarchists and socialists alike: ranging from Karl Marx to Carlo Cafiero and Benoit Malon to Gnocchi Viani. From that time forward, the word communism has always been taken to mean a system for the production and distribution of wealth in a socialist society, the practical guidelines for which were set down in the formula: FROM EACH ACCORDING TO HIS RESOURCES AND ABILITY – TO EACH ACCORDING TO HIS NEEDS.[9] The communism of anarchists, built on the political terrain of the negation of the state, was and is understood to have this meaning, to signify precisely a practical system of socialist living after the revolution, in keeping with both the derivation of the word and the historical tradition.

In contrast, what the neo-communists understand by "communism" is merely or mostly a set of methods of struggle and the theoretical criteria they stand by in discussion and propaganda. Some talk of violence or state terrorism which has to be imposed by the socialist regime; others want the word "communism" to signify the complex of theories that are known as marxism (class struggle, historical materialism, seizure of power, dictatorship of the proletariat, etc.); still others quite purely and simply a method of philosophical reasoning, like the dialectical approach. So some—harnessing together words that have no logical connection between them—call it *critical communism* while others opt for *scientific communism.*

As we see it, they are all mistaken; for the ideas and tactics mentioned above can be shared and used by communists too, and be more or less made compatible with communism, but they are not in themselves communism—nor are they enough to set it apart, whereas they could very well be made compatible with other, quite different systems, even those contrary to communism. If we want to amuse ourselves with word games, we could say that there is

---

9. In contrast, the collectivists' formula was "to each the fruits of his labour" or even "to each according to his work." Needless to say, these formulae must be taken in their approximate meaning, as a general guideline, and absolutely not as dogma, as however they were employed at one time.

quite a lot to the doctrines of authoritarian communists, but what is most strikingly absent is nothing other than communism.

Let it be clearly understood that in no way do we dispute the right of authoritarian communists to adopt whatever title they see fit, whatever they like, and adopt a name that was our exclusive property for almost half a century and that we have no intention of giving up. It would be ridiculous to contest that right. But whenever the neo-communists come to discuss anarchy and hold discussions with anarchists there is a moral obligation on them not to pretend they know nothing of the past, and they have the basic duty not to appropriate that name to such a degree as to monopolise it, to such a degree that an incompatibility is created between the term communism and the term anarchy that is artificial and false.

Whenever they do these things they reveal themselves to be devoid of all sense of political honesty.

Everyone knows how our ideal, expressed in the word *anarchy*, taken in the programmatic sense of a socialism organised in a libertarian way, has always been known as anarchist communism. Almost all anarchist literature has, since the end of the First International, belonged to the communist school of socialism. Up until the outbreak of the Russian Revolution in 1917 the two chief schools into which socialism was divided were, on the one hand, legalistic, statist collectivism, and, on the other, anarchist, revolutionary communism. What number of polemics, between 1880 and 1918, have we not engaged in with the Marxist socialists, today's neo-communists, in support of the communist ideal as against their German-barrack-room collectivism!

And so, their ideal view of the reorganisation to come has remained the same, and its authoritarian overtones have even become more pronounced. The only difference between the collectivism that we criticised in the past and the dictatorial communism of today is a tactical one and a slight theoretical difference, and not the question of the immediate goal to be reached. True, this links up with the state communism of the pre-1880 German socialists—the *Volksstaat* or people's State—against which

Bakunin directed such vitriolic criticism; and likewise the government socialism of Louis Blanc, so brilliantly demolished by Proudhon. But the connection with the revolutionary statist approach is only on the secondary level of politics, and not on the level of its particular economic viewpoint—that is, the organisation of production and the distribution of the products—of which Marx and Blanc had a rather broader, more general view than their latest heirs.

In contrast, the dichotomy is not between anarchy and a more or less "scientific" communism, but rather between AUTHORITARIAN OR STATE COMMUNISM, rushing headlong towards a despotic dictatorship, and ANARCHIST OR ANTI-STATE COMMUNISM with its libertarian vision of revolution.

If one has to talk about contradiction in terms, it must be not between the term communism and the term anarchy, which are so compatible that the one is not possible in the absence of the other, but rather between communism and state. Where there is state or government, no communism is possible. At least, it is so difficult to reconcile them, and so demanding of the sacrifice of all human freedom and dignity, that one can surmise that it is impossible when today the spirit of revolt, autonomy and initiative is so widespread among the masses, hungering not only for bread but also for freedom.

V The Russian Revolution and the Anarchists

When they run out of arguments against our unshakable reasoning, the parting shot authoritarian communists loose at us is to portray us as "enemies of the Russian Revolution."

From our position of fighting against the dictatorial conception of revolution—a position we share with our Russian comrades—to back up our arguments we cite the baneful results of the dictatorial direction of revolutionary Russia, and hold up to the light the grave errors of the government there; in this sense alone are we fighting against the Russian Revolution.

This is more than a question of unfair accusations: it is at once a lie and a slander. If the cause of the Revolution is the cause of freedom and justice, in a PRACTICAL and not in any abstract sense, that is to say, if it is the cause of the proletariat and its emancipation from all political and economic servitude, all state or private exploitation and oppression; if the Revolution is the cause of social equality, then it is with justice that we can insist that the only ones still faithful today to the Russian Revolution, the revolution made by the working people of Russia, are the anarchists.

We appreciate that, for some considerable period, in time of revolution, all that anyone—and especially revolutionaries—has a right to expect is thorns and very few roses. Let us have no illusions about that. But revolution ceases to be revolution when it is not and does not signify an improvement, however slight, for the broad masses, and fails to assure to the proletarians a greater well-being or at least, if they cannot clearly see that, once certain temporary difficulties can be surmounted, well-being will come about. It ceases to be revolution if, in practical terms, it does not mean an increase in freedom to think and act—in whatever ways do not restrict the freedom of others—for all those who were oppressed under the old regime.

Such are the views and feelings that act as our guides in our propaganda and polemics. In no way are propaganda and polemic prompted by a spirit of sectarianism, much less by a spirit of competition or by personal interest; and we do not in the least engage in them as an exercise in criticism and doctrinairism. Rather we are aware of fulfilling a double obligation, of immediate political relevance.

On the one hand, the study of the Russian Revolution, the shedding of light on the errors made by those in government, and the criticism of the bolshevik system that won the day are, as far as we are concerned, a duty imposed by political solidarity with our Russian comrades who, because they share our thinking and hold our point of view—which, we believe, are the thoughts and viewpoint most compatible with the interests of the revolution of the proletariat—are deprived of all liberty, persecuted, imprisoned, exiled, and, some of them, put to death by that government. On the other hand, we have a duty to show up the bolshevik error, so that if a similar crisis arose in the western countries the proletariat would take care not to set out along a road, to take a direction, that we now know from first-hand experience means the wrecking of the revolution.

If that is what we think, if we are deeply convinced that that is the case—and our opponents cannot doubt it, for there are no other interests or strong feelings that could turn our mind away from such an undertaking—then it is our duty, as anarchists and revolutionaries, to break our silence. But does all that mean that we are against the Russian Revolution?

The Russian Revolution is the most earth-shaking event of our day. Brought on and made easier by an enormous cause, the world war, it has surpassed that world war in magnitude and importance. Had it managed, if it manages or should it manage in the future—as, in spite of everything, we still hope—to break the bonds of wage slavery that bind the working class, or should the advances made by earlier revolutions be expanded to include economic and social equality, freedom for all in fact as well as in theory, that is to say with the material possibility of enjoying it, then the Russian Revolution will surpass in historical importance even the French Revolution of 1789—93.

If the world war failed to extinguish all hope of resurrection by the oppressed people of the world, if despite it men are not to be set back centuries to the animal existence of their ancestors, but only a little way, it is beyond dispute that we owe it to the Russian Revolution. It is the Russian Revolution that has raised the moral and ideal values of humanity and which has impelled our aspirations and the collective spirit of all peoples forwards towards a higher humanity.

In that sad dawn of 1917, while the whole world seemed to be rushing headlong into horror, death, falsehood, hatred and blackest obscurity, the Russian Revolution suddenly flooded those of us who were suffering from that endless tragedy with the searching light of truth and brotherhood, and the warmth of life and love began to flow again along withered veins to the parched hearts of the workers' international. For as long as that memory persists, all the peoples of the earth will be obliged to the Russian people for an effort that, not only in Russia and Europe but in the most distant corners of the globe inhabited by men, succeeded in lifting the hopes of the oppressed.

We absolutely do not conceal the cost of the Russian people's feat in terms of fatigue, heroism, sacrifice and martyrdom.

We anarchists have not followed the progress of the revolution with mental reservations or in a spirit of sectarianism. We never talked this way, in public or in private: up till now, but no more. So long as the revolution was moving forward we did not concern ourselves with whichever party it was that won the most fame. Then no one, or practically no one, spoke of the Russian anarchists. We knew—and later news proved we were right—that they must be in the forefront of the battle, unknown but nonetheless important factors in the revolution. And for us that was enough.

We have no partisan interests, nor have we any need to exploit our fallen to secure privileges for the future; and for that reason our silence on the work of our comrades did not dampen our joy. And, between the months of March and November, before they seized power (and even for a few months after they had, until bitter experience confirmed what our doctrine had given us an inkling of in advance) the bolsheviks seemed to be the most energetic foes of the old oppressors, of the war policy, of all truck with the bourgeoisie; and fought against democratic radicalism with its roots in capitalism and, along with it, against the social patriots, reformists, right socialist revolutionaries and mensheviks; and later, when after a little hesitation they co-operated to scatter to the winds the equivocation of the constituent Assembly, the anarchists, without any senseless rivalry, stood at their side.

They stood at their side ideally, spiritually, outside Russia and, more practically, in the sphere of propaganda and political activity against the slander and calumnies of the bourgeoisie. And, even more practically, they stood there still (and that even after they had begun to oppose at the polemical level), against the bourgeois governments when, so far as was possible, an effort was made to use direct action to prevent the infamous blockade of Russia and to stop the supply of war materials to her enemies. Every time the interests of the revolution and the Russian people seemed to be at stake, the anarchists held their ground, even when they knew that they could indirectly be giving help to their opponents.

The same thing, on a much larger scale, with a greater expenditure of energies and more sacrifices in ruthless armed struggle, happened inside Russia where our comrades have been fighting for the revolution against tsarism since before 1917, with dogged opposition to the war and after that with weapons in hand in March; then later against bourgeois democracy and social reformism in July and October; fighting at last on all fronts, giving up their lives in the fight against Yudenich, Denikin and Wrangel, against the Germans in Riga, the English in Archangel, the French in Odessa and the Japanese in Siberia. Many of them (and this is not the place to see if or to what extent they were mistaken in so doing) have collaborated with the Bolsheviks in internal civil or military organisation, wherever they could, with least conflict with their own conscience, to the advantage of the revolution. And if today Russian anarchists are among the opposition inside Russia and fight against bolshevik policy and the bolshevik government, all they are doing is pressing on—a heroic few—with the struggle for revolution begun in March 1917.

Not only is today's government not the Russian Revolution, but it has become its very negation. On the other hand, that was inevitable by virtue of the fact that it is a government. Not only does fighting the Russian government, at the level of polemic, with revolutionary arguments—that have nothing in common with the arguments of the revolution's enemies—not only does this not make one a foe of the revolution, but it defends it, clarifies it and frees it of the stains which the bulk of the public sees in it—stains that are not of it, but come from the government party, the new ruling caste that is growing, parasite-like on its trunk, to the detriment of the great bulk of the proletariat.

This in no way prevents us from understanding the grandiosity of the Russian Revolution, and appreciating the renewal it has meant for a good half of Europe. The only thing we oppose is the claim of a single party to monopolise the credit and the benefits of such an enormous event, which they certainly did have a hand in, but in a proportion one might reasonably expect from their numbers and organisation. The Russian Revolution was not the work of a party—it was the work of a whole people: and the people is the real leading actor of the real Russian Revolution. The grandeur of the Revolution comes not in the form of government ordinances, laws and military feats, but in the form of the profound change wrought in the moral and material life of the population.

That change is irrefutable. Tsarism in Russia has died, and with it a whole endless series of monstrosities. The old noble and bourgeois ruling class is destroyed and along with it many things, from the roots up, especially a lot of prejudices, the removal of which was once thought impossible. Should Russia, as appears to be the case, be unfortunate enough to see a new ruling class formed there, then the demolition of the old annihilated one leads to the expectation that the rule of the new power will in its turn be overthrown without difficulty. The original libertarian idea behind the "Soviets" did not win the souls of Russians over in vain, even if the bolsheviks have maimed it and turned it into a cog in the bureaucracy of the dictatorship; inside that idea lies the seed of the new revolution which will be the only one that acts out real communism, communism with freedom.

No government can lay claim of the moral renewal of Russia in the wake of revolution, nor can it destroy it; and that renewal is the merit of the popular revolution alone, not of a political party. And of course, in spite of everything (a comrade wrote to me who had just returned from Russia, after some criticisms of the bolshevik maladministration), "the impression that the life of the Russian people makes all in all is so grand that everything here in capitalist Europe seems a wretched, stupid 'petit bourgeois' imitation. No vulgarity there; one never hears those vulgar songs sung by drunks; there the off-putting atmosphere of Sundays and those places where people *amuse themselves* in western countries does not exist.

Amid sacrifice and unspeakable suffering, the people really do live a better, more intense moral life."

In real terms the Russian Revolution lives on in the Russian people. That is the revolution we love, that we celebrate with enthusiasm and with a heart filled with hope. But, as we never tire of repeating, the revolution and the Russian people are not the government that, in the eyes of superficial folk, represents them abroad. A friend of mine, returning from Russia in 1920 burning with enthusiasm, when I warned him that the soviets there were a humiliating sort of subordination and that government agents even manipulated their elections "fascistically," replied some-what rashly: "But if the majority of the proletarians were really able to elect the soviets of their choice, the Bolshevik government would not remain in government another week!"

If that is so, then when we criticise—not persons, not individuals, whom we have often defended against slanderers in the kept press of capitalism—when we, prompted by our constant concern not to fall into the mistaken, exaggerated form of criticism, attack the ruling party in Russia and those of its supporters anxious to follow in its footsteps in Italy—because we see that its methods are harmful to the revolution and bring about a real counter-revolution—how can anyone say that "we are taking up a stand against the Russian Revolution"?

The proletariat, which knows and heeds us, knows that this is an evil, ridiculous assertion, as evil and ridiculous as the way the hacks of the bourgeoisie try to pass off as insults and charges against the whole Italian people the justly harsh criticisms—which we support—that foreign revolutionaries level at the government and the ruling class of Italy.

The Soviet System or the Dictatorship of the Proletariat?

RUDOLF ROCKER

Perhaps the reader thinks he has found a flaw in the above title and that the soviet system and the dictatorship of the proletariat are one and the same thing? No. They are two radically different ideas which, far from being mutually complementary, are mutually opposed. Only an unhealthy party logic could accept a fusion when what really exists is an irreconcilable opposition.

The idea of "soviets" is a well defined expression of what we take to be social revolution, being an element belonging entirely to the constructive side of socialism. The origin of the notion of dictatorship is wholly bourgeois and as such, has nothing to do with socialism. It is possible to harness the two terms together artificially, if it is so desired, but all one would get would be a very poor caricature of the original idea of soviets, amounting, as such, to a subversion of the basic notion of socialism.

The idea of soviets is not a new one, nor is it one thrown up, as is frequently believed, by the Russian Revolution. It arose in the most advanced wing of the European labour movement at a time when the working class emerged from the chrysalis of bourgeois radicalism to become independent. That was in the days when the International Workingmen's Association achieved its grandiose plan to gather together workers from various countries into a single huge union, so as to open up to them a direct route towards their real emancipation. Although the International has been thought of as a broad based organisation composed of professional bodies, its statutes were drafted in such a way as to allow all the socialist tendencies of the day to join with the sole proviso that they agree with the ultimate objective of the organisation: the complete emancipation of the workers.

Naturally enough, at the time of its foundation, the ideas of this great Association were far from being as clearly defined as they were at the Geneva Congress in 1866 or the Lausanne in 1867. The more experienced the International became the more it matured and spread throughout the world as a fighting organisation, the clearer and more objective the thinking of its adepts appeared. The practical activity arising out of the day to day battle between capital and labour led, of itself, to a deeper understanding of basic principles.

After the Brussels congress of 1868 the International had come out in favour of collective ownership of the soil, the subsoil and the instruments of labour, and the groundwork had been laid down for the further development of the International.

At the Basel congress of 1869 the internal evolution of the great workers' association reached its zenith. Apart from the issue of the soil and subsoil, freshly considered by the congress, the chief issue was how workers' unions were to be set up, run and used. A report on this issue, presented by the Belgian Hins and his friends, excited a lively interest at the congress. On this occasion, for the first time, the tasks which the workers' unions were to tackle as well as the importance of those unions was set out in an utterly unmistakable way, reminiscent, to a degree, of the thinking of Robert Owen. Thus it was announced at Basel in clear and unmistakable terms that the trades union, the local federation, was more than merely an ordinary and temporary body whose only reason to exist was capitalist society, and which was fated to disappear when it did. According to what Hins set out, the state socialist view that the workers' unions ought to confine their activities to improving the living conditions of the workers in terms of wages, no more and no less, was radically amended.

The report by Hins and his friends shows how the workers' organisations for the economic struggle can be regarded as cells of the socialist society of the future, and that the International's task is to educate these local organisations to equip them to carry out their historic mission Indeed, the congress did adopt the Belgian view; but we know today that many delegates, especially those from the German labour organisations, never had any wish to put the resolution into practice within the bound of their influence.

After the Basel congress, and especially after the war of 1870, which thrust the European social movement along quite a different route, it became obvious that there were two tendencies inside the International, tendencies so irreconcilably opposed to one another that this opposition went as far as a split. Later an attempt was made to reduce their disagreements to the level of a personal squabble between Michael Bakunin and Karl Marx, the latter with his General Council in London. There could not be a more mistaken, groundless account than this one, which is based on utter ignorance of the facts. Of course, personal considerations did have a role to play in these clashes, as they usually do in such situations. In any event, it was Marx and Engels who resorted to every conceivable impropriety in their attacks on Bakunin. As a matter of fact, Karl Marx's biographer, the author Franz Mehring, was unable to keep silent on this fact, since, basically, it was not a question of vain silly squabbling, but of a clash between two ideological outlooks which did and do have a certain natural importance.

In the Latin countries, where the International found its principal support, the workers were active through their organisations of economic struggle. To their eyes, the state was the political agent and defender of the possessing classes, and, this being the case, the seizure of political power was not to be pursued in any guise for it was nothing other than a prelude to a new tyranny and a survival of exploitation. For that reason, they avoided imitating the bourgeoisie by setting up yet another political party that would spawn a new ruling class captained by professional politicians. Their objective was to get control of machines, industry, the soil and the subsoil; and they foresaw correctly that this approach divided them radically from the Jacobin politicians of the bourgeoisie who sacrificed everything for the sake of political power. The Latin internationalists realised that monopoly of ownership had to go, as well as monopoly of power; that the whole life of the society to come had to be founded upon wholly new bases. Taking as their starting point the fact that "man's domination over his fellow man" was a thing of the past, these comrades tried to get to grips with the idea of "the administration of things." They replaced the politics of parties inside the state with the economic politics of labour. Furthermore, they realised that the reorganisation of society in a socialist sense had to be undertaken inside industry itself, this being the root idea behind the notion of the councils (or soviets).

In an extremely clear and precise way, the congresses of the Spanish Regional Federation went more deeply into these ideas of the anti-authoritarian wing of the International, and developed them. That is where the terms "juntas" and "workers' councils" (meaning the same thing as soviets) came from.

The libertarian socialists of the First International realised full well that socialism cannot be decreed by a government, but has to grow, organically, from the bottom up. They understood, also, that it was for the workers alone to undertake the organisation of labour and production and, similarly, distribution for equal consumption. This was the overriding idea which they have opposed to the state socialism of parliamentary politicians.

As the years have passed, and even today, the labour movements of these Latin countries have undergone savage persecutions. This bloody policy can be traced back to the repression of the Paris Commune in 1871. Later, reactionary excesses of that sort spread to Spain and Italy. As a result, the idea of "councils" has receded into the background, since all open propaganda was suppressed and in the clandestine movements the workers' organisation had to set up, militants were constrained to deploy all their energies, all their resources, to fighting the reaction and defending its victims.

Revolutionary Syndicalism and the Idea of Councils

The development of revolutionary syndicalism has unearthed this idea and breathed new life into it. During the most active period of French revolutionary syndicalism between 1900 and 1907 the councils idea was pursued in its most comprehensive, well defined form.

A glance at the writings of Pouget, Griffuelhes, Monatte, Yvetot and some others, especially Pelloutier, is enough to persuade one that neither in Russia nor anywhere else has an iota been added to what the propagandists of revolutionary syndicalism formulated fifteen or twenty years before the Russian events of 1917.

Throughout those years the socialist workers' parties rejected the idea of councils out of hand. Most of those who today are advocates of the idea of soviets (especially in Germany) scorned it yesterday as some "new utopia." Lenin, no less, stated to the president of the St. Petersburg delegates' council in 1905 that the councils system was an outmoded institution with which the party had nothing in common.

And so this notion of councils, the credit for which is due to the revolutionary syndicalists, marks the most important point and constitutes the keystone of the international labour movement, thanks to which we shall be permitted to add that the councils system is the only institution likely to lead to socialism becoming a reality, since any other path will be a mistaken one. "Utopia" has won over "sciencificism."

Equally, it is beyond question that the council idea arises naturally out of a libertarian socialist vision which has so taken root in a large part of the international labour movement, as opposed to the state idea with its wake of bourgeois ideological traditions.

The "Dictatorship of the Proletariat," an Inheritance from the Bourgeoisie

That is all that can be said of dictatorship, since it is not a product of socialist thinking. Dictatorship is no child of the labour movement, but a regrettable inheritance from the bourgeoisie, passed into the proletarian camp to guarantee its "happiness." Dictatorship is closely linked with the lust for political power, which is likewise bourgeois in its origin.

Dictatorship is one of the forms which the state, ever greedy for Power, is apt to assume. It is the state on a war footing. Like

51

other advocates of the state idea, the supporters of dictatorship would—provisionally (?)—impose their will upon the people. This concept alone is an impediment to social revolution, the very life's blood of which is precisely the constructive participation and direct initiative of the masses.

Dictatorship is the denial, the destruction of the organic being, of the natural form of organisation, which is from the bottom upwards. Some claim that the people are not yet sufficiently mature to take charge of their own destiny. So there has to be a ruler over the masses, tutelage by an "expert" minority. The supporters of dictatorship could have the best intentions in the world, but the logic of Power will oblige them always to take the path of the most extreme despotism.

Our state socialists adopted the notion of dictatorship from that pre-bourgeois party, the Jacobins. That party damned striking as a crime and banned workers' organisations under pain of death. The most active spokesmen for this overbearing conduct were Saint-Just and Couthon, while Robespierre operated under the same influence.

The false, onesided way that bourgeois historians usually depict the Great Revolution has heavily influenced most socialists, and contributed mightily to giving the Jacobin dictatorship an ill deserved prestige, while the martyrdom of its chief leaders seems to have increased. Generally, folk are easy prey for the cult of martyrs, which disables them from studied criticism of ideas and deeds.

The creative labour of the French Revolution is well known— it abolished feudalism and the monarchy. Historians have glorified this as the work of the Jacobins and revolutionaries of the Convention, but nonetheless, with the passage of time that picture has turned out to be an absolute falsification of the whole history of the Revolution.

Today we know that this mistaken interpretation is based on the wilful ignorance of historical fact, especially the truth that the bona fide creative work of the Revolution was carried out by the peasants and the proletariat from the towns in defiance of the National Assembly and the Convention. The Jacobins and the Convention were always rather vigorously opposed to radical changes, up until they were a fait accompli, that is, until popular actions imposed such changes upon them. Consequently, the convention's proclamation that the feudal system was abolished was nothing more than an official recognition of inroads made directly by the revolutionary peasants into the old oppressive system, in spite of the fierce opposition they had had to face from the political parties of the day.

As late as 1792, the National Assembly had not touched the feudal system. It was only the following year that the said revolutionary Assembly condescended to prove "the mob of the country-side" right by sanctioning the abolition of feudal rights, something the people had already accomplished by popular decision. The same thing, or almost, goes for the official abolition of the monarchy.

Jacobin Traditions and Socialism

The first founders of a popular socialist movement in France came from the Jacobin camp, so it is natural that the political inheritance of 1792 should weigh heavily upon them.

When Babeuf and Darthey set up the conspiracy of "The Equals," they aimed to turn France, by means of dictatorship, into an agrarian communist state and, as communists. they appreciated that they would have to set about solving the economic question if they were ever to attain the ideal of the Great Revolution. But, as Jacobins, "The Equals" believed they could attain their objective by reinforcing the state, conferring vast powers on it. With the Jacobins, belief in the omnipotence of the state reached its acme and so thoroughly permeated them that they were incapable of conceiving any alternative scheme to follow.

Half-dead, Babeuf and Darthey were dragged to the guillotine, but their ideas lived on among the people, taking refuge in secret societies, like the "Egalitarians" during the reign of Louis Philippe. Men like Barbes and Blanqui worked along the same lines, fighting for a dictatorship of the proletariat designed to make the aims of the communists a reality.

It was from these men that Marx and Engels inherited the notion of a dictatorship of the proletariat, which they set out in their Communist Manifesto. By that means they were to arrive at a central power with uncontested capabilities, the task of which it would be to crush the potential of the bourgeoisie through radical coercive laws and, when the time was ripe, reorganise society in the spirit of state socialism.

Marx and Engels abandoned bourgeois democracy for the socialist camp, their thinking profoundly shaped by Jacobin influence. What is more, the socialist movement was, at that time, insufficiently developed to come up with an authentic path of its own. The socialism of both of the two leaders was more or less subject to bourgeois traditions going back to the French Revolution.

Everything for the Councils

Thanks to the growth of the labour movement in the days of the international, socialism found itself in a position to shrug off the last remnants of bourgeois traditions and to become entirely independent. The concept of councils abandoned the notion of the state and of power politics under any guise whatever. Similarly, it was diametrically opposed to any suggestion of dictatorship. In fact, it not only attempted to strip away the instruments of power from the forces that possessed them and from the state, but it also tended to increase its own sway as far as possible.

The forerunners of the council system appreciated well that along with the exploitation of man by man would have to vanish also the domination of man by man. They realised that the state, being the organised power of the ruling classes, cannot be transformed into an instrument for the emancipation of labour. Likewise, it was their view that the primary task of the social revolution has to be the demolition of the old power structure, to remove the possibility of any new form of exploitation and retreat.

Let no one object that the "dictatorship of the proletariat" cannot be compared to run of the mill dictatorship because it is the dictatorship of a class. Dictatorship of a class cannot exist as such, for it ends up, in the last analysis, as being the dictatorship of a given party which arrogates to itself the right to speak for that class. Thus, the liberal bourgeoisie, in their fight against despotism, used to speak in the name of the "people." In parties which have never enjoyed the use of power, the lust for power or the desire to wield it assume an extremely dangerous form.

Those who have recently won power are even more obnoxious than those who possessed it. The example of Germany is illuminating in this respect: the Germans are currently living under the powerful dictatorship of the professional politicians of the social democracy and the centralistic functionaries of the trade unions. They find no measure too base or brutal to apply and subdue the members of their "own" class who dare to take issue with them. When these gentlemen, reneging on socialism, "went under" they tossed away even those gains made by bourgeois revolutions guaranteeing a certain degree of freedom and personal inviolability. What's more they have also fathered the most horrendous police system, going so far as to arrest anyone who is ungrateful to the authorities and rendering him harmless for a time at least. The celebrated "lettres de cachet" of the French despots and the administrative deportation of the Russian tsarist system have been exhumed and applied by these unique champions of democracy.

Needless to say, these new despots pratel on insistently about support for a constitution that guarantees every possible right to good Germans; but that constitution exists only on paper. Even the French republican constitution of 1793 suffered from the same flaw—it was never put into effect. Robespierre and his henchmen tried to explain themselves by stating that the fatherland was in danger. Consequently, the "Incorruptible" and his men maintained a dictatorship which led to Thermidor, the disgraceful rule of the Directory, and, ultimately, the dictatorship of the sword under Napoleon. At the present time we in Germany have reached our Directory: the only thing missing is the man who will play the role of Napoleon.

We already know that a revolution cannot be made with rose-water. And we know, too, that the owning classes will never yield up their privileges spontaneously. On the day of victorious revolution the workers will have to impose their will on the present owners of the soil, of the subsoil and of the means of production, which cannot be done—let us be clear on this—without the workers taking the capital of society into their own hands, and, above all, without their having demolished the authoritarian structure which is, and will continue to be, the fortress keeping the masses of the people under dominion. Such an action is, without doubt, an act of liberation; a proclamation of social justice; the very essence of social revolution, which has nothing in common with the utterly bourgeois principle of dictatorship.

The fact that a large number of socialist parties have rallied to the idea of councils, which is the proper mark of libertarian socialist and revolutionary syndicalists, is a confession, recognition that the tack they have taken up until now has been the product of a falsification, a distortion, and that with the councils the labour movement must create for itself a single organ capable of carrying into effect the unmitigated socialism that the conscious proletariat longs for. On the other hand, it ought not to be forgotten that this abrupt conversion runs the risk of introducing many alien features into the councils concept, features, that is, with no relation to the original tasks of socialism, and which have to be eliminated because they pose a threat to the further development of the councils. These alien elements are able only to conceive things from the dictatorial viewpoint. It must be our task to face up to this risk and warn our class comrades against experiments which cannot bring the dawn of social emancipation any nearer, which indeed, to the contrary, positively postpone it.

Consequently, our advice is as follows: Everything for the councils or soviets! No power above them! A slogan which at the same time will be that of the social revolutionary.

The Idea of Equality and the Bolsheviks

NESTOR MAKHNO

The 14th Congress of the Russian Communist Party has roundly condemned the notion of equality. Prior to the congress, Zinoviev had mentioned the idea in the course of his polemic against Ustrialov and Bukharin. He declared then that the whole of contemporary philosophy was sustained by the idea of equality. Kalinin spoke up forcefully at the congress against that contention, taking the line that any reference to equality could not help but be harmful and was not to be tolerated. His reasoning was as follows:

"Can we talk to peasants about equality? No, that is out of the question, for in that case, they would set about demanding the same rights as workers, which would be in complete contradiction with the dictatorship of the proletariat. Likewise, can we talk of equality to workers? No, that is out of the question too, for if, say, a communist and a non-party member do the same job, the difference resides in the former being paid twice the wage of the latter. To concede equality would allow non-party members to demand the same pay as is paid out to a communist. Is that acceptable, comrades? No, it is not. Can we call for equality among communists then? No, that is not on either, for they too occupy different positions, in terms of their rights and their material circumstances alike."

On the basis of such considerations, Kalinin concluded that Zinoviev's use of the term "equality" could only have been demagogic and harmful. In his reply, Zinoviev in turn told the congress that, whilst he had spoken of equality, he had meant it in quite a different sense. As for himself, all he had had in mind was "socialist equality," that is, the equality that would one day come to pass in a more or less distant future. For the time being, until such time as the world revolution had taken place and as there was no way of knowing when it would, there could be no question of any equality. In particular, there could be no equality of rights, for that would risk dragging us in the direction of very dangerous "democratic" deviations.

This understanding on the notion of equality was not spelled out in a resolution from the congress. But, essentially, the two camps that clashed at the congress were agreed in regarding the idea of equality as intolerable.

Formerly, and not all that long ago, the Bolsheviks spoke quite a different language. It was under the banner of equality that they operated during the great Russian revolution, to overthrow the bourgeoisie, in concert with the workers and peasants, at whose expense they rose to political control over the country. It was under those colors that, after eight years of ruling over the lives and liberties of the toilers of the former Russia—henceforth to be known as the "Union of Soviet Socialist Republics" the Bolshevik tsars sought to persuade the toilers of that "Union," (oppressed by them), as well as the toilers from other countries (which they do not yet control), that if they have persecuted, left to rot in prison or deported and murdered their political enemies, this has been done exclusively in the name of the revolution, its egalitarian foundations (which they allegedly had introduced into the revolution) which their enemies supposedly wished to destroy.

It shall soon be eight years since the blood of anarchists began to flow because of their refusal to servilely bow before the violence or effrontery of those who have seized power, nor before their famously lying ideology and their utter irresponsibility.

In that criminal act, an act that cannot be described as other than a bloodlust of the Bolshevik gods, the finest offspring of the revolution have perished because they were the most loyal exponents of revolutionary ideals and because they could not be bribed into betraying them. In honestly defending the precepts of the revolution, these children of the revolution sought to fend off the madness of the Bolshevik gods and find a way out of their dead end, so as to forge a path to real freedom and genuine equality of the toilers.

The Bolshevik potentates quickly realized that the aspirations of these children of the revolution would spell doom for their madness and above all for the privileges they adroitly inherited from the toppled bourgeoisie, then treacherously beefed up to their advantage. On these grounds they condemned the revolutionaries to death. Men with the souls of slaves supported them in this and the blood flowed. For the past eight years it has gone on flowing, and in the name of what, we might ask? In the name of freedom and equality of the toilers, say the Bolsheviks, continuing to exterminate thousands of nameless revolutionaries, fighters for the social revolution, labeled as "bandits" and "counter-revolutionaries."

With that shameless falsehood, the Bolsheviks have hidden the true state of affairs in Russia from the eyes of toilers the world over, particularly their utter bankruptcy in the matter of building socialism, when this is all too apparent to all who have the eyes to see.

Anarchists alerted toilers of every country in time to the Bolsheviks' crimes in the Russian revolution. Bolshevism, embodying the ideal of a centralizing State, has shown itself as the deadly enemy of the free spirit of revolutionary toilers. Resorting to unprecedented measures, it has sabotaged the development of the revolution and besmirched the honor of its finest aspect. Successfully disguised, it concealed its real face from the gaze of the toilers, passing itself off as the champion of their interests. Only now, after an eight years' reign, increasingly flirting with the international bourgeoisie, does it begin to cast aside its mask of revolution and expose to the world of labor the face of a rapacious exploiter.

The Bolsheviks have jettisoned the idea of equality, not just in practice but also in theory, for the very enunciation of it strikes them as dangerous now. This is quite understandable, for their entire rule depends on a diametrically contrasting notion, on a screaming inequality, the entire horror and evils of which have battened upon the backs of the workers. Let us hope that the toilers of every country may draw the necessary conclusions and, in turn, finish with the Bolsheviks, those exponents of the idea of slavery and oppressors of Labor.

The State and Revolution: Theory and Practice

Iain McKay

There were three Revolutions in 1917—the February revolution which started spontaneously with strikes on International Women's Day; the October revolution when the majority of the Second All-Russian Congress of Soviets voted to elect a Bolshevik government; and what the Russian anarchist Voline termed "The Unknown Revolution" in between when the workers and peasants started to push the revolution from a mere political change into a *social* transformation.

This Unknown Revolution saw the recreation of the soviets first seen during the revolution of 1905 based on delegates elected from workplaces subject to recall, workers creating unions and factory committees and peasants seizing land back from the landlords while unprecedented political freedoms were taken for granted after the tyranny of Tsarism. Hope for a better future spread around the globe and the October Revolution was welcomed by many on the revolutionary left—anarchists included—as the culmination of this process.

Yet by 1921 anarchists had broken with the regime after the crushing of the Kronstadt rebellion for soviet freedom. The Bolshevik State was, rightly, denounced politically as being a party dictatorship and economically as state-capitalist. How did this happen?

It would be impossible to cover all aspects of Leninist ideology and practice as well as the anarchist alternative, so here I will indicate the main factors at work in the process. Lenin's *The State and Revolution*[1] is taken as the focus for, written during 1917, it expresses the aspirations of Bolshevism in its best light—as shown by the

---

[1]. V.I. Lenin, "The State and Revolution: The Marxist Theory of the State and the Tasks of the Proletariat in the Revolution," in *The Lenin Anthology*, Robert C. Tucker, ed. (New York: W. W. Norton, 1975), 311–398.

fact that even today Leninists recommend we read it in order to see why we should join their party. We will compare the rhetoric of Lenin's work to the reality of the regime that was created, the theory to the practice. By doing that we can see why the revolution degenerated and better understand—to use Alexander Berkman's expression—"the Bolshevik myth" in order to learn from history rather than repeat it.[2]

Theory

When Lenin returned to Russia in April 1917, he quickly came into conflict with his colleagues by taking a radical position. Instead of arguing—in line with Marxist orthodoxy—that Russia faced a bourgeois revolution and so required the creation of a republic and capitalism, he argued that the revolution be intensified and pushed toward *social* transformation by means of the creation of a new State based on the soviets. This and continued opposition to the Imperialist war saw the Bolsheviks gain more and more influence, going from a small sect to a mass party in the space of a few months.

He wrote *The State and Revolution* during this heady period aiming to theoretically justify this change in perspective. It was primarily directed at those within the Marxist movement who disagreed with Lenin as well as, to a lesser degree, anarchists. The two are related because Lenin's positions on the need for *social* transformation and opposition to both sides in capitalist conflicts had previously only been advocated by anarchists.[3]

---

2. Excellent anarchist analyses of the Russian Revolution include: Emma Goldman, *My Disillusionment in Russia* (New York: Thomas Y. Crowell Company, 1970); Alexander Berkman, *The Bolshevik Myth* (London: Pluto Press, 1989); Voline, *The Unknown Revolution* (Detroit/Chicago: Black & Red/Solidarity, 1974); GP Maximoff, *The Guillotine At Work: The Leninist Counter-Revolution* (Sanday: Cienfuegos Press, 1979); Ida Mett, *The Kronstadt Uprising* (London: Solidarity, 1967); Goldman and Berkman, *To Remain Silent is Impossible: Emma Goldman and Alexander Berkman in Russia*, Andrew Zonneveld, ed. (Atlanta: On Our Own Authority!, 2013).

3. For the 1905 revolution, see Peter Kropotkin's articles "The Revolution in Russia," "The Russian Revolution and Anarchism," and "Enough of Illusions" in *Direct Struggle Against Capital: A Peter Kropotkin Anthology*, Iain McKay, ed. (Edinburgh/Oakland/Balti-

The "bourgeoisie and the opportunists within the labour movement concur in this doctoring of Marxism. They omit, obscure, or distort the revolutionary side of this theory, its revolutionary soul" and so "our prime task is to re-establish what Marx really taught on the subject of the state." Lenin does, as he promised, provide "a number of long quotations from the works of Marx and Engels themselves" yet has to provide commentary in order to ensure that the reader interprets them correctly.[4] This is because Marx and Engels argued differently than Lenin suggests. Similarly, his comments on anarchism—as well as distorting it—fail to address the real issues between it and Marxism.[5]

Lenin argued that "[o]nly he is a Marxist who extends the recognition of the class struggle to the recognition of the dictatorship of the proletariat."[6] The revolution requires "that the 'special coercive force' for the suppression of the proletariat by the bourgeoisie, of millions of working people by handfuls of the rich, must be replaced by a 'special coercive force' for the suppression of the bourgeoisie by the proletariat (the dictatorship of the proletariat)."[7] The aim was "to overthrow the bourgeoisie, to destroy bourgeois parliamentarism, for a democratic republic after the type of the [Paris] Commune, or a republic of Soviets of Workers' and Soldiers' Deputies, for the revolutionary dictatorship of the proletariat."[8] For the "proletariat needs state power, a centralised organisation of force, an organisation of violence, both to crush the resistance of the exploiters and to *lead* the enormous mass of the population—the peasants, the petty bourgeoisie, and semi-proletarians—in the work of organising a socialist economy."[9]

The current State was bourgeois and had to be smashed and replaced by a new kind of State and "it is precisely this

more: AK Press, 2014). For his refusal to take sides in the imperialist Russo-Japanese War, see "La Guerre russo-japonaise," *Les Temps Nouveaux*, 5 March 1904.

4. Lenin, *The Lenin Anthology*, 313.

5. Space precludes discussing every aspect of this, for further discussion see section H of *An Anarchist FAQ (AFAQ)* Vol. 2 (Edinburgh/Oakland: AK Press, 2012).

6. Lenin, *The Lenin Anthology*, 334.

7. Ibid., 322.

8. Ibid., 396.

9. Ibid., 328.

fundamental point which has been completely ignored by the dominant official Social-Democratic parties and, indeed, distorted [...] by the foremost theoretician of the Second International, Karl Kautsky."[10] According to Lenin, the anarchists fail to understand that this new State is needed just as they fail to understand that the "organ of suppression" is "the majority of the population, and not a minority, as was always the case under slavery, serfdom, and wage slavery. And since the majority of people itself suppresses its oppressors, a 'special force' for suppression is no longer necessary! In this sense, the state begins to wither away."[11] Therefore the State cannot be abolished as anarchists claim but it can and will disappear.

The practice of the Bolshevik regime did not match the theory but first we need to discuss the theoretical problems of Lenin's argument in order to understand why this happened, for bad theory produces bad practice.

The Paris Commune

The core of Lenin's argument rests on the Paris Commune of 1871 and the lessons Marx and Engels drew from it. Yet he fails to mention key aspects of this event and, like Marx and Engels, provides a superficial analysis of it. This is in stark contrast to some anarchists, for example Kropotkin wrote far more on the Commune than Marx or Engels.

The key aspect of the Commune for Lenin is summarized by this quote from Marx: "One thing especially was proved by the Commune, viz., that 'the working class cannot simply lay hold of the ready-made state machinery and wield it for its own purposes.'"[12] Marx is also quoted on how it "was to be a working, not a parliamentary, body, executive and legislative at the same time." It, Lenin summarised, "replaced the smashed state machine 'only' by

---

10. Ibid., 329.
11. Ibid., 340.
12. Ibid., 336.

fuller democracy: abolition of the standing army; all officials to be elected and subject to recall" and "was ceasing to be a state since it had to suppress, not the majority of the population, but a minority (the exploiters). It had smashed the bourgeois state machine. In place of a special coercive force the population itself came on the scene. All this was a departure from the state in the proper sense of the word."[13]

Yet the Paris Commune was not a new State structure at all but rather was a transformed municipal council. Indeed, Lenin quotes Marx on how the Commune "was formed of the municipal councillors, chosen by universal suffrage in the various wards of the town, responsible and revocable at any time."[14] After the initial (spontaneous) insurrection on March 18th the Central Committee of the Paris National Guard refused to take power itself and instead called elections to the *existing* municipal council with its members elected from the *existing* municipal wards by means of (male) universal suffrage. The Commune, then, was no soviet.[15]

The *practical* conclusions that Marx and Engels drew from it were—as before it—that workers should organise in political parties and take part in "political action" to capture the State on the national level in the same way as the Communards had locally. Lenin confuses smashing the State *machine* with smashing the State itself.

It is also important to note that Marx's *The Civil War in France* is his most appealing work because it is mostly reporting what had happened during a revolution inspired by anarchist ideas. While Marx failed to mention it, the driving force behind the Commune's proclamations were Internationalists influenced by Proudhon. To see this we need simply compare Proudhon's position during the 1848 Revolution to that applied—and praised by Marx—in 1871:

---

13. Ibid., 341, 339, 357.
14. Ibid., 339.
15. Marx later suggested (in 1881) that it was "merely the rising of a city under exceptional conditions, the majority of the Commune was in no wise socialist, nor could it be." Karl Max and Friedrich Engels, *Marx-Engels Collected Works* (MECW) Vol. 46 (London: Lawrence & Wishart, 1992), 66

We do not want the government of man by man any more than the exploitation of man by man [...] It is up to the National Assembly, through organisation of its committees, to exercise executive power, just the way it exercises legislative power through its joint deliberations and votes. [...] socialism is the contrary of governmentalism. [...] Besides universal suffrage and as a consequence of universal suffrage, we want implementation of the imperative mandate [*mandat impératif*]. Politicians balk at it! Which means that in their eyes, the people, in electing representatives, does not appoint mandatories but rather abjure their sovereignty!... That is assuredly not socialism: it is not even democracy.[16]

Lenin, like Marx, forgets to mention that the Communards called themselves *Fédérés* ("Federals"). As such, his complaint "that the renegade [Eduard] Bernstein" suggested "as far as its political content" went Marx's programme "displays, in all its essential features, the greatest similarity to the federalism of Proudhon" ignores the awkward fact that in-so-far-as Marx reports accurately on the revolt, he cannot help but appear to be a federalist.[17]

Lenin seems ignorant of what federalism means. The whole point of federalism is to co-ordinate activity *at the appropriate level* (and so cannot be anything other than bottom-up). Centralism, in contrast, co-ordinates *everything* at the centre (and so cannot be anything other than top-down). So when Lenin proclaims that when Marx "purposely used" certain words (such as "National unity was... to be organised") to "oppose conscious, democratic, proletarian centralism to bourgeois, military, bureaucratic centralism" he was completely missing the point.[18]

Likewise, Proudhon wrote of how "to create national unity [...] from the bottom to the top, from the circumference to the centre" and under federalism "the attributes of the central authority

---

16. *Property is Theft!: A Pierre-Joseph Proudhon Anthology* (Edinburgh/Oakland/Baltimore: AK Press, 2011), 378–9; he had argued this from the very first days of the revolution: "we are all voters [...] We can do more; we can follow them step-by-step in [...] their votes; we will make them transmit our arguments [...]; we will suggest our will to them, and when we are discontented, we will recall and dismiss them," 273.
17. Lenin, *The Lenin Anthology*, 346.
18. Ibid., 348.

become specialised and limited" to "concerning federal services."[19] So the Communards talking of organising national unity and (to quote Marx) how a "few but important functions which would still remain for a central government were not to be suppressed, as had been deliberately mis-stated, but were to be transferred to communal, i.e., strictly responsible, officials" is an *expression* of federalism and *not* its denial.[20] That Marx confuses the highest federal body with "a central government" does not change this.

Similarly, Proudhon also argued that it was "necessary to disarm the powers that be" by ending military conscription and "organis[ing] a citizens' army." It "is the right of the citizens to appoint the hierarchy of their military chiefs, the simple soldiers and national guards appointing the lower ranks of officers, the officers appointing their superiors." In this way "the army retains its civic feelings" while the People "organise its military in such a way as to simultaneously guarantee its defence and its liberties." Moreover, he predated Lenin on "the replacement of bourgeois democracy by proletarian democracy"[21] by contrasting "labour democracy" to existing forms.[22]

Given this obvious influence, it is not the case that "[t]o confuse Marx's view on the 'destruction of state power, a parasitic excrescence', with Proudhon's federalism is positively monstrous!"[23] For the Communards *were* federalists and while Lenin proclaimed that there is "not a trace of federalism in Marx's above-quoted observation on the experience of the Commune" there had to be if his account were remotely accurate.[24] That before and after the Commune Marx was a centralist does not distract from his reporting on the Communards but it does mean we cannot, as Lenin wishes, take *The Civil War in France* as the definitive account of his ideas on social transformation.

While for Lenin Marx had "tried to draw practical lessons" from and so "'learned' from the Commune," in fact anarchists

19. *Property is Theft!*, 447, 698.
20. Lenin, *The Lenin Anthology*, 346.
21. Ibid., 388.
22. Proudhon, *Property is Theft!*, 407, 443–4, 724, 750, 763.
23. Lenin, *The Lenin Anthology*, 347.
24. Ibid.

provided a deeper analysis of the revolt.[25] For Kropotkin, by "proclaiming the free Commune, the people of Paris proclaimed an essential anarchist principle" but "they stopped mid-course" and gave "themselves a Communal Council copied from the old municipal councils." Thus the Paris Commune did not "break with the tradition of the State, of representative government, and it did not attempt to achieve within the Commune that organisation from the simple to the complex it inaugurated by proclaiming the independence and free federation of the Communes." The elected revolutionaries were isolated from the masses and shut-up in the town hall which lead to disaster as the Commune council became "immobilised, in the midst of paperwork," lost "the inspiration that comes from continual contact with the masses" and so "they themselves paralysed the popular initiative."[26] This is confirmed by one Marxist account of the Commune which admitted (in passing!) that the communal council was "overwhelmed" by suggestions from other bodies, the "sheer volume" of which "created difficulties" and it "found it hard to cope with the stream of people who crammed into the offices."[27]

Regardless of Lenin's assertions, the anarchists were right "to claim the Paris Commune as [...] a collaboration of their doctrine" and it is the Marxists who have "completely misunderstood its lessons."[28]

Opportunism

Lenin's work was directed against two main opponents in the Marxist movement, the Opportunists and the Kautskyites. The former were the reformist wing of the Social Democratic parties and most associated with Eduard Bernstein. The latter were their main opponents in the Second International and most associated

---

25. Ibid., 344.
26. Kropotkin, *Direct Struggle against Capital*, 446.
27. Donny Gluckstein, *The Paris Commune: A Revolutionary Democracy* (London: Bookmarks, 2006), 47–8.
28. Lenin, *The Lenin Anthology*, 385.

with Karl Kautsky. Until the outbreak of World War One Lenin considered himself a follower of Kautsky and repeatedly invoked his writings to show his Marxist orthodoxy (most infamously in *What is to be Done?* when he says, "socialist consciousness is something introduced into the proletarian class struggle from without" by "the *bourgeois intelligentsia*").[29]

Even as late as 1913 he praised the "fundamentals of parliamentary tactics" of German Social Democracy, which was "implacable on questions of principle and always directed to the accomplishment of the final aim."[30] As is well known, Lenin originally disbelieved news reports on German Social Democrat politicians voting for war credits in 1914 such was his faith in that party.

So while he was surprised that it had "turned out that in reality the German Social-Democratic Party was much more moderate and opportunist than it appeared to be"[31] anarchists were not for we had predicted and repeatedly denounced the obvious reformism in Social Democracy for decades.[32] Lenin doesn't discuss *why* "opportunism" developed in the first place, namely the Marxist tactic of *political* action by parties in elections rather than the anarchist one of *direct* action by workers' unions. As such, it was a striking confirmation of Bakunin's warnings that when "common workers" are sent "to Legislative Assemblies" the result is that the "worker-deputies, transplanted into a bourgeois environment, into an atmosphere of purely bourgeois ideas, will in fact cease to be workers and, becoming Statesmen, they will become bourgeois" for "men do not make their situations; on the contrary, men are made by them."[33] Indeed, "opportunism" existed in Social Democracy *from the start*—as can be seen from Lenin's admission that Bakunin's attacks were "justified" as the "people's state" was as "an absurdity" and "a departure from socialism" and so Engels

---

29. Ibid., 28.
30. Lenin, *Collected Works* Vol. 19 (Moscow: Progress Publishers, 1963), 298.
31. Lenin, *The Lenin Anthology*, 390.
32. See Kropotkin's "Socialism and Politics" and other texts included in *Direct Struggle Against Capital*.
33. *The Basic Bakunin: Writings 1869–71* (Buffalo: Prometheus Books, 1994), 108. That there was no real possibility of electioneering in Tsarist Russia allowed the Bolsheviks to avoid the fate of their sister parties in the Second International.

sought to "rid" German Social Democracy "of opportunist prejudices"[34] concerning the State... in 1875![35]

So while much of Lenin's book is commentary upon numerous quotes from Marx and Engels and contrasting his interpretation to the then-orthodox position, he fails to mention that he, like all Marxists before 1917, were "opportunists" in the sense of after having read Marx and Engels they concluded that "political action" would be used to capture "political power" which would then, in turn, be used to transform both State and society.[36]

The reason for this is obvious: Lenin confuses smashing the State machine with smashing the State itself. He is right that "it was Marx who taught that the proletariat cannot simply win state power in the sense that the old state apparatus passes into new hands, but must smash this apparatus, must break it and replace it by a new one."[37] He is wrong in that Marx thought it would be achieved without first securing universal suffrage and then a majority in the legislature. As such, when Lenin states that Kautsky "speaks of the winning of state power—and no more" and so "has chosen a formula which makes a concession to the opportunists, inasmuch as it admits the possibility of seizing power without destroying the state machine" he misses the point.[38] This can be seen in quotes from Marx and Engels that Lenin himself provides and to which he feels the need to add commentary to what should be self-evident comments.[39]

34. Lenin, *The Lenin Anthology*, 357.
35. It may be the case that "every state is not 'free' and not a 'people's state'" but "Marx and Engels explained this repeatedly to their party comrades in the seventies" (Lenin, *The Lenin Anthology*, 323) only in *private* letters. Publicly, *Der Volksstaat* (*The People's State*) was the central organ of the *Social Democratic Workers Party of Germany* between 1869 and 1876 and Marx and Engels regularly contributed to it. So the "opportunist" notion of a *Volkstaat* was associated with the party most influenced by Marx and Engels. Moreover, "People's State" was used in the same way that modern-day Leninists use the term "Workers' State" to describe their new regime. Opportunism does not lie, surely, in the *words* used?
36. As Kautsky noted in 1919. Karl Kautsky and John H. Kautsky, *The Road to Power: Political Reflections on Growing into the Revolution* (Atlantic Highlands: Humanities Press, 1996), 34, xlviii.
37. Lenin, *The Lenin Anthology*, 392.
38. Ibid., 387.
39. This, by necessity, is just a selection of the evidence. See section H.3.10 of *AFAQ* for further analysis. For a similar account but from a more-or-less orthodox Marxist perspective, see Binay Sarker and Adam Buick, *Marxism-Leninism—Poles Apart* (Memari:

Thus, after providing a long quote by Engels, Lenin has to add "Engels speaks here of the proletariat revolution 'abolishing' the *bourgeois* state, while the words about the state withering away refer to the remnants of the *proletarian* state *after* the socialist revolution" when Engels himself makes no such distinction and just talks of the State. Similarly, he quotes Engels on how, "If one thing is certain it is that our party and the working class can only come to power in the form of the democratic republic" and that this "is even the specific form for the dictatorship of the proletariat, as the Great French Revolution has already shown" before feeling the need to add—presumably hoping his readers would not notice that Engels said no such thing—that "Engels realised here in a particularly striking form the fundamental idea which runs through all of Marx's works, namely, that the democratic republic is the nearest approach to the dictatorship of the proletariat."[40] Thus "the specific form" becomes "the nearest approach"![41]

Engels repeatedly suggested that "the republic" is "the ready-made political form for the future rule of the proletariat" which in France "is already in being"[42] and did so in the text Lenin quotes:

> So, then, a unified republic [...] From 1792 to 1798 each French department, each commune [*Gemeinde*], enjoyed complete self-government on the American model, and this is what we too must have. How self-government is to be organised and how we can manage, without a bureaucracy has been shown to us by America and the first French Republic, and is being shown even today by Australia, Canada and the other English colonies.[43]

There is no mention of the Paris Commune *at all* in Engels's critique of the draft of the Erfurt Programme, which is significant given Lenin proclaims that it "cannot be ignored; for it is with

Avenel Press, 2012).

40. Lenin, *The Lenin Anthology*, 322, 360.

41. Julius Martov, leader of the Menshevik-Internationalists, noted this in his important critique of Lenin in "Decomposition or Conquest of the State," *The State and The Socialist Revolution* (New York: International Review, 1938), 40–1.

42. Marx-Engels, *MECW* Vol. 50 (London: Lawrence & Wishart, 2004), 276.

43. Lenin, *The Lenin Anthology*, 362.

the *opportunist* views of the Social-Democrats on questions of *state* organisation that this criticism is mainly concerned."[44]

This position is consistent with Marx's comments on "smashing" the State machine which Lenin thinks is so important. This is because it is possible to argue that political action can be used to capture political power and that the first action of the victorious party is to smash the State bureaucracy—as Engels confirmed in an 1884 letter when asked to clarify this precise point by Bernstein:

> It is simply a question of showing that the victorious proletariat must first refashion the old bureaucratic, administrative centralised state power before it can use it for its own purposes: whereas all bourgeois republicans since 1848 inveighed against this machinery so long as they were in the opposition, but once they were in the government they took it over without altering it and used it partly against the reaction but still more against the proletariat.[45]

Which reflects Marx's earlier comment (quoted by Lenin) on the "executive power with its enormous bureaucratic and military organisation, with its vast and ingenious state machinery, with a host of officials numbering half a million, besides an army of another half million, this appalling parasitic body [...] All revolutions perfected this machine instead of smashing it."[46] So unlike anarchists—who, from Proudhon onwards, had argued that it was "inevitably enchained to capital and directed against the proletariat"[47]—Marxists had viewed the bourgeois State as not only able to be captured but reformed in the interests of the working class.

The fundamental difference between the Opportunists and Kautskyites was that the former simply wished the party to revise the rhetoric used to bring it in line with its (reformist) practice

---

44. Ibid., 358.
45. Marx-Engels, *MECW* Vol. 47 (London: Lawrence & Wishart, 1995), 74; This perspective is reflected a passage in a draft of Marx's *The Civil War in France* found in Marx-Engels, *MECW* Vol. 22 (London: Lawrence & Wishart, 1986), 533.
46. Lenin, *The Lenin Anthology*, 329.
47. Proudhon, *Property is Theft!*, 226.

while the latter insisted that the rhetoric remain revolutionary. However, both utilised the same tactics and aimed for the same thing—a Social Democratic majority. The former wished to use the existing State machine to implement reforms to the system and saw no need to smash that machinery or quickly transform the system. The latter remained true to Marx and argued that to secure the proletariat as the ruling class, parliament would have to smash that machine in order to replace capitalism with socialism.

Given that the Paris Commune had utilised a part of the current State—the Parisian municipal council—to abolish the State machine, it is easy to see why Lenin's interpretation of Marx and Engels took until 1917 to be formulated, particularly given their well-known support for electioneering and opposition to anarchist calls to smash the State and replace it with a new form of social organisation based on federations of workers' groupings.

Before turning to this, I must note that Lenin, while finding the time to berate Bernstein for having "more than once repeated the vulgar bourgeois jeers at 'primitive' democracy" and how he "combats the ideas of 'primitive' democracy"—"binding mandates, unpaid officials, impotent central representative bodies, etc."—to "prove" that this "is unsound" and "refers to the experience of the British trade unions, as interpreted by the Webbs,"[48] he failed to note how he refers to the same book in *What is to be Done?* in order to prove "the absurdity of such a conception of democracy."[49]

Anarchism

If Lenin's account of Marxism leaves much to be desired, this is nothing compared to the nonsense he inflicts on anarchism. To describe Lenin's understanding of Anarchism as superficial would be generous. He summarises what he considers the differences between Marxists and anarchists:

---

48. Lenin, *The Lenin Anthology*, 340, 394.
49. Ibid., 90.

(1) The former, while aiming at the complete abolition of the state, recognise that this aim can only be achieved after classes have been abolished by the socialist revolution, as the result of the establishment of socialism, which leads to the withering away of the state. The latter want to abolish the state completely overnight, not understanding the conditions under which the state can be abolished. (2) The former recognise that after the proletariat has won political power it must completely destroy the old state machine and replace it by a new one consisting of an organisation of the armed workers, after the type of the Commune. The latter, while insisting on the destruction of the state machine, have a very vague idea of what the proletariat will put in its place and how it will use its revolutionary power. The anarchists even deny that the revolutionary proletariat should use the state power, they reject its revolutionary dictatorship. (3) The former demand that the proletariat be trained for revolution by utilising the present state. The anarchists reject this.[50]

First, regardless of Lenin's suggestions of "overnight" revolutions, anarchists had never viewed social revolution in that way. Quite the opposite, as anarchists have *always* stressed that revolutions are difficult and take time, as well they *explicitly* reject the notion of "one-day" revolutions. Kropotkin argued that while it may be possible to "topple and change a government in one day," a revolution, "if it is to achieve a tangible outcome [...] *takes three or four years of revolutionary upheaval*."[51] Then the working class would be in a position to finally smash the State and capitalism its revolt had weakened, and so be free to start constructing a new society.

The element of truth in Lenin's statement is that anarchists *do* reject the Marxist notion that we need a State to rebuild and defend society after a successful revolution. This is because of our differing analyses of what the State is. Both agree that all

---

50. Ibid., 392.
51. Kropotkin, *Direct Struggle against Capital*, 553; also see sections H.3.5 and I.2.2 of *AFAQ*.

States, current and previous, are instruments of class rule, that class being the minority of oppressors and exploiters who have monopolised social wealth. Marxists think that a State—whether a suitably transformed republic (Kautsky, Lenin before 1917) or a new soviet-State (Lenin in 1917)—can be the instrument of the majority, of the working class, for it is simply "a special force for the suppression of a particular class."[52] Anarchists reject this analysis and argue that the State institution is marked by certain structures that allow it to do its task and that the State develops its own interests. The "dictatorship of the proletariat" would soon become the "dictatorship *over* the proletariat."

This is because the State is an "organisation of hierarchical centralisation" and is "necessarily hierarchical, authoritarian—or it ceases to be the State." It is "the absorption of the whole national life, concentrated into a pyramid of functionaries."[53] This structure did not appear by accident. What is striking about Lenin's account of the State is that he never, ever wonders *why* this social structure has taken the form it has. The bourgeois State is centralised and the proletarian State will likewise be—and any attempts to suggest Marx was a federalist are dismissed (albeit, correctly!) for he "upheld democratic centralism, the republic—one and indivisible."[54]

Yet hierarchical and centralised structures are needed for a minority to rule. They exclude the masses from participation in social life. As Proudhon argued:

And who benefits from this regime of unity? The people? No, the upper classes [...] Unity [...] is quite simply a form of bourgeois exploitation under the protection of bayonets. Yes, political unity, in the great States, is bourgeois: the positions which it creates, the intrigues which it causes, the influences which it cherishes, all that is bourgeois and goes to the bourgeois.[55]

52. Lenin, The Lenin Anthology, 340.
53. Kropotkin, La Science moderne et l'anarchie (Paris : Stock, 1913), 135, 164, 329.
54. Lenin, The Lenin Anthology, 361.
55. La fédération et l'unité en Italie (Paris: E. Dentu, 1862), 27–8.

The centralised, hierarchical, state is "the cornerstone of bourgeois despotism and exploitation."[56] Under the rising bourgeoisie, Kropotkin noted, "the State was the sole judge" which meant that "all the local, insignificant disputes [...] piled up in the form of documents in the offices" and "parliament was literally inundated by thousands of these minor local squabbles. It then took thousands of functionaries in the capital—most of them corruptible—to read, classify, evaluate all these, to pronounce on the smallest detail" and "the flood [of issues] always rose!"[57] The same process would be at work in the new so-called semi-State as it, too, was centralised and so had "a whole new administrative network in order to extend its writ and enforce obedience."[58] This was why anarchists sought to decentralise decision making away from one central body into federations of workplace and community associations and wondered why Marxists had "adopted the ideal of the *Jacobin State* when this ideal had been designed from the viewpoint of the bourgeois, in direct opposition to the egalitarian and communist tendencies of the people which had arisen during the [French] Revolution."[59]

Lenin confuses social organisation with the State and misses the point by saying we "cannot imagine democracy, even proletarian democracy, without representative institutions, but we can and must imagine democracy without parliamentarism"[60] for while *any* organisation requires delegates to co-ordinate decisions it is a mistake to confuse this with representative—and so centralised—government. So if "[u]nder socialism *all* will govern in turn and

---

56. Proudhon, *La fédération et l'unité en Italie*, 33.
57. Kropotkin, *La Science moderne et l'anarchie*, 219–220.
58. Kropotkin, *Direct Struggle against Capital*, 509.
59. Kropotkin, *La Science moderne et l'anarchie*, 329; "Attacks upon the central authorities, stripping these of their prerogatives, de-centralisation, dispersing authority would have amounted to abandoning its affairs to the people and would have run the risk of a genuinely popular revolution. Which is why the bourgeoisie is out to strengthen the central government still further" and why the working class, "not about to abdicate their rights to the care of the few, will seek some new form of organisation that allows them to manage their affairs for themselves," from Kropotkin, *Direct Struggle against Capital*, 232, 228.
60. Lenin, *The Lenin Anthology*, 343–44.

will soon become accustomed to no one governing"[61] under Anarchism, rather than having a series of rulers, all would participate in decision making and the "centralistic, bureaucratic and military organisation" of the State which operates "from the top down and from centre to periphery" will be replaced "with a federal organisation" of associations and communes "from the bottom up, from periphery to centre" with "elective officials answerable to the people, and with arming of the nation."[62]

The question is whether these elected bodies are focused on specific tasks at appropriate levels or whether they, like Parliaments, dictate all social matters from the centre. In both cases "representative" institutions remain, in the sense that specific individuals are elected to specific bodies. But Lenin confused the matter by saying the "way out of parliamentarism is not, of course, the abolition of representative institutions and the elective principle, but the conversion of the representative institutions from talking shops into 'working' bodies."[63] This is only part of what is needed, as the question of centralisation is key for it greatly decreases popular participation and vastly increases bureaucratic tendencies.

For Lenin, the "exploiting classes need political rule to maintain exploitation, i.e., in the selfish interests of an insignificant minority against the vast majority of all people" while the "exploited classes need political rule in order to completely abolish all exploitation."[64] Anarchists agree with the first part but disagree with the second. Political rule—a State—*is* needed for a minority class to dominate society and is structured appropriately (hierarchical, centralised, top-down). It is not needed—indeed, defeats the aim—when we are talking about formerly exploited classes ("the vast majority") running society simply because it is not structured to allow that. By creating a new centralised social structure, Marxists create the conditions for the birth of a new ruling

61. Ibid., 395.
62. Bakunin, *No Gods, No Masters: An Anthology of Anarchism*, Daniel Guérin, ed. (Edinburgh/San Francisco: AK Press 2005), 162.
63. Lenin, *The Lenin Anthology*, 342.
64. Ibid., 327.

class—*the bureaucracy*. This is why anarchists reject the notion of using a State to build socialism:

> The State, with its hierarchy of functionaries and the weight of its historical traditions, could only delay the dawning of a new society freed from monopolies and exploitation [...] what means can the State provide to abolish this monopoly that the working class could not find in its own strength and groups? [...] what advantages could the State provide for abolishing these same [class] privileges? Could its governmental machine, developed for the creation and upholding of these privileges, now be used to abolish them? Would not the new function require new organs? And these new organs would they not have to be created by the workers themselves, in *their* unions, *their* federations, completely outside the State?[65]

Lenin is also keen to confuse the need to defend a revolution with the State and quotes from a polemic Marx addressed to the reformist mutualists, generalising it to all anarchists:

> Marx chooses the sharpest and clearest way of stating his case against the anarchists: After overthrowing the yoke of the capitalists, should the workers 'lay down their arms', or use them against the capitalists in order to crush their resistance? But what is the systematic use of arms by one class against another if not a 'transient form' of state?[66]

So, according to Marx and Engels, the anarchists urged the working class to rise in insurrection against the bourgeoisie and its State and, once victorious, then simply put down its arms? It is difficult to take this seriously—particularly as it confuses defence of a revolution (of freedom) with the State. Lenin, like Marx and Engels, join those who "believe that after having brought down government and private property we would allow both to be

---

65. Kropotkin, *La Science moderne et l'anarchie*, 91–2.
66. Lenin, *The Lenin Anthology*, 353.

quietly built up again, because of a respect for the *freedom* of those who might feel the need to be rulers and property owners. A truly curious way of interpreting our ideas!"[67] Lenin suggests that the "armed workers who proceed to form a militia involving the entire population" is "a more democratic state machine."[68] Yet if the State were simply this then there would be no disagreement between Anarchism and Marxism:

> Immediately after established governments have been overthrown, communes will have to reorganise themselves along revolutionary lines [...] In order to defend the revolution, their volunteers will at the same time form a communal militia. But no commune can defend itself in isolation. So it will be necessary to radiate revolution outward, to raise all of its neighbouring communes in revolt [...] and to federate with them for common defence.[69]

Lenin's innovation was to move away from the orthodox Marxist position on the State toward the anarchist position that socialism must be built by the workers' themselves using the organisations they themselves create in the struggle against capitalism. However, he linked this to a continued Marxist prejudice in favour of centralised structures and so his assertion that the new regime "is no longer the state proper" was simply not true for in a centralised structure power rests at the top, in the hands of a minority—with its own (class) interests.[70] So when Lenin argued that "we shall fight for the complete destruction of the old state machine, in order that the armed proletariat itself *may become the government*"[71] anarchists simply note that in a centralised structure it would be the Marxist party leadership who would become the government, *not* the armed proletariat:

---

67. Errico Malatesta, *Anarchy* (London: Freedom Press, 2001) 42–3.
68. Lenin, *The Lenin Anthology*, 383.
69. Bakunin, *No Gods, No Masters*, 164; also see section H.2.1 of *AFAQ*.
70. Lenin, *The Lenin Anthology*, 340; also see section H.3.9 of *AFAQ*.
71. Lenin, *The Lenin Anthology*, 396.

By popular government the marxians mean government of the people by means of a small number of representatives elected through universal suffrage [...] government of the vast majority of the masses of the people by a privileged minority. But this minority, the marxians argue, will be made up of workers. Yes, to be sure, of former workers who, as soon as they become the people's governors and representatives, will stop being workers and will begin to look down upon the proletarian world from the heights of the State: they will then represent, not the people, but themselves and their ambitions to govern it. Anyone who queries that does not know human nature.[72]

In a centralised "one and indivisible" republic, electing, mandating, and recalling become increasingly meaningless—it would require millions of electors at the base across the country to simultaneously act in the same manner to have any impact. This means that there is substantial space for the interests of the State to diverge from the people and, as Bakunin warned, "the State cannot be sure of its own self-preservation without an armed force to defend it against its own *internal enemies*, against the discontent of its own people."[73]

Which is why, while recognising the need for insurrection and defence of the revolution, anarchists seek to abolish the State and replace it with a social structure more appropriate for building socialism—for "whenever a new economic form emerges in the life of a nation—when serfdom, for example, came to replace slavery, and later on wage-labour for serfdom—a new form of political grouping always had to develop" and so "economic emancipation will be accomplished by smashing the old political forms represented by the State. Man will be forced to find new forms of organisation for the social functions that the State apportioned between its functionaries."[74]

Second, the claim that anarchists have only a "vague" notion of what will replace the State is simply wrong. Proclaiming that

---

72. Bakunin, *No Gods, No Masters*, 195.
73. *Michael Bakunin: Selected Writings* (London: Jonathan Cape, 1973), 265.
74. Kropotkin, *La Science moderne et l'anarchie*, 98–9.

anarchists argue that we "must think only of destroying the old state machine" and "it is no use probing into the concrete lessons of earlier proletarian revolutions and analysing what to put in the place of what has been destroyed, and how," flies in the face of the many articles and books in which anarchists did precisely that.[75] To quote Bakunin:

> Workers, no longer count on anyone but yourselves [...] Abstain from all participation in bourgeois radicalism and organise outside of it the forces of the proletariat. The basis of that organisation is entirely given: the workshops and the federation of the workshops; the creation of funds for resistance, instruments of struggle against the bourgeoisie, and their federation not just nationally, but internationally. The creation of Chambers of Labour [...] the liquidation of the State and of bourgeois society [...] Anarchy, that it to say the true, the open popular revolution [...] organisation, from top to bottom and from the circumference to the centre.[76]

The "Chambers of Labour" were federations of local unions grouped by territory. Bakunin's visions of revolution predicted the workers' councils of 1905 and 1917. Likewise, Kropotkin argued that "independent Communes for the *territorial* groupings, and vast federations of trade unions for groupings *by social functions*—the two interwoven and providing support to each to meet the needs of society—allowed the anarchists to conceptualise in a real, concrete way the possible organisation of a liberated society"—based on an analysis of both the workers' movement and the Paris Commune as well as the history of the State.[77]

Yet, Lenin claimed that "anarchists dismissed the question of political forms altogether."[78]

Similarly, he was wrong to proclaim that if the workers and peasants "organise themselves quite freely in communes, and *unite*

---

75. Lenin, *The Lenin Anthology*, 395.
76. "Letter to Albert Richard," *Anarcho-Syndicalist Review* no. 62, 18.
77. Kropotkin, *La Science moderne et l'anarchie*, 92.
78. Lenin, *The Lenin Anthology*, 349.

the action of all the communes in striking at capital, in crushing the resistance of the capitalists, and in transferring the privately-owned railways, factories, land and so on to the *entire* nation, to the whole of society" then that would "be the most consistent democratic centralism."[79] In fact it would be *federalism*:

> All productive capital and instruments of labour are to be confiscated for the benefit of toilers' associations [...] the Alliance of all labour associations [...] will constitute the Commune [...] there will be a standing federation of the barricades and a Revolutionary Communal Council [... made up of] delegates [...] invested with binding mandates and accountable and revocable at all times [...] all provinces, communes and associations [... will] delegate deputies to an agreed place of assembly (all [...] invested with binding mandated and accountable and subject to recall), in order to found the federation of insurgent associations, communes and provinces.[80]

Unsurprisingly then, it was Kropotkin and not Lenin who in 1905 saw the soviets as the means of both fighting and replacing the State as well as comparing them to the Paris Commune. Thus "the Council of workers [...] were appointed by the workers themselves—just like the insurrectional Commune of August 10, 1792." The council "completely recalls [...] the Central Committee which preceded the Paris Commune in 1871 and it is certain that workers across the country must organise themselves on this model [...] these councils represent the revolutionary strength of the working class. [...] Let no one come to proclaim to us that the workers of the Latin peoples, by preaching the general strike and direct action, were going down the wrong path. [...] A new force is thus constituted by the strike: the force of workers asserting themselves for the first time and putting in motion the lever of any revolution—direct action." The "urban workers [...] imitating the rebellious peasants [...] will likely be asked to put their hands on all that

---

79. Ibid., 348.
80. Bakunin, *No Gods, No Masters*, 181.

is necessary to live and produce. Then they can lay in the cities the initial foundations of the communist commune."[81]

In contrast, the Bolsheviks in 1905 could "find nothing better to do than to present the Soviet with an ultimatum: immediately adopt a Social-Democratic program or disband."[82] Nor did the Bolsheviks seek to transform or extend the revolution from bourgeois to socialist aims—unlike the anarchists. Given this, perhaps it was for the best that the October Revolution meant Lenin never wrote the second part of *The State and Revolution* that was to deal with the events of 1905.[83]

All of which makes a mockery of Lenin's assertion that "Anarchism has given nothing even approximating true answers to the concrete political questions: Must the old state machine be smashed? And what should be put in its place?"[84] Anarchism had advocated workers' councils as a means of both fighting and replacing capitalism and the State since Bakunin clashed with Marx in the International.

Third, those paying attention would have concluded that the fate of Social Democracy and its degeneration into "opportunism" would have shown why anarchists reject taking part in the State by contesting elections. This only "trains" workers in letting others act for them and so "disaccustom the people to the direct care of their own interests and schools the ones in slavishness and the others in intrigues and lies."[85] As Kropotkin stressed:

We see in the incapacity of the statist socialist to understand the true historical problem of socialism a gross error of judgement [...] To tell the workers that they will be able to introduce the socialist system *while retaining the machine of the State* and only

---

81. "L'Action directe et la Grève générale en Russie," *Les Temps Nouveaux*, 2 December 1905.

82. Trotsky, *Stalin: An Appraisal of the man and his influence* (London: Panther History, 1969), 106; Anweiler, *The Soviets: The Russian Workers, Peasants, and Soldiers Councils 1905–1921* (New York: Random House, 1974), 77–9.

83. Lenin, *The Lenin Anthology*, 397.

84. Ibid., 385.

85. Errico Malatesta, *The Method of Freedom: An Errico Malatesta Reader* (Oakland/Edinburgh: AK Press, 2014), 210; also see section J.2 of *AFAQ*.

changing the men in power; to prevent, instead of aiding, the mind of the workers progressing towards *the search for new forms of life* that would be *their* own—that is in our eyes a historic mistake which borders on the criminal.[86]

Instead of electioneering, "anarchists, since the beginnings of the International to the present, have taken an active part in the workers organisations formed for the direct struggle of Labour against Capital. This struggle, while serving far more power- fully than any indirect action to secure some improvements in the life of the worker and opening up the eyes of the workers to the evil done to society by capitalist organisation and by the State that upholds it, this struggle also awakes in the worker thoughts concerning the forms of consumption, production and direct exchange between those concerned, without the intervention of the capitalist and the State."[87]

Finally, Lenin's work is the source of the common assertion by Marxists that most anarchists supported their ruling class during the First World War. Regardless of his comment about "the few anarchists" who "preserved a sense of honour and a conscience"[88] by opposing the war, in reality pro-war anarchists in spite of having "amongst them comrades whom we love and respect most" were "not numerous" and "almost all" of the anarchists "have remained faithful to their convictions."[89] Nor does Lenin mention that these few—which, sadly, included Kropotkin—had rejected Bakunin's position (turn the imperialist war into a revolution) in favour of Engels's defence of the fatherland while, ironically, Lenin went the opposite way.[90]

---

86. Kropotkin, *La Science moderne et l'anarchie*, 124–5.
87. Kropotkin, *La Science moderne et l'anarchie*, 99–100.
88. Lenin, *The Lenin Anthology*, 380.
89. Malatesta, *The Method of Freedom*, 379, 385. Similarly, of the syndicalist unions only the CGT in France supported the war—unlike the vast the majority of Marxist parties and unions (significantly, the CGT was a member of the Marxist Second International).
90. As regards Lenin's rejection of Engels position, see "What Lenin Made of the Tes- tament of Engels" by the ex-communist Bertram D. Wolfe, *Marxism: One Hundred Years in the Life of a Doctrine* (New York: The Dial Press, 1965).

Socialism

The State and Revolution is primarily a study of political structures and an ideological defence for Lenin's new positions. There is very little in it on socialism or, more correctly, the initial steps the socialist State would take once power had been seized but those few words are significant.

The key factor for Lenin is not who manages production but rather who owns property. "The means of production are no longer the private property of individuals" but rather they would "belong to the whole of society" and while there would, initially, be differences in wealth "the *exploitation* of man by man will have become impossible because it will be impossible to seize the *means of production*—the factories, machines, land, etc.—and make them private property."[91]

Yet it is perfectly possible for exploitation to exist without private property—it depends on how society "owns" the means of production. Do workers manage their own labour or does someone else—the State—do that? Lenin's vision of socialism sets up the latter possibility by equating socialism with universal wage-labour rather than its abolition:

> *All* citizens are transformed into hired employees of the state [...] *All* citizens becomes employees and workers of a *single* country-wide state 'syndicate' [...] The whole of society will have become a single office and a single factory, with equality of labour and pay.[92]

There is some talk of how we "must *start* with the expropriation of the capitalists, with the establishment of workers' control over the capitalists" but why workers would need to control capitalists who have had their property expropriated is not immediately obvious. A closer read shows that Lenin had no desire to *immediately* expropriate the capitalists and introduce workers' management of production. Instead the capitalists would remain and

---

91. Lenin, *The Lenin Anthology*, 376, 377.
92. Ibid., 383.

control "must be exercised not by a state of bureaucrats, but by a state of *armed workers.*"[93]

While the political structures created by capitalism had to be smashed, the economic ones had to be used as the "economic foundation" for socialism[94]:

> A witty German Social-Democrat [...] called the *postal service* an example of the socialist economic system. This is very true. At the present the postal service is a business organised on the lines of state-*capitalist* monopoly. Imperialism is gradually transforming all trusts into organisations of a similar type, in which [...] one has the same bourgeois bureaucracy. But the mechanism of social management is here already to hand. Once we have overthrown the capitalists [...] and smashed the bureaucratic machinery of the modern state, we shall have a splendidly-equipped mechanism, freed from the 'parasite', a mechanism which can very well be set going by the united workers themselves, who will hire technicians, foremen and accountants, and pay them *all*, as indeed *all* 'state' officials in general, workmen's wages. Here is a concrete, practical task which can immediately be fulfilled in relation to all trusts, a task whose fulfilment will rid the working people of exploitation.[95]

The Bolshevik's "immediate aim" was to "organise the whole economy on the lines of the postal service" and "on the basis of what capitalism has already created."[96] So the structures created by the capitalists and *their* State—fitting for *their* priorities and interests—would be extended with "the conversion of all citizens into workers and other employees of one huge 'syndicate'—the whole state—and the complete subordination of the entire work of this syndicate to a genuinely democratic state, *the state of the Soviets of Workers' and Soldiers' Deputies.*"[97]

---

93. Ibid., 380. Also see section H.3.14 of *AFAQ.*
94. Ibid., 340.
95. Ibid., 345.
96. Ibid., 345.
97. Ibid., 380.

Control, then, would be by the State—initially over the capitalists but eventually of State employees. Lenin is well aware of Engels' infamous article "On Authority"[98] in which he "ridicules the muddled ideas of the Proudhonists, who call themselves 'anti-authoritarians', i.e., repudiated all authority, all subordination, all power. Take a factory, a railway, a ship on the high seas, said Engels: is it not clear that not one of these complex technical establishments, based on the use of machinery and the systematic co-operation of many people, could function without a certain amount of subordination and, consequently, without a certain amount of authority or power?"[99] Yet Engels argues much more strongly than that:

> Organisation [...] means that questions are settled in an authoritarian way. The automatic machinery of the big factory is much more despotic than the small capitalists who employ workers ever have been [...] If man, by dint of his knowledge and inventive genius, has subdued the forces of nature, the latter avenge themselves upon him by subjecting him, in so far as he employs them, to a veritable despotism independent of all social organisation.[100]

Lenin's aim was to turn the new economy into a single factory under the control of the State and yet did not conclude that this would be "more despotic" than capitalism. He completely fails to realise that without workers' management of production when "equality is achieved for all members of society *in relation* to ownership of the means of production, that is, equality of labour and wages" it is just turning them into wage-slaves of the State bureaucracy.[101] Capitalism—individual ownership by the few—turns into State-Capitalism—collective ownership by the few in the new centralised structures of the State and the institutions inherited from capitalism.[102]

---

98. For a critique of Engels's article, see section H.4 of *AFAQ*.
99. Lenin, *The Lenin Anthology*, 353.
100. Marx-Engels, *MECW* 23 (London: Lawrence & Wishart, 1988), 423.
101. Lenin, *The Lenin Anthology*, 381.
102. See section H.3.13 of *AFAQ*.

There is nothing in Lenin's work that suggests anything like Proudhon's vision of socialism built by workers themselves using their own organisations:

> Under universal association, ownership of the land and of the instruments of labour is *social* ownership [...] We do not want expropriation by the State [...] it is still monarchical, still wage-labour. We want [...] democratically organised workers' associations [...] the pioneering core of that vast federation of companies and societies woven into the common cloth of the democratic and social Republic.[103]

Similarly, there is no notion that a "strongly centralised Government" could "*command* that a prescribed quantity" of a good "be sent to such a place on such a day" and be "received on a given day by a specified official and stored in particular warehouses" was not only "undesirable" but also "wildly Utopian" not least because it could not utilise "the co-operation, the enthusiasm, the local knowledge" of the people.[104] Hence the anarchist prediction "that to hand over to the State all the main sources of economic life" and "also the management of all the main branches of industry" would "create a new instrument of tyranny. State capitalism would only increase the powers of bureaucracy and capitalism." This "new bureaucracy would end by making expropriation hateful in the eyes of all."[105]

The Party

The most obvious difference between the theory of *The State and Revolution* and the practice of the new regime is that the book makes next-to-no mention of the vanguard party and its role. The most significant mention is ambiguous:

103. Proudhon, *Property is Theft!*, 377–8.
104. Kropotkin, *Direct Struggle against Capital*, 32.
105. Ibid., 165, 527.

By educating the workers' party, Marxism educates the vanguard of the proletariat, capable of assuming power and leading the whole people to socialism, of directing and organising the new system, of being the teacher, the guide, the leader of all the working and exploited people in organising their social life without the bourgeoisie and against the bourgeoisie.[106]

Is it the proletariat or its vanguard that assumes power? Lenin's other writings during 1917 make it clear—it is the vanguard, the party, which assumes power.[107] Given this, we need to understand the nature of the party Lenin spent his life building and whose ideology would necessarily shape the decisions being made and structures being built.

The first thing to note about the vanguard is how important it is for socialism. Without the right kind of party, socialism would be impossible. As Lenin stressed in 1902 *"there could not have been* Social-Democratic consciousness among the workers" as it must "be brought to them from without. The history of all countries shows that the working class, exclusively by its own effort, is able to develop only trade union consciousness" while the "theory of socialism, however, grew out of the philosophic, historical, and economic theories elaborated by educated representatives of the propertied classes, by intellectuals."[108] The party was needed to educate a class that could never develop socialist ideas by itself:

There can be no talk of an independent ideology formulated by the working masses themselves in the process of their movement, the *only* choice is—either bourgeois or socialist ideology. There is no middle course [...] Hence, to belittle the socialist ideology *in any way, to turn aside from it in the slightest degree* means to strengthen bourgeois ideology. There is much talk of spontaneity. But the *spontaneous* development of the working-class movement leads to its subordination to bourgeois ideology [...] Hence, our task,

---

106. Lenin, *The Lenin Anthology*, 328.
107. See section H.3.11 of *AFAQ*.
108. Lenin, *The Lenin Anthology*, 24.

the task of Social-Democracy, is *to combat spontaneity, to divert* the working-class movement from this spontaneous, trade-unionist striving to come under the wing of the bourgeoisie, and to bring it under the wing of revolutionary Social Democracy.[109]

Ignoring the obvious point that "history" shows no such thing—as an obvious counter-example, in 1917 "the masses were incomparably more revolutionary than the Party, which in turn was more revolutionary than its committeemen"[110]—this perspective cannot help give the party and more particularly its leadership a privileged position. The obvious conclusion is that to disagree with the party and its leadership was to show the absence of socialist consciousness. The party, then, substitutes itself for the working class.[111] This perspective helps explain one of Lenin's stranger comments in *The State and Revolution*:

> We are not utopians, we do not 'dream' of dispensing at once with all administration, with all subordination. These anarchist dreams, based upon incomprehension of the tasks of the proletarian dictatorship, are totally alien to Marxism, and, as a matter of fact, serve only to postpone the socialist revolution until people are different. No, we want the socialist revolution with people as they are now, with people who cannot dispense with subordination, control, and 'foremen and accountants.'[112]

Ignoring the awkward fact administration no more equates to subordination than organisation equates to authority and so these "anarchist dreams" existed only in Lenin's head, this statement flows naturally from the perspective that the working class cannot by their own struggles change themselves.[113] At best the majority can recognise that the party embodies its interests and vote for

109. Ibid., 28–9.
110. Trotsky, *Stalin*, 305.
111. For a critique of vanguardism, see section H.5 of *AFAQ*.
112. Lenin, *The Lenin Anthology*, 344.
113. While recognising the need for anarchists to organise to influence the class struggle, Bakunin also recognised that people learn through struggle and draw socialist conclusions, see *Basic Bakunin*, 101–3.

it (and even join it, if the party considers them suitable). Some will object since Lenin does add that this "subordination, however, must be to the armed vanguard of all the exploited and working people, i.e., to the proletariat" but this is question begging—for surely the proletariat are people too?[114] How can that class also dispense "at once with all administration, with all subordination"? But then Lenin talks about "establishing strict, iron discipline backed by the state power of the armed workers."[115]

This is significant since during the 1905 revolution he mocked the Mensheviks for only wanting "pressure from below" which was "pressure by the citizens on the revolutionary government." Instead, Lenin argued for pressure "from above as well as from below," where "pressure from above" was "pressure by the revolutionary government on the citizens." He notes that Engels "appreciated the importance of action from above" and that he saw the need for "the utilisation of the revolutionary governmental power" for "[l]imitation, in principle, of revolutionary action to pressure from below and renunciation of pressure also from above is *anarchism*."[116]

The 1905 revolution also saw this deep-rooted suspicion of working class self-activity surface in the St. Petersburg Bolsheviks. They were convinced that "only a strong party along class lines can guide the proletarian political movement and preserve the integrity of its program, rather than a political mixture of this kind, an indeterminate and vacillating political organisation such as the workers council represents and cannot help but represent."[117] So the soviets could not reflect workers' interests because they were elected by the workers. Lenin, to his credit, fought against this position when he returned from exile but support for the soviets was, as he put it in 1907, "for the purpose of developing and strengthening the Social-Democratic Labour Party" and "if Social-Democratic activities among the proletarian masses are properly, effectively and

---

114. Lenin, *The Lenin Anthology*, 345.
115. Ibid.
116. V.I. Lenin, *Collected Works* Vol. 8 (London: Lawrence & Wishart, 1962), 474, 478, 480, 481.
117. Quoted by Anweiler, 77.

widely organised, such institutions may actually become super-fluous."[118] Building the party remains the end and working class self-organisation merely a means.

As well as privileging the party over the class, the leadership is privileged over the membership. The leadership naturally substitutes itself for the membership as required by "the transformation of the power of ideas into the power of authority, the subordination of lower Party bodies to higher ones."[119] A centralised, top-down perspective becomes a necessity:

> It is the organisational principle of revolutionary Social-Democracy as opposed to the organisational principle of opportunist Social-Democracy. The latter strives to proceed from the bottom upward [...] The former strives to proceed from the top downward.[120]

The need for centralisation flows from the assumptions of vanguardism—if socialist consciousness comes from outside the working class then that also applies within the party. Hence the need for central control, beyond the notion that it is more efficient and effective than federalism.[121] So the vanguard party is centralised like the capitalist system it claims to oppose. Anarchists have long argued that the centralisation of the State structure produced around it a bureaucracy and, unsurprisingly, the Bolshevik party likewise produced a caste of officials. Discussing the Bolsheviks in 1905 Trotsky points out this tendency existed from the start:

> The habits peculiar to a political machine were already forming in the underground. The young revolutionary bureaucrat was already emerging as a type. The conditions of conspiracy, true enough, offered rather meagre scope for such formalities of democracy as electiveness, accountability and control. Yet,

---

118. Lenin, *Collected Works* Vol. 12 (London: Lawrence & Wishart, 1962), 43–4.
119. Lenin, *Collected Works* Vol. 7 (London: Lawrence & Wishart, 1962), 367.
120. Ibid., 396–7.
121. Space excludes a discussion of the false nature of such notions as shown by the limitations of the Bolshevik Party in 1917, see section H.5.12 of *AFAQ*.

undoubtedly the committeemen narrowed these limitations considerably more than necessity demanded and were far more intransigent and severe with the revolutionary workingmen than with themselves, preferring to domineer even on occasions that called for lending an attentive ear to the voice of the masses.[122]

Unsurprisingly, Lenin also spent a lot of energy fighting the bureaucracy of his own party in 1917 to push the revolution forward. As Trotsky reported:

> As often happens, a sharp cleavage developed between the classes in motion and the interests of the party machines. Even the Bolshevik Party cadres, who enjoyed the benefit of exceptional revolutionary training, were definitely inclined to disregard the masses and to identify their own special interests and the interests of the machine on the very day after the monarchy was overthrown. What, then, could be expected of these cadres when they became an all-powerful state bureaucracy?[123]

And it is now to that question, the reality of the Bolshevik regime that we turn.

Practice

Of course, the anarchist position may be wrong and Lenin's right. We need to look at what happened after the Bolshevik party seized power and started to implement their vision of socialism to see who was correct.[124]

While often portrayed as a *coup d'état*, in reality the Bolsheviks did have significant popular support in the main industrial centres and

---

122. Trotsky, *Stalin*, 101.
123. Ibid., 298.
124. We quote exclusively from academic accounts of the new regime as these confirm the analysis presented by anarchists. For example, compare the accounts of bureaucratic paralysis presented below to the summaries by Goldman in *My Disillusionment in Russia* on pages 99 and 253 and Kropotkin in *Direct Struggle against Capital* on 490 and 584.

the October Revolution took place only once the party had a majority in the Petrograd and Moscow soviets. They then gained a majority of votes in the Second All-Russian Soviet Congress for ratifying the overthrow of the provisional government and its replacement by some-kind of soviet system. The question is, what happened next?

We concentrate on the Bolshevik's relations with the urban working class as this was their favoured class, the one the new State was meant to ensure was the ruling class.[125] We cannot cover everything and will by necessity focus on certain key developments, which historian S.A. Smith summarises well:

> The Bolsheviks established their power in the localities through soviets, soldiers' committees, factory committees, and Red Guards. Numbering less than 350,000 in October 1917, the party had little option but to allow such independent organisations extensive leeway. Yet the same desperate problems of unemployment and lack of food and fuel that helped turn the workers against the Provisional Government soon began to turn workers against the Bolsheviks. In the first half of 1918, some 100,000 to 150,000 workers across Russia took part in strikes, food riots and other protests, roughly on a par with labour unrest on the eve of the February Revolution. In this context, the Bolsheviks struggled to concentrate authority in the hands of the party and state organs. [...] In spring 1918, worker discontent translated into a renewal of support for the Mensheviks and, to a lesser extent, the SRs, causing the Bolsheviks to cancel soviet elections and close

---

125. Given the size of Russian peasantry within the population, it would have been impossible for the Bolsheviks to gain a majority in the republic they had supported previously (and, indeed, they received 25% of the vote to the Constituent Assembly while the peasant party, the SRs, received 57%). Gaining a majority in the urban soviets elected by workers and soldiers was feasible and may explain Lenin's new perspective in 1917. The new regime gave priority to urban workers and built in an institutional bias in voting of approximately five-to-one against the peasants. While fitting for a Marxist party and its prejudices against the peasantry, this helped to alienate the bulk of the population against the new regime—an alienation reinforced by numerous other Bolshevik policies such as the creation of "poor peasants' committees" and the forced requisition of food (driven, in part, due to lack of goods to trade with the peasants, a lack Bolshevik economic policies made worse). Bolshevik attitudes to the peasants undoubtedly made the situation worse.

down soviets that proved uncooperative, thus initiating the process whereby soviets and trade unions were turned into adjuncts
to a one-party state. When the Whites seized leadership of the
anti-Bolshevik movement in the latter months of 1918, however,
most workers swung back in support of the government. During
the civil war, labour unrest continued [...] the Bolsheviks generally reacted by rushing in emergency supplies and by arresting the
leaders of the protest, who were often Mensheviks or Left SRs
[...] they did not scruple when they deemed it necessary to deploy
armed force to suppress strikes, to confiscate ration cards or even
to dismiss strikers en masse and then rehire them selectively. The
Bolsheviks expected the working class to speak with one voice—
in favour of the regime—and when they didn't they, who had once
excoriated the Mensheviks for their refusal to accept that a true
proletariat existed in Russia, charged the working class with being
no more than a mass of uprooted peasants with a thoroughly petty-bourgeois psychology.[126]

These developments did not come out of the blue. They
reflected the clash of Bolshevik ideology and prejudices with reality, a clash in which the former made the latter worse. They also
reflected the changed perspectives of those who found themselves
in positions of power within a centralised, hierarchical, top-down
social organisation—the State.

While such factors as economic crisis, civil war, imperialist
intervention, and a "declassed" or "disappeared" working class were
later invoked by Leninists (starting with Trotsky in the 1930s) to
rationalise and justify the anti-socialist decisions of the Bolsheviks—that so obviously paved the way for Stalinism—we will show
it was primarily the combination of ideology and the realities of
the centralised political and economic structures the Bolsheviks
favoured that proved the anarchist position correct and showed
the naiveté of *The State and Revolution*.

---

126. S.A. Smith, *Revolution and the People in Russia and China: A Comparative History* (Cambridge, Cambridge University Press, 2008), 201. Also see section H.6 of *AFAQ* for a
fuller discussion of these events.

The State and the Soviets

Lenin had stressed the need for "working bodies" and the fusion of legislative and executive bodies yet the Second All-Russian Congress of Soviets elected a new Central Executive Committee (VTsIK, with 101 members) and created the Council of People's Commissars (Sovnarkom, with 16 members). A mere four days later the Sovnarkom unilaterally gave itself legislative power by simply issuing a decree to this effect. This made clear the party's pre-eminence over the soviets.

However, this should not have come as a surprise since throughout 1917 Lenin argued that the "Bolsheviks must assume power" and "can and *must* take state power into their own hands."[127] The Bolshevik Central Committee admitted to doing so just after the October Revolution: "it is impossible to refuse a purely Bolshevik government without treason to the slogan of the power of the Soviets, since a majority at the Second All-Russian Congress of Soviets [...] handed power over to this government."[128] So in the "new" State, it was not the people nor the soviets which governed but rather the Bolsheviks.

Thus the VTsIK, in theory the highest organ of soviet power, was turned into little more than a rubber stamp for a Bolshevik executive. This was aided by the activities of its Bolshevik-dominated presidium that circumvented general meetings, postponed regular sessions and presented it with policies which had already been implemented by the Sovnarkom.[129] In addition, "[e]ffective power in the local soviets relentlessly gravitated to the executive committees, and especially their presidia. Plenary sessions became increasingly symbolic and ineffectual."[130]

Combined with the rise of executive power, the "new" State also saw an increase in bureaucracy that started immediately with the seizure of power by the Bolsheviks:

127. Lenin, *Collected Works* Vol. 26 (Moscow: Progress Publishers, 1964), 19.
128. Robert V. Daniels (ed.), *A Documentary History of Communism* Vol. 1 (New York: Vintage Books, 1960), 128–9.
129. Charles Duval, "Yakov M. Sverdlov and the All-Russian Central Executive Committee of Soviets (VTsIK)," *Soviet Studies*, XXXI, 1.
130. Carmen Sirianni, *Workers' Control and Socialist Democracy* (London: Verso/NLB, 1982), 204.

The old state's political apparatus was 'smashed,' but in its place a new bureaucratic and centralised system emerged with extraordinary rapidity. After the transfer of government to Moscow in March 1918 it continued to expand [....] As the functions of the state expanded so did the bureaucracy, and by August 1918 nearly a third of Moscow's working population were employed in offices. The great increase in the number of employees [...] took place in early to mid-1918 and, thereafter, despite many campaigns to reduce their number, they remained a steady proportion of the falling population.[131]

Bureaucracy "grew by leaps and bounds. Control over the new bureaucracy constantly diminished" while "alienation between 'people' and 'officials,' which the soviet system was supposed to remove, was back again. Beginning in 1918, complaints about 'bureaucratic excesses,' lack of contact with voters, and new proletarian bureaucrats grew louder and louder."[132] In stark contrast to the promise to "take immediate steps to cut bureaucracy down to the roots" it swiftly and dramatically increased.[133] Perhaps Lenin was right to assert that the notion of "[a]bolishing the bureaucracy at once, everywhere and completely, is out of the question" and "a utopia" but to massively *increase* that bureaucracy is something else—particularly when the opposite had been so confidently proclaimed.[134]

Alongside the ever-increasing bureaucracy, the new "semi-State" also gained "special bodies" of armed forces. On 20th of December 1917 the Sovnarkom decreed the formation of a political police force, the Cheka. For all the talk of "smashing" the old State machine, the Cheka's first headquarters was at Gorokhovaia 2

---

131. Richard Sakwa, "The Commune State in Moscow in 1918," *Slavic Review* 46, 3/4: 437–8.

132. Anweiler, *The Soviets*, 242.

133. Lenin, *The Lenin* Anthology, 389.

134. Ibid., 344. As Kropotkin noted, "It is often thought that it would be easy for a revolution to economise in the administration by reducing the number of officials. This was certainly not the case during the Revolution of 1789–1793, which with each year extended the functions of the State, over instruction, judges paid by the State, the administration paid out of the taxes, an immense army, and so forth," from *The Great French Revolution* (Montreal/New York: Black Rose Books, 1989), 440.

which had housed the Tsar's notorious security service the Okhrana. In March 1918, Trotsky replaced the militia with a regular army by eliminating the soldier's committees and elected officers: "the principle of election is politically purposeless and technically inexpedient, and it has been, in practice, abolished by decree."[135]

This shifting of power territorially to the centre and functionally to executives, the rise of a "new" bureaucracy and specialised armed forces—while all expected by anarchists—did not automatically mean dictatorship as other parties could, in theory, win elections to soviets, become the majority and replace the executives. This is precisely what the Mensheviks decided to do and they achieved significant success by the spring of 1918 as the working class was "becoming increasingly disillusioned with the Bolshevik regime, so much so that in many places the Bolsheviks felt constrained to dissolve Soviets or prevent re-elections where Mensheviks and Socialist Revolutionaries had gained majorities."[136]

As well as delaying elections and disbanding soviets elected with non-Bolshevik majorities by force, the Bolsheviks also took to packing soviets with representatives of organisations they controlled. So, for example, in Petrograd the Bolshevik Soviet confirmed new regulations "to help offset possible weaknesses" in their "electoral strength in factories." The "most significant change" was the "numerically decisive representation" given "to agencies in which the Bolsheviks had overwhelming strength, among them the Petrograd Trade Union Council, individual trade unions, factory committees in closed enterprises, district soviets, and district non-party workers' conferences." This ensured that "[o]nly 260 of roughly 700 deputies in the new soviet were to be elected in factories, which guaranteed a large Bolshevik majority in advance" and so the Bolsheviks

135. Leon Trotsky, *How the Revolution Armed: The Military Writings and Speeches of Leon Trotsky*, Vol. 1 (London: New Park Publications, 1979), 47.

136. Israel Getzler, *Martov: A Political Biography of a Russian Social Democrat* (Carlton: Melbourne University Press, 1967) 179; Vladimir Brovkin, "The Mensheviks' Political Comeback: The Elections to the Provincial City Soviets in Spring 1918," *The Russian Review* 42, 1; Leonard Schapiro, *The Origin of the Communist Autocracy: Political Opposition in the Soviet State: The First Phase, 1917–1922* (New York: Frederick A. Praeger, 1965), 191; Silvana Malle, *The Economic Organisation of War Communism, 1918–1921* (Cambridge: Cambridge University Press, 2002), 366–7; Duval, *Soviet Studies* XXXI, 13–14.

"contrived a majority" in the new Soviet long before gaining 127 of the 260 factory delegates. This, moreover, ignores the repression of opposition parties and press on the results. Overall, the Bolshevik election victory "was highly suspect, even on the shop floor."[137]

So much for Lenin's promise of "sovereign, all-powerful Soviets of Workers' and Soldiers' Deputies."[138]

Such activities would have been hard with a State dependent on the armed people—but by then the Bolsheviks had a regular army and political police force to do their bidding. The Bolshevik regime confirmed Engels description of the State as quoted by Lenin:

> The establishment of a public power which no longer directly coincides with the population organising itself as an armed force. This special, public power is necessary because a self-acting armed organisation of the population has become impossible since the split into classes.... This public power exists in every state; it consists not merely of armed men but also of material adjuncts, prisons, and institutions of coercion of all kinds.[139]

The irony is that it was Engels's own ideology that produced this as society had split between the working class and the new party-bureaucratic ruling class. As anarchists predicted, function and organ are inseparable and the centralised State produced around it a new minority class. The State did not begin to "wither away" but rather enlarged and strengthened. If, "according to Marx, the proletariat needs only a state which is withering away, i.e., a state so constituted that it begins to wither away immediately, and cannot but wither away" then Lenin's regime failed to provide it.[140]

---

137. Alexander Rabinowitch, *The Bolsheviks in Power: The first year of Soviet rule in Petrograd* (Bloomington: Indiana University Press, 2007) 248–252; also see Vladimir N. Brovkin, *The Mensheviks After October: Socialist Opposition and the Rise of the Bolshevik Dictatorship* (Ithaca: Cornell University Press, 1987), 238–43.

138. Lenin, *The Lenin Anthology*, 393.

139. Ibid., 316.

140. Ibid., 326. This is not to suggest that Lenin and the Bolsheviks were happy with the bureaucracy they failed to anticipate. Quite the reverse as they denounced it repeatedly while flailing around for some kind of solution. Yet blinded by simplistic Marxist notions, they could think of nothing better than organisational and police methods—new bodies are organised to oversee the existing bureaucratic ones, only to become bureaucratic

The State and Socialism

Throughout 1917 the Bolsheviks had argued that the economic problems facing Russia were the fault of the Provisional Government as it was bourgeois in origin and therefore unwilling to take the measures needed against speculators and vested interests. The creation of a new "soviet" power would quickly end the problems. This proved to be optimistic in the extreme. The economic crisis continued once the Bolsheviks seized power and got worse as Bolshevik ideology started to play its part.

The Bolsheviks did what Lenin had indicated in *The State and Revolution*—build "socialism" on the structures created by capitalism. In December 1917, the VTsIK decreed the creation of the Supreme Council of the National Economy (Vesenka). This "was an expression of the principle of centralisation and control from above which was peculiar to the Marxist ideology." This body utilised the "chief committees" (*glavki*) formed during the war by the Tsarist regime and were intended by the Bolsheviks "to provide good grounds and prerequisites for nationalisation and price control" and so "were kept on and assigned increasing functions." More were created and these "became the foundation of the organisation of production" based on "a ready-made institutional framework for further policies of coordination and control."[141] Alternatives based on workers' own organisations were rejected:

> On three occasions in the first months of Soviet power, the [factory] committee leaders sought to bring their model into being. At each point the party leadership overruled them. The result was to vest both managerial *and* control powers in organs of the state which were subordinate to the central authorities, and formed by them.[142]

themselves; other bodies are enlarged or workers added to them, only for the problems to worsen; more centralisation is implemented, resulting in more bureaucracy. The conflict with the bureaucracy is finally resolved after Lenin's death—with the complete victory of the bureaucrats under Stalin who then uses the repressive techniques perfected under Lenin against the left-wing opposition and the working class *within the party itself*.
141. Malle *The Economic Organisation of War Communism, 1918–1921*, 95, 45–6, 218.
142. Thomas F. Remington, *Building Socialism in Bolshevik Russia: Ideology and Industrial Organ-*

Indeed, it is "likely that the arguments for centralisation in economic policy, which were prevalent among Marxists, determined the short life of the All-Russian Council of Workers' Control."[143] Moreover, attempts by the factory committees to organise themselves were systematically hindered by the Bolsheviks using unions under their control to prevent, amongst other things, a planned All-Russian Congress.

Lenin initially rejected calls for nationalisation and left the capitalists in place, subject to "workers' control" (or rather supervision) by the workers' State. Direct workers' control of production was not seen as essential and, indeed, was rejected. By April 1918, faced with the growing economic crisis, Lenin turned on the factory committees by channelling Engels's article "On Authority"—with its confusion of agreement with authoritarianism, co-operation with coercion—and demanded "[o]bedience, and unquestioning obedience at that, during work to the one-man decisions of Soviet directors, of the dictators elected or appointed by Soviet institutions, vested with dictatorial powers."[144] In short, *capitalist* relations in production in which workers were once again mere order-takers:

Firstly, the question of principle, namely, is the appointment of individuals, dictators with unlimited powers, in general compatible with the fundamental principles of Soviet government? [...] concerning the significance of individual dictatorial powers from the point of view of the specific tasks of the present moment, it must be said that large-scale machine industry—which is precisely the material source, the productive source, the foundation of socialism—calls for absolute and strict unity of will, which directs the joint labours of hundreds, thousands and tens of thousands of people [...] But how can strict unity of will be ensured? By thousands subordinating their will to the will of one [...] *unquestioning subordination* to a single will is absolutely necessary for the success of processes organised on the pattern

isation 1917–1921 (London: University of Pittsburgh Press, 1984), 38.
143. Malle, *The Economic Organisation of War Communism, 1918–1921*, 94.
144. Lenin, *The Collected Works* Vol. 27 (Moscow: Progress Publishers, 1965), 316.

of large-scale machine industry. [...] revolution demands—precisely in the interests of its development and consolidation, precisely in the interests of socialism—that the people *unquestioningly obey the single will* of the leaders of labour.[145]

This was part of "our task" which was "to study the state capitalism of the Germans, to spare *no effort* in copying it and not to shrink from adopting *dictatorial* methods to hasten the copying of it" and prefigured in *The State and Revolution* (as Lenin himself latter stressed against opponents within the Party).[146]

The State and Civil War

A standard response to the anarchist critique of the Bolshevik regime by modern-day Leninists is that it fails to mention the terrible Civil War and imperialist invasion. These, they argue, caused the degeneration of the regime from the ideals of *The State and Revolution.*

Yet the anarchist critique remains valid: the usurpation of soviet power by executives, abolition of democracy in the armed forces, "dictatorial" one-man management, creation of a highly centralised economic structure based on the institutions inherited from Tsarism, packing and disbanding of soviets, expanding bureaucracy, and so on—all these occurred *before* Civil War broke-out in late May 1918.

The State and Revolution made clear that Lenin—unlike anarchists—expected the Revolution to be an easy affair, with minimal resistance. His hopes seemed justified initially. As he noted in March 1918, "victory was achieved" with "extraordinary ease" and the "revolution was a continuous triumphal march in the first months."[147] Yet signs of authoritarianism—some consistent with

145. Ibid., 267–9.
146. Ibid., 340, 341, 354; Also see Maurice Brinton's classic "The Bolsheviks and Workers' Control" for an excellent discussion of this subject in Maurice Brinton, *For Workers' Power: The Selected Writings of Maurice Brinton* (Edinburgh/Oakland: AK Press, 2004).
147. Lenin, *The Collected Works* Vol. 27, 88–9.

The State and Revolution, some not—were present from the first day and increased during the next six months. The outbreak of civil war in late May 1918 merely accelerated them.

The Bolsheviks had already packed and disbanded soviets at the local level for some months before acting on the national level at the Fifth All-Russian Soviet Congress in July 1918. With the Mensheviks and Right-SRs banned from the soviets, popular disenchantment with Bolshevik rule was expressed by voting for the Left-Social-Revolutionaries (SRs). The Bolsheviks ensured their majority in the congress and so a Bolshevik government by "electoral fraud [which] gave the Bolsheviks a huge majority of congress delegates" by means of "roughly 399 Bolsheviks delegates whose right to be seated was challenged by the Left SR minority in the congress's credentials commission." Without these dubious delegates, the Left SRs and SR Maximalists would have outnumbered the Bolsheviks by around 30 delegates and this ensured "the Bolshevik's successful fabrication of a large majority."[148] Deprived of their democratic majority the Left SRs assassinated the German ambassador to provoke a revolutionary war with Germany. The Bolsheviks labelled this an uprising against the soviets and made the Left-SRs, like the Mensheviks and Right-SRs, illegal.

So by July 1918, the regime was a de facto Bolshevik dictatorship. It took some months for this reality to be reflected in the rhetoric. The ex-anarchist Victor Serge recalled in the 1930s that "the degeneration of Bolshevism" was apparent "at the start of 1919" for he "was horrified to read an article" by Zinoviev "on the monopoly of the party in power."[149] By 1920 Zinoviev was proclaiming this conclusion to the assembled revolutionaries of the world at the Second Congress of the Communist International:

---

148. Rabinowitch, *The Bolsheviks in Power*, 396, 288, 442, 308; The Bolsheviks "allowed so-called committees of poor peasants to be represented at the congress" and this "blatant gerrymandering ensured a Bolshevik majority" according to Geoffrey Swain, *The Origins of the Russian Civil War* (London/New York: Longman, 1996), 176.

149. Victor Serge and Leon Trotsky, *The Serge-Trotsky Papers*, David Cotterill, ed. (London: Pluto Press, 1994), 188; it must be noted that Serge kept his horror well-hidden throughout this period—and well into the 1930s (see my "The Worst of the Anarchists," *Anarcho-Syndicalist Review* No. 61).

Today, people like Kautsky come along and say that in Russia you do not have the dictatorship of the working class but the dictatorship of the party. They think this is a reproach against us. Not in the least! We have a dictatorship of the working class and that is precisely why we also have a dictatorship of the Communist Party. The dictatorship of the Communist Party is only a function, an attribute, an expression of the dictatorship of the working class [...] the dictatorship of the proletariat is at the same time the dictatorship of the Communist Party.[150]

It is within the context of secure one-party rule that we must view the fate of the opposition parties. The Bolsheviks banned the Mensheviks from the soviets in June 1918 and rescinded it in November 1918 and they, like other left-wing parties, experienced periods of tolerance and repression.[151] This reflected a general pattern—when the civil war was at its most intense, the Bolsheviks legalised opposition parties for they knew they could be counted upon to work with the regime against the White threat. Once the danger had receded, they were once again banned—so they could not influence nor benefit from the inevitable return of popular discontent and protest that accompanied these victories against the Whites. Unsurprisingly, then, oppositional parties—like factions within the party—were finally banned *after* the end of the Civil War.

Economically, the same building upon the authoritarian tendencies already present before the civil war continued. Faced with the predictable resistance by the capitalists, at the end of June 1918 wide-scale nationalisation was decreed—although many local soviets had already decided to do this under workforce pressure. This

---

150. *Workers of the World and Oppressed Peoples, Unite! Proceedings and Documents of the Second Congress of the Communist International, 1920*, Vol. 1, John Ridell, ed. (New York: Pathfinder, 1991), 151–2; Lenin made similar comments in the work *Left-Wing Communism* written for that Congress see *The Lenin Anthology*, 567–8, 571–3.
151. Space excludes a detailed discussion of Menshevik and other opposition to the Bolsheviks beyond noting that the Menshevik's official position was to oppose armed rebellions in favour of winning a majority in the soviets (any party members who participated in such revolts were swiftly expelled): "The charge that the Mensheviks were not prepared to remain within legal limits is part of the Bolsheviks' case; it does not survive an examination of the facts," Schapiro, 355.

simply handed the economy to the ever-growing bureaucracy—the apparatus of the Vesenka grew from 6,000 in September 1918 to 24,000 by the end of 1920, with over half its budget consumed by personnel costs by the end of 1919.[152]

April 1920 saw what appeared to be victory against the Whites and with peace the Bolsheviks started to concentrate on building socialism. Whatever limited forms of workers' control or management remained were replaced by one-man management and so the perspective of 1918 continued with Lenin in 1920 stressing that "domination of the proletariat consists in the fact that the landowners and capitalists have been deprived of their property." The "victorious proletariat has abolished property" and "therein lies its domination as a class. The prime thing is the question of property."[153] Workers' self-management of production—in other words, basic economic power—was considered as irrelevant.

Looking back at April 1918, Lenin reiterated his position ("Dictatorial powers and one-man management are not contradictory to socialist democracy") while also stressing that this was not forced upon the Bolsheviks by civil war. Discussing how, again, the civil war had ended and it was time to build socialism he argued that the "whole attention of the Communist Party and the Soviet government is centred on peaceful economic development, on problems of the dictatorship and of one-man management [...] When we tackled them for the first time in 1918, there was no civil war and no experience to speak of." So it was "not only experience" of civil war, argued Lenin "but something more profound" that has "induced us now, as it did two years ago, to concentrate all our attention on labour discipline."[154] The Bolsheviks "took victory as a sign of the correctness of its ideological approach and set about the task of economic construction on the basis of an intensification of War Communism policies."[155]

---

152. Remington, *Building Socialism in Bolshevik Russia*, 153—4.
153. Lenin, *The Collected Works*, Vol. 30 (Moscow: Progress Publishers, 1965), 456.
154. Ibid., 503—4.
155. Jonathan Aves, *Workers Against Lenin: Labour Protest and the Bolshevik Dictatorship* (London: Tauris Academic Studies, 1996), 37.

Even such abominations as the "militarisation of labour" were defended not as desperate measures provoked by necessity—which, while wrong, would at least indicate some awareness of what socialism meant—but *ideologically* in terms of appropriate tools for building socialism. Thus Trotsky as well as defending the "substitution" of "the dictatorship of the Soviets" by "the dictatorship of the party" also defended one-man management ("I consider if the civil war had not plundered our economic organs of all that was strongest, most independent, most endowed with initiative, we should undoubtedly have entered the path of one-man management in the sphere of economic administration much sooner and much less painfully") and the militarisation of labour ("the only solution to economic difficulties from the point of view of both principle and of practice is to treat the population of the whole country as the reservoir of the necessary labour power [...] and to introduce strict order into the work of its registration, mobilisation and utilisation").[156] These perspectives were bolstered by Engels's position in "On Authority" and the reference to "industrial armies" in the *Communist Manifesto*. They failed.[157]

So rather than being driven by civil war, "for the leadership, the principle of maximum centralisation of authority served more than expedience. It consistently resurfaced as the image of a peacetime political system as well."[158] This was to be expected for Lenin had long argued that centralised, top-down organisation was the model for the revolutionary State and, once in power, he did not disappoint.

---

156. *Terrorism and Communism: A Reply to Karl Kautsky* (Ann Arbor, MI: University of Michigan Press, 1961), 109, 162–3, 135.
157. Trotsky applied his ideas on the railway workers which led to the "ignorance of distance and the inability to respond properly to local circumstances [...] 'I have no instructions' became all the more effective as a defensive and self-protective rationalisation as party officials vested with unilateral power insisted all their orders be strictly obeyed. Cheka ruthlessness instilled fear, but repression [...] only impaired the exercise of initiative that daily operations required." William G. Rosenberg, "The Social Background to Tsektran," *Party, State, and Society in the Russian Civil War*, Diane P. Koenker, William G. Rosenberg and Ronald Grigor Suny, eds. (Indiana: Indiana University Press, 1989), 369. Militarisation was imposed in September 1920 which was followed by a disastrous collapse of the railway network in the winter. "The revolutionary tribunal and the guillotine could not make up for the lack of a constructive communist theory," Kropotkin, *The Great French Revolution*, 499.
158. Remington, *Building Socialism in Bolshevik Russia*, 91.

However, by its very nature centralism, cannot help but produce bureaucracy—how else will the central bodies gather and process the needed information and implement its decisions? Thus "red tape and vast administrative offices typified Soviet reality" for as the "functions of the state expanded, so did the bureaucracy" and so "following the revolution the process of institutional proliferation reached unprecedented heights."[159]

If the Paris Commune had been "overwhelmed" by the demands placed on it, the new institutions in Russia covering a greater territory and set of responsibilities experienced far worse. Thus the Commissariat of Finance was "not only bureaucratically cumbersome, but [it] involved mountainous accounting problems" and "the various offices of the Sovnarkhoz and commissariat structure [were] literally swamped with 'urgent' delegations and submerged in paperwork."[160] The Vesenka "was deluged with work of an ad hoc character," as demands "for fuel and supplies piled up" and factories "demanded instructions." Its presidium "scarcely knew what its tasks were."[161] In short:

> The most evident shortcoming [...] was that it did not ensure central allocation of resources and central distribution of output, in accordance with any priority ranking [...] materials were provided to factories in arbitrary proportions: in some places they accumulated, whereas in others there was a shortage. Moreover, the length of the procedure needed to release the products increased scarcity at given moments, since products remained stored until the centre issued a purchase order on behalf of a centrally defined customer. Unused stock coexisted with acute scarcity. The centre was unable to determine the correct proportions among necessary materials and eventually to enforce implementation of the orders for their total quantity. The gap between theory and practice was significant.[162]

---

159. Richard Sakwa, *Soviet Communists in Power: a study of Moscow during the Civil War, 1918–21* (Basingstoke: Macmillan, 1987), 190-1.
160. William G. Rosenberg, "The Social Background to Tsektran," 357.
161. Remington, *Building Socialism in Bolshevik Russia*, 61–2.
162. Malle, *The Economic Organisation of War Communism, 1918–1921*, 233.

To ensure centralism, customers had to go via a central orders committee, which would then past the details to the appropriate *glavki* and, unsurprisingly, it was "unable to cope with these enormous tasks" and the "shortcomings of the central administrations and *glavki* increased together with the number of enterprises under their control."[163] The "centre lacked basic information about the performance of the economy" and "lacked the knowledge on which to judge the costs or effects of the policies it proposed." Elementary information about the state of production "could not be gathered" and "[l]acking information about the availability of fuel, raw materials, and labour and about the state of repair of equipment, the *glavki* issued blind production orders."[164]

Faced with the realities rather than rhetoric of centralised, top-down structures even the most committed Bolshevik ended up acting independently of the formal structures just to get things done.[165] Such local initiative came into conflict with orders from above but repeated demands for change were ignored for they "challenged" the "central directives of the party" which "approved the principles on which the *glavki* system was based" and "the maximum centralisation of production." So "the failure of *glavkism* did not bring about a reconsideration of the problems of economic organisation [...] On the contrary, the ideology of centralisation was reinforced."[166]

While the situation was pretty chaotic in early 1918, this does not prove that the factory committees' socialism was not the most efficient way of running things under the circumstances.[167] Unless,

---

163. Ibid., 232, 250.

164. Remington, *Building Socialism in Bolshevik Russia*, 154.

165. Ironically, the "run-down of large-scale industry and the bureaucratic methods applied to production orders and financial estimates" made the supply system based on *glavki* "unreliable" and instead the Red Army "started relying directly" on craft co-operatives, a sector which "developed to a large extent because it involved a smaller amount of bureaucratic procedure," Malle *The Economic Organisation of War Communism, 1918–1921*, 477–8.

166. Malle, *The Economic Organization of War Communism, 1918–1921*, 271, 275.

167. Rates of "output and productivity began to climb steadily after" January 1918, "[i]n some factories, production doubled or tripled in the early months of 1918" and "[m]any of the reports explicitly credited the factory committees for these increases," Sirianni, *Workers' Control and Socialist Democracy*, 109. There is "evidence that until late 1919, some factory committees performed managerial tasks successfully. In some regions factories

like the Bolsheviks, you have a dogmatic belief that centralisation is *always* more efficient and, moreover, a principle of socialism.

Lenin's vision of socialism was impoverished but very much in the orthodox Marxist tradition. So rather than being unclear on what socialism was, the Bolsheviks had very strong opinions on the subject and sought to implement them. The net effect of *The State and Revolution*'s vision of socialism was to build state-capitalism and make the economic crisis worse.

In short, "[f]rom the first days of Bolshevik power there was only a weak correlation between the extent of 'peace' and the mildness or severity of Bolshevik rule, between the intensity of the war and the intensity of proto-war communist measures" while "[c]onsidered in ideological terms there was little to distinguish the 'breathing space' (April–May 1918) from the war communism that followed." The "breathing space of the first months of 1920 after the victories over Kolchak and Denikin" saw their "intensification and the militarisation of labour" and "no serious attempt was made to review the aptness of war communist policies." Ideology "constantly impinged on the choices made at various points of the civil war" and so "Bolshevik authoritarianism cannot be ascribed simply to the Tsarist legacy or to adverse circumstances." Indeed, "in the soviets and in economic management the embryo of centralised and bureaucratic state forms had already emerged by mid-1918."[168]

Finally, there is a major irony in this standard defence of the Bolsheviks. Leninists usually (and falsely) attack anarchists for not recognising the need to defend a revolution. Yet here we have them rationalising Bolshevik authoritarianism by referring to something—Civil War—that they proclaim is an *inevitable* aspect of any revolution. So even if we ignore the awkward fact that before May 1918 the regime was well on its way to a one-party state-capitalist dictatorship, we can only conclude that if Leninism cannot

---

were still active thanks to their workers' initiatives in securing raw materials," Malle, *The Economic Organisation of War Communism, 1918–1921*, 101. While this may be dismissed as speculation based on a few examples, we cannot avoid recognising that turning the economy over to the bureaucracy coincided with the deepening of the economic crisis.
168. Sakwa, *Soviet Communists in Power*, 24, 27, 30, 96–7.

experience what it (rightly) proclaims is inevitable without degenerating then it is best avoided.

The State and the Masses

The privileged position of the party—unspoken of in *The State
and Revolution*—both in terms of ideology and in terms of holding
and exercising power, played its role in Bolshevik attitudes to the
masses in whose name they ruled. Lenin quotes Engels:

> As the state is only a transitional institution which is used in
> the struggle, in the revolution, to hold down one's adversaries by
> force, it is sheer nonsense to talk of a 'free people's state'; so long
> as the proletariat still needs the state, it does not need it in the
> interests of freedom but in order to hold down its adversaries.[169]

The problem is that in a State it is *not* the people who rule but
rather those who make up the government and these, in turn, need
bodies to implement their decisions. The transformation of the
Red Army and the creation of the Cheka confirm anarchist pre-
dictions that the ruling party would need an armed force to defend
it against the people. So Engels confused the need to defend a revolution with the ruling party supressing those who oppose it—
including the proletariat. As Lenin explained in 1920:

> Without revolutionary coercion directed against the avowed
> enemies of the workers and peasants, it is impossible to break
> down the resistance of these exploiters. On the other hand, rev-
> olutionary coercion is bound to be employed towards the waver-
> ing and unstable elements among the masses themselves.[170]

Who determines what these "elements" are? The party, of
course. The party which was built on the assertion that the working

169. Lenin, *The Lenin Anthology*, 356.
170. Lenin, *Collected Works*, Vol. 42 (Moscow: Progress Publishers, 1971), 170.

class cannot reach socialist consciousness by its own efforts and which pledged to combat spontaneity as this reflected bourgeois influences. Thus "the Party, shall we say, absorbs the vanguard of the proletariat, and this vanguard exercises the dictatorship of the proletariat" for "in all capitalist countries" the proletariat "is still so divided, so degraded, and so corrupted in parts" that the dictatorship "can be exercised only by a vanguard." The lesson of the revolution was clear: "the dictatorship of the proletariat cannot be exercised by a mass proletarian organisation."[171]

Yet, as Lenin argued in 1917, "it is clear that there is no freedom and no democracy where there is suppression and where there is violence." He was talking of the "freedom of the oppressors, the exploiters, the capitalists" but it equally applies to the working class—if the so-called "dictatorship of the proletariat, i.e., the organisation of the vanguard of the oppressed as the ruling class" is suppressing the working class itself then that class cannot be the ruling class, then its self-proclaimed "vanguard" is in fact the ruling class and just like "under capitalism we have the state in the proper sense of the word, that is, a special machine for the suppression of one class by another, and, what is more, of the majority by the minority."[172]

Lenin did mention this in 1917 for he talks of the "organised control over the insignificant capitalist minority" and "over the workers who have been thoroughly corrupted by capitalism" but he failed to indicate that this latter category was defined by how much they agreed with the party leadership.[173] Soon it amounted to the bulk of the working class—and pressure "from above" by the "revolutionary government" unsurprisingly was stronger than that "from below" by the citizens. That this minority was the class of the State bureaucracy—armed with political *and* economic power—did not make it any less exploitative or oppressive.

This is the grim reality of Engels's comment that a "revolution is certainly the most authoritarian thing there is; it is an act

---

171. Lenin, *Collected Works*, Vol. 32 (Moscow: Progress Publishers, 1966), 20–1.
172. Lenin, *The Lenin Anthology*, 373, 374.
173. Ibid., 383.

whereby one part of the population imposes its will upon the other part by means of rifles, bayonets and cannon, all of which are highly authoritarian means. And the victorious party must maintain its rule by means of the terror which its arms inspire in the reactionaries."[174] Ignoring the obvious point that it is hardly authoritarian to destroy an authoritarian system in which a minority continuously imposes it will on the majority, Engels failed to see that in a State the "victorious party" will need to maintain its rule against the many as well as the few.

Space precludes a comprehensive account of labour protest under—and State repression by—the Bolsheviks. Suffice to say, from the spring of 1918 both were a regular feature of life in "revolutionary" Russia. Workers protested and struck and the Bolsheviks sent in troops and the Cheka, withheld rations, made mass firings, and selective rehirings—all throughout the civil war period when, according to Leninists, the working class had become "declassed," "atomised," or had "disappeared."[175] Indeed, this argument was first raised by Lenin himself to "justify a political clamp-down" and as "discontent amongst workers became more and more difficult to ignore," he argued that the consciousness of the working class had deteriorated such that "workers had become 'declassed.'"[176] While self-serving, this argument reflected the notions raised in *What is to Be Done?* and the privileged position the party holds in Leninism— as the workers disagreed with the party by definition they were lacking class consciousness and "declassed."

---

174. Ibid., 354.

175. See section H.6.3 of AFAQ for an account of the massive and frequent labour protests—and subsequent repression—under the Bolsheviks. The Bolsheviks also clamped down even advisory bodies they themselves set up. In his 1920 diatribe against Left-wing Communism, Lenin pointed to "non-Party workers' and peasants' conferences" and Soviet Congresses as means by which the party secured its rule. Yet, *if* the congresses of soviets were "*democratic* institutions, the like of which even the best democratic republics of the bourgeois have never known," the Bolsheviks would have no need to "support, develop and extend" non-Party conferences "to be able to observe the temper of the masses, come closer to them, meet their requirements, promote the best among them to state posts," see *The Lenin Anthology*, 573. Yet even these were too much for the Bolsheviks for during the labour protests and strikes of late 1920 "they provided an effective platform for criticism of Bolshevik policies" and they "were discontinued soon afterward," see Sakwa, *Soviet Communists in Power*, 203.

176. Aves, *Workers against Lenin*, 18, 90.

In short, Lenin was right when he argued that the "essence of the matter" was *has the oppressed class arms?*[177] This was the case with new State and its various actions to dispossess the working class of its arms, to replace democratic militias with regular standing armies, to create a political police force. When workers' organisations, protests, and strikes are being repeatedly and systematically repressed, it is nonsense to suggest that the working class is the ruling class—particularly when this repression began so soon into the new regime.

Alternatives

It may be objected that we are indulging in armchair theorising and the fact that it was the Bolsheviks and not the anarchists who were facing civil war and imperialist intervention shows that anarchism should, as Trotsky proclaimed, be consigned into the dustbin of history. Except for two facts. First, the Bolshevik descent into authoritarianism *preceded* the civil war and, second, anarchists *did* face those challenges and did not succumb as the Bolsheviks did.

We have shown the former and space precludes a detailed account of the latter beyond indicating that the Makhnovist movement in the Ukraine faced the same (arguably worse) pressures and encouraged soviet democracy, freedom of speech, workers' management, and so on while the Bolsheviks repressed them. After helping to defeat the Whites, the Bolsheviks betrayed the Makhnovists and crushed them after yet more months of fighting.[178]

This counter-example—flawed as any real movement would be compared to the ideal, undoubtedly—shows that ideas and structures *matter*. Thus prejudices in favour of centralisation, notions that "top-down" structures reflect "revolutionary Social-Democracy," impoverished visions of socialism, the privileged position of

---

177. Lenin, *The Lenin Anthology*, 364.

178. Peter Arshinov, *The History of the Maknovist Movement* (London: Freedom Press, 1987); Michael Malet, *Nestor Makhno in the Russian civil war* (London: MacMillan Press, 1982.); Alexandre Skirda, *Nestor Makhno: Anarchy's Cossack - The Struggle for Free Soviets in the Ukraine 1917–1921* (Edinburgh/Oakland: AK Press, 2004).

the party, the confusion of defending freedom with "authoritarian" methods, all played their part in the failure of the Russian Revolution and the degeneration of the Bolshevik regime.

Regardless of Lenin's claims, anarchists do not envision "overnight" revolutions. Emma Goldman, for example, did not come to Russia "expecting to find Anarchism realised" nor did she "expect Anarchism to follow in the immediate footsteps of centuries of despotism and submission." Rather, she "hope[d] to find in Russia at least the beginnings of the social changes for which the Revolution had been fought" and that "the Russian workers and peasants as a whole had derived essential social betterment as a result of the Bolshevik regime."[179] Both hopes were dashed.

So anarchists did not and do not contrast the reality of Bolshevik Russia with an impossible ideal of a swiftly created utopia. Rather, the issue is whether the masses were building a better world or whether they were subject to a new minority regime. Regardless of Lenin's claims in 1917, the latter was the case in the new "soviet" system with its ruling party, marginalised soviets, centralisation, bureaucracy, appointed from above dictatorial managers, nationalisation, and so forth. The Bolsheviks may have won the Civil War but they lost the Revolution.

The continued mass working class protests from the spring of 1918 onward (that is, during and after the civil war) indicate that there *was* a social base upon which an alternative could be built. This would involve—as anarchists argued at the time—keeping the soviets as delegates from workplaces and actually eliminating executive bodies; supporting the factory committees and their federations; supporting customer co-operatives; keeping democratic armed forces; protecting freedom of press, assembly and organisation; implementing socialisation rather than nationalisation. In short, recognising that freedom is not an optional extra during a revolution but its only guarantee, by recognising the validity of anarchism—for it did not correctly predict the failures of Marxism by accident.

Finally, while the Russian Revolution shows the bankruptcy of vanguardism, it also shows the pressing need for anarchists to

179. Goldman, *My Disillusionment in Russia*, xlvii.

organise as anarchists to influence the class struggle.[180] The Russian anarchists—unlike their Ukrainian comrades—did not organise sufficiently and paid the price. Rising anarchist influence in 1917 could not make-up for the previous lack of systematic organisation and activity within the labour movement. Only anarchists having a firm social basis would have meant victory for the "unknown revolution" against both Red and White authority.

Conclusions

If, as Lenin argued, the State is "a power which arose from society but places itself above it and alienates itself more and more from it" and "consists of special bodies of armed men having prisons, etc., at their command" then the Bolshevik regime was most definitely a State... *in the normal sense of the term*.[181] The notion that it was a semi-State or some-such cannot be sustained for from the moment of the Bolsheviks seizing power the soviets were marginalised from decision making and transformed from "working bodies" into talking shops while all around them a "new" bureaucracy grew at a staggering rate and the regime created regular armed forces, a specialised armed political police force with its own prisons, etc.

The key difference is that rather than being an instrument of the bourgeoisie or feudal aristocracy, as had the Tsarist State it replaced, it was the instrument of a new minority—the Party leadership and the State bureaucracy. This ruling class combined political and economic power in its own hands, the latter slowly but surely replacing the former as the real power within the new social hierarchy.

While many anarchists concentrate on the Kronstadt Rebellion of early 1921 (presumably because noted anarchists like Goldman and Berkman arrived in Russia in 1920), the fate of the revolution was made much earlier. The Unknown Revolution had been fighting for its life from the start as the anti-Socialist

---

180. See section J.3 of *AFAQ*.
181. Lenin, *The Lenin Anthology*, 316.

tendencies of the regime expressed themselves rapidly—within six months of the October Revolution the so-called "semi-State" had all the features of the State in the "proper sense of the word" and well on its way to one-party dictatorship and state-capitalism. By early 1919 the reality of, and necessity, for party dictatorship became official ideology. Zinoviev proclaimed it at the Second Congress of the Communist International while Trotsky was still arguing for the "objective necessity" of the "dictatorship of a party" into the late 1930s.[182] The so-called workers' State was needed to repress the workers:

> The very same masses are at different times inspired by different moods and objectives. It is just for this reason that a centralised organisation of the vanguard is indispensable. Only a party, wielding the authority it has won, is capable of overcoming the vacillation of the masses themselves [...] if the dictatorship of the proletariat means anything at all, then it means that the vanguard of the proletariat is armed with the resources of the state in order to repel dangers, including those emanating from the backward layers of the proletariat itself.[183]

As everyone is, *by definition*, "backward" compared to the vanguard and "vacillations" get expressed by elections, mandates, and recall, we have the logical conclusion of the vanguardism of Lenin's *What is to be Done?* in Trotsky's implicit acknowledgment that the party needs a State in "the proper sense of the word," that the working class is not the "ruling class" in the "new" State.

The reality of the Revolution did not reflect the promises made in 1917. Yet looking closely at these promises, at Lenin's *The State and Revolution*, we can see the role ideology played in the degeneration. Ideas matter—particularly the ideas of those at the highest levels of the State. Structures matter—as these are not neutral but reflect class interests and needs and they shape the decisions made

---

182. Leon Trotsky, *Writings of Leon Trotsky 1936–37* (New York: Pathfinder Press, 1978), 513–4.

183. Leon Trotsky, "The Moralists and Sycophants against Marxism," *Their Morals and Ours* (New York: Pathfinder, 1973), 59.

by those in power and by either fostering or hindering meaningful mass participation in society. Both the ideas and structures advocated by Lenin in 1917 had their (negative) impact.

That the Bolsheviks were initially elected did not undermine the dynamics inherent in the centralised political and economic structures they favoured and built. A bloated bureaucratic State and a state-capitalist economy were inevitable. The combination of Bolshevik ideology and its favoured (centralised, top-down) structures produced this outcome—and confirmed anarchist theory.

Lenin was right when he said, "[s]o long as the state exists there is no freedom. When there is freedom, there will be no state."[184] His error was thinking that a State—a centralised, hierarchical structure developed by the few to secure their rule—could be utilised in a different way. Even when based on workers' organisations it quickly reverted to its role—of securing minority rule, in this case that of the party leadership and the bureaucracy which any centralised structure generates. Anarchist warnings were proven right and only anarchism offers a solution: in the form of a federalist, self-managed, bottom-up social organisation.

The Russian Revolution shows that it was not a case of the State *and* Revolution but rather the State *or* Revolution.

---

184. Lenin, *The Lenin Anthology*, 379.

A Decade of Bolshevism

ALEXANDER BERKMAN

The communist dictatorship in Russia has completed its first decade. It may therefore be interesting and instructive to sum up the achievements of the Bolsheviki during that time, to visualize the results of their rule.

But "results" are a relative matter. One can form an estimate of them only by comparing them with the things that were to be achieved, with the objects sought.

What were the objects of the Russian Revolution? What have the Bolsheviki achieved?

The Romanov regime was an absolutism; Russia under the tsars was the most enslaved country in Europe. The people hungered for liberty.

The February–March Revolution, 1917, abolished that absolutism. The people became free.

But that freedom was only negative. The people were free from the chains that had held them bound for centuries. Now their liberated arms and spirit longed to apply themselves, sought the opportunity to do, to act. But THAT freedom had not yet been achieved. The people were free FROM some things, but not TO do the things they wanted.

They wanted positive freedom. The workers wanted the opportunity to use the tools and machinery they had themselves made; they wanted to use them to create more wealth and to enjoy that wealth. The peasant wanted free access to the land and a chance to cultivate it without being robbed of the products of his hard toil. The people at large wanted to apply their new-won freedom to the pursuit of life and happiness.

The negative liberty of the February–March Revolution was therefore quite unsatisfactory, unconvincing, and inadequate. That is why the people soon began to continue the revolution, to deepen it into a social transformation. To make the revolution, in short. The soldiers dropped their guns and left the fronts en masse. They knew they had nothing to fight for in foreign countries. They returned to their fathers and brothers, the peasants, and together they drove the landlords away and went to work on their own mother-land. The industrial proletariat at the same time expropriated the lords of industry and possessed themselves of the mills, mines, and factories. Thus the laboring masses of Russia came into their own, for the first time in the history of the world.

As always during the revolution, this activity of the Russian masses proceeded outside the sphere of governmental influence. The struggle against oppression—whether political, economic, or social—against the exploitation of man by man, is always at the same time also a struggle against government itself, against government as such.

The Russian Revolution, like every revolution, faced this alternative: to build freely, independent of government and even despite it; or to choose government with all the limitation and stagnation that it involves. The path of the Russian Revolution lay in the constructive self-reliance of the masses, in the direction of no-government, of Anarchism.

Between February and October of 1917, the Revolution instinctively followed that path. It destroyed the old State mechanism and proclaimed the principle of the federation of Soviets. It used the method of direct expropriation to abolish private capitalistic ownership. In the field of economic reconstruction it employed the principle of the federation of shop and factory committees for the management of production. Proletarian and peasant organisations attended to distribution and exchange. House committees looked after the proper assignment of living quarters. Street and district committees secured public safety.

This was the course of the October–November revolution. In that spirit it kept growing and developing.

But this development of the Revolution was not in consonance with the philosophy of Marx and the purpose of the Communist Party. The latter sought to gain control of the movement of the masses, and gradually succeeding, it gave an entirely different turn to the work of social reconstruction.

Under cover of the motto, "the dictatorship of the proletariat," it began to build a centralized, bureaucratic State. In the name of the "defence of the Revolution," it abolished popular liberties and instituted a system of new oppression and terror.

The Bolshevik idea was, in effect, that the Social Revolution must be directed by a special staff, vested with dictatorial powers. The fundamental characteristics of that idea was a deep distrust of the masses. According to the Bolsheviki, the masses must be made free by force. "Proletarian compulsion in all its forms," wrote Bukharin, the foremost Communist theoretician, "beginning with summary execution and ending with compulsory labor, is a method of reworking the human material of the capitalist epoch into Communist humanity."

The Communist Party proceeded "reworking" the human material. Compulsion and terrorism became the main means toward it. Freedom of thought, freedom of the press, of public assembly, self-determination of the worker and his unions, the initiative and freedom of labor—all this was declared old rubbish, "bourgeois prejudices." The "dictatorship of the proletariat" became the absolutism of a handful of Bolsheviki in the Kremlin.

Practically the Communist dictatorship worked out as follows: free exchange of opinion was suppressed; the initiative of the individual as well as of the collectivity, so vital in life, and particularly in revolutionary times, was eliminated; voluntary co-operation and organized free efforts were wiped out; every revolutionary element, not Bolshevik, was exterminated or imprisoned. The people's Soviets were transformed into sections of the ruling political party; the labor organizations found themselves deprived of all power and activity, serving only as the official mouthpieces of the Party orders. Each and every citizen became the servant of the Bolshevik State, its obedient functionary, unquestioningly executing the will of his master, the all-powerful Kremlin dictators.

The inevitable results did not fail soon to manifest themselves. The Bolshevik policies corrupted and disintegrated the Revolution, slayed its soul and destroyed its moral and spiritual significance. By its bloody despotism, by its tyrannous paternalism, both petty and stupid, by the perfidy which replaced its former revolutionary idealism, by its deadening formalism and criminal indifference to the interests and aspirations of the laboring masses, by its cowardly suspicion and distrust of the people and by its mania of persecution, the "dictatorship of the proletariat" hopelessly cut itself off from the masses.

Thrust back from direct participation in the constructive work of the Revolution, harassed at every step, the victim of constant control and supervision by the Party, the proletariat got to feel that the Revolution and its further fortunes were the private, personal affair of the Bolsheviki. Constructive energy and active interest on the part of the people were paralised. The factories were deserted, the peasant refused to feed his new oppressors.

Lenin was compelled to introduce the "new economic policy." It meant the return of capitalism, "for long and in earnest," as Lenin himself put it. The return of capitalism in 1921, which the social revolutionary work of the laboring masses of Russia had abolished in 1917! The return of capitalism, as the direct result of Bolshevik methods; of capitalism partly State and partly private.

And today, after ten years of Bolshevik rule? Growing and inevitable disintegration of the Party itself, with the threat of a Napoleonic shadow in the background. While the country at large is groaning under the heel of a Tsarist Socialism.

Social antagonisms, the exploitation of labor, the enslavement of the worker and peasant, the cancellation of the citizen as a free human being and his transformation into a microscopic part of the economic mechanism owned by the government; the creation of privileged groups favored by the State; a multitudinous and corrupt bureaucracy; a system of labor service with its degrading and brutalising rewards and punishments—these are the characteristic features of Russia of today.

Only blind fanaticism or unpardonable hypocrisy can see in this, the most grievous form of slavery, the emancipation of labor or even the least approach to it.

The so-called "proletarian dictatorship" in Russia today is the worst betrayal of all that the Russian Revolution stood for. It is black reaction and counter-revolution.

There is no hope for Russia except in the speedy return of the principles and purposes of October. The first step toward it is the termination of the dictatorship, the re-establishment of real, free Soviets, of freedom of speech, press, and assembly, the absolute abolition of persecution for opinion's sake, and the immediate and unconditional liberation of all labor and political prisoners.

A.B.

Preface to Ida Mett's
"The Kronstadt Commune"

MAURICE BRINTON

The fiftieth anniversary of the Russian Revolution will be assessed, analyzed, celebrated or bemoaned in a variety of ways.

To the peddlers of religious mysticism and to the advocates of "freedom of enterprise," Svetlana Stalin's sensational (and well-timed) defection will "prove" the resilience of their respective doctrines, now shown as capable of sprouting on what at first sight would appear rather barren soil.

To incorrigible liberals, the recent, cautious reintroduction of the profit motive into certain sectors of the Russian economy will "prove" that laissez-faire economics is synonymous with human nature and that a rationally planned economy was always a pious pipe-dream.

To those "lefts" (like the late Isaac Deutscher) who saw in Russia's industrialization an automatic guarantee of more liberal attitudes in days to come, the imprisonment of Daniel and Sinyavsky for thought-crime (and the current persecution of those who stood up for them) will have come as a resounding slap in the face.

To the "Marxist-Leninists" of China (and Albania), Russia's rapprochement with the USA, her passivity in the recent Middle East crisis, her signing of the Test Ban Treaty and her reactionary influence on revolutionary developments in the colonial countries will all bear testimony to her headlong slither into the swamp of revisionism, following the Great Stalin's death. (Stalin, it will be remembered, was the architect of such revolutionary, non-revisionist, measures as the elimination of the Old Bolsheviks, the Moscow Trials, the Popular Front, the Nazi-Soviet Pact, the Tehran and Yalta Agreements and the dynamic struggles of the French and Italian Communist Parties in the immediate post-war years, struggles which led to their direct seizure of power in their respective countries.)

To the Yugoslavs, reintegrated at last after their adolescent wandering from the fold, the re-emergence of "sanity" in Moscow will be seen as corroboration of their worst suspicions. The 1948 "troubles" were clearly all due to the machinations of the wicked Beria. Mihajlo Mihajlov now succeeds Djilas behind the bars of a people's prison ... just to remind political heretics that, in Yugoslavia too, "proletarian democracy" is confined to those who refrain from asking awkward questions.

To the Trotskyists of all ilk—at least to those still capable of thinking for themselves—the mere fact of the fiftieth anniversary celebrations should be food for thought. What do words mean? How "transitional" can a transitional society be? Aren't four decades of "Bonapartism" in danger of making the word a trifle meaningless? Like the unflinching Christians carrying their cross, will unflinching Trotskyists go on carrying their question mark (concerning the future evolution of Russian society) for the rest of their earthly existence? For how much longer will they go on gargling with the old slogans of "capitalist restoration or advance towards socialism" proposed by their mentor in his *Revolution Betrayed* ... thirty years ago! Surely only the blind can now fail to see that Russia is a class society of a new type, and has been for several decades.

Those who have shed these mystifications—or who have never been blinded by them—will see things differently. They will sense that there can be no vestige of socialism in a society whose rulers can physically annihilate the Hungarian Workers' Councils, denounce equalitarianism and workers' management of production as "petty-bourgeois" or "anarcho-syndicalist" deviations, and accept the cold-blooded murder of a whole generation of revolutionaries as mere "violations of socialist legality," to be rectified—oh so gingerly and tactfully—by the technique of "selective posthumous rehabilitation." It will be obvious to them that something went seriously wrong with the Russian Revolution. *What was it? And when did the "degeneration" start?*

Here again the answers differ. For some the "excesses" or "mistakes" are attributable to a spiteful paranoia slowly sneaking up on the senescent Stalin. This interpretation (apart from tacitly accepting the very "cult of the individual" which its advocates would claim to decry) fails, however, to account for the repressions of revolutionaries and the conciliations with imperialism perpetrated at a much earlier period. For others the "degeneration" set in with the final defeat of the Left Opposition as an organized force (1927), or with Lenin's death (1924), or with the abolition of factions at the tenth Party Congress (1921). For the Bordigists the proclamation of the New Economic Policy (1921) irrevocably stamped Russia as "state capitalist." Others, rightly rejecting this preoccupation with the minutiae of revolutionary chronometry, stress more general factors, albeit in our opinion some of the less important ones.

Our purpose in publishing this text about the Kronstadt events of 1921 is not to draw up an alternative timetable. Nor are we looking for political ancestors. The construction of an orthodox apostolic succession is the least of our preoccupations. (In a constantly changing world it would only testify to our theoretical sterility.) Our occupation is simply to document some of the real—but less well-known—struggles that took place against the growing bureaucracy during the early post-revolutionary years, at a time when most of the later critics of the bureaucracy were part and parcel of the apparatus itself.

The fiftieth anniversary of the Russian Revolution presents us with the absurd sight of a Russian ruling class (which every day resembles more its Western counterpart) solemnly celebrating the revolution which overthrew bourgeois power and allowed the masses, for a brief moment, to envisage a totally new kind of social order.

What made this tragic paradox possible? What shattered this vision? How did the Revolution degenerate?

Many explanations are offered. The history of how the Russian working class was dispossessed is not, however, a matter for an esoteric discussion among political cliques, who compensate for their own irrelevance by mental journeys into the enchanted world of the revolutionary past. An understanding of what took place is essential for every serious socialist. It is not mere archivism.

127

No viable ruling class rules by force alone. To rule it must succeed in getting its own vision of reality accepted by society at large. The concepts by which it attempts to legitimize its rule must be projected into the past. Socialists have correctly recognized that the history taught in bourgeois schools reveals a particular, distorted, vision of the world. It is a measure of the weakness of the revolutionary movement that *socialist* history remains for the most part unwritten.

What passes as socialist history is often only a mirror image of bourgeois historiography, a percolation into the ranks of the working class movement of typically bourgeois methods of thinking. In the world of this type of "historian" leaders of genius replace the kings and queens of the bourgeois world. Famous congresses, splits or controversies, the rise and fall of political parties or unions, the emergence or degeneration of this or that leadership replace the internecine battles of the rulers of the past. The masses never appear independently on the historical stage, making their own history. At best they only "supply the steam," enabling others to drive the locomotive, as Stalin so delicately put it.

"Most of the time, 'official' historians don't have eyes to see or ears to hear the acts and words which express the workers' spontaneous activity ... They lack the categories of thought—one might even say the brain cells—necessary to understand or even to perceive this activity as it really is. To them an activity that has no leader or programme, no institutions and no statutes, can only be described as 'troubles' or 'disorders.' The spontaneous activity of the masses belongs by definition to what history suppresses."[1]

This tendency to identify working class history with the history of its organizations, institutions and leaders is not only inadequate—it reflects a typically bourgeois vision of mankind, divided in almost preordained manner between *the few* who will manage and decide, and the *many*, the malleable mass, incapable of acting consciously on its own behalf, and forever destined to remain the object (and never the subject) of history. Most histories of the degeneration of the Russian Revolution rarely amount to more than this.

---

1. Paul Cardan, *From Bolshevism to the Bureaucracy* (Solidarity Pamphlet 24).

The Stalinist bureaucracy was unique in that it presented a view of history based on outright lies rather than on the more usual mixture of subtle distortion and self-mystification. But Khrushchev's revelations and subsequent developments in Russia have caused official Russian versions of events (in all their variants) to be questioned even by members of the Communist Party. Even the graduates of what Trotsky called "the Stalin school of falsification" are now beginning to reject the lies of the Stalinist era. Our task is to take the process of demystification a little further.

Of all the interpretations of the degeneration of the Russian Revolution that of Issac Deutscher is the most widely accepted on the Left. It echoes most of the assumptions of the Trotskyists. Although an improvement on the Stalinist versions, it is hardly sufficient. The degeneration is seen as due to strictly conjunctural factors (the isolation of the revolution in a backward country, the devastation caused by the Civil War, the overwhelming weight of the peasantry, etc.). These factors are undoubtedly very important. But the growth of the bureaucracy is more than just an accident in history. It is a worldwide phenomenon, intimately linked to a certain stage in the development of working class consciousness. It is the terrible price paid by the working class for its delay in recognizing that the true and final emancipation of the working class can only be achieved by the working class itself, and cannot be entrusted to others, allegedly acting on its behalf. If "socialism is Man's total and positive self-consciousness" (Marx, 1844), the experience (and rejection) of the bureaucracy is a step on that road.

The Trotskyists deny that early oppositions to the developing bureaucracy had any revolutionary content. On the contrary they denounce the Workers' Opposition and the Kronstadt rebels as basically counter-revolutionary. Real opposition, for them, starts with the proclamation—within the Party—of the Left Opposition of 1923. But anyone in the least familiar with the period will know that by 1923 the working class had already sustained a decisive defeat. It had lost power in production to a group of managers appointed from above. It had also lost power in the Soviets, which were now only ghosts of their former selves, only a rubber stamp for the emerging bureaucracy. The Left Oppostion fought within the confines of the Party, which was itself already highly bureaucratized. No substantial number of workers rallied to its cause. Their will to struggle had been sapped by the long struggle of the preceding years.

Opposition to the anti-working-class measures being taken by the Bolshevik leadership in the years immediately following the revolution took many forms and expressed itself through many different channels and at many different levels. It expressed itself *within* the Party itself, through a number of oppositional tendencies of which the Workers' Opposition (Kollontai, Lutovinov, Shlyapnikov) is the best known.[2] Outside the Party the revolutionary opposition found heterogenous expression, in the life of a number, often illegal groups (some anarchist, some anarcho-syndicalist, some still professing their basis faith in Marxism).[3] It also found expression in spontaneous, often "unorganized" class activity, such as the big Leningrad strikes of 1921 and the Kronstadt uprising. It found expression in the increasing resistance of the workers to Bolshevik industrial policy (and in particular to Trotsky's attempts to militarize the trade unions). It also found expression in proletarian opposition to Bolshevik attempts to evict all other tendencies from the Soviets, thus effectively gagging all those seeking to re-orient socialist construction along entirely different lines.

At an early stage several tendencies had struggled against the bureaucratic degeneration of the Revolution. By posthumously excluding them from the ranks of the revolutionary, Trotskyists, Leninists and others commit a double injustice. Firstly they excommunicate all those who foresaw and struggled against the nascent bureaucracy *prior to 1923*, thereby turning a deaf ear to some of the most pertinent and valid criticisms ever voiced against the bureaucracy. Secondly they weaken their own case, for if the demands for freely elected Soviets, for freedom of expression

---

2. For information concerning their programme see *The Workers' Opposition* by Alexandra Kollontai. This was first published in English in Sylvia Pankhurst's *Workers' Dead-nought* in 1921 and republished in 1961 as Solidarity Pamphlet 8.
3. The history of such groups as the Workers' Truth group or the Workers' Struggle group still remains to be written.

(proletarian democracy) and for workers' management of production were wrong in 1921, why did they become partially correct in 1923? Why are they correct now? If in 1921 Lenin and Trotsky represented the "real interests" of the workers (against the actual workers), why couldn't Stalin? Why couldn't Kadar in Hungary in 1956? The Trotskyist school of hagiography has helped to obscure the real lessons of the struggle against the bureaucracy.

When one seriously studies the crucial years after 1917, when the fate of the Russian Revolution was still in the melting pot, one is driven again and again to the tragic events of the Kronstadt uprising of March 1921. These events epitomize, in a bloody and dramatic manner, the struggle between two concepts of the Revolution, two revolutionary methods, two types of revolutionary ethos. Who decides what is or is not in the long term interests of the working class? What methods are permissible in settling differences between revolutionaries? And what methods are double-edged and only capable in the long run of harming the Revolution itself?

There is remarkably little of a detailed nature available in English about the Kronstadt events. The Stalininst histories, revised and re-edited according to the fluctuating fortunes of Party functionaries, are not worth the paper they are written on. They are an insult to the intelligence of their readers, deemed incapable of comparing the same facts described in earlier and later editions of the same book.

Trotsky's writings about Kronstadt are few and more concerned at retrospective justification and at scoring debating points against the Anarchists than at seriously analyzing this particular episode of the Russian Revolution.[4] Trotsky and the Trotskyists

---

4. An easy enough task after 1936, when some well-known anarchist "leaders" (*sic!*) entered the Popular Front government in Catalonia at the beginning of the Spanish Civil War—and were allowed to remain there by the anarchist rank and file. This action—in an area where the anarchists had a mass basis in the labour movement—irrevocably damned them, just as the development of the Russian Revolution had irrevocably damned the Mensheviks, as incapable of standing up to the test of events.

are particularly keen to perpetuate the myth that they were the first and only coherent anti-bureaucratic tendency. All their writings seek to hide how far the bureaucratization of both Party and Soviets had already gone by 1921—i.e. how far it had gone during the period when Lenin and Trotsky were in full and undisputed control. The task for serious revolutionaries today is to see the link between Trotsky's attitudes and pronouncements during and before the "great trade union debate" of 1920–21 and the healthy hostility to Trotskyism of the most advanced and revolutionary layers of the industrial working class. This hostility was to manifest itself—arms in hand—during the Kronstadt uprising. It was to manifest itself again two or three years later—this time by folded arms—when these advanced layers failed to rally to Trotsky's support, when he at last chose to challenge Stalin, within the limited confines of a Party machine, towards whose bureaucratization he had signally contributed.[5]

Deutscher in *The Prophet Armed* vividly depicts the background of Russia during the years of Civil War, the suffering, the economic dislocation, the sheer physical exhaustion of the population. But the picture is one-sided, its purpose to stress that the "iron will of the Bolsheviks" was the only element of order, stability and

5. Three statements from Trotsky's *Terrorism and Communism* (Ann Arbor: University of Michigan Press, 1961), first published in June 1920, will illustrate the point:
"The creation of a socialist society means the organization of the workers on new foundations, their adaptation to those foundations and their labour re-education, with the one *unchanging* end of the increase in the productivity of labour ..." (p. 146).
"I consider that if the Civil War had not plundered our economic organs of all that was strongest, most independent, most endowed with initiative, we should undoubtedly have *entered the path of one-man management* in the sphere of economic administration much sooner and much less painfully" (pp. 162-163).
"We have been more than once accused of having substituted for the dictatorship of the Soviets the dictatorship of our own Party ... In the substitution of the power of the Party for the power of the working class there is nothing accidental, and in reality there is no substitution at all. The Communists express the fundamental interests of the working class ..." (p. 109).
So much for the "anti-bureaucratic" antecedents of Trotskyism. It is interesting that the book was highly praised by Lenin. Lenin only took issue with Trotsky on the trade union question at the Central Committee meeting of November 8 and 9, 1920. Throughout most of 1920 Lenin had endorsed all Trotsky's bureaucratic decrees in relation to the unions.

continuity in a society that was hovering on the brink of total collapse. He pays scant attention to the attempts made by groups of
workers and revolutionaries—both within the Party and outside
its ranks—to attempt social reconstruction on an entirely different basis, from below.[6] He does not discuss the sustained opposition and hostility of the Bolsheviks to workers' management of
production or in fact to any large-scale endeavour which escaped
their domination or control.[7] Of the Kronstadt events themselves,
of the Bolshevik calumnies against Kronstadt and of the frenzied
repression that followed the events of March 1921, Deutscher says
next to nothing, except that the Bolshevik accusations against the
Kronstadt rebels were "groundless." Deutscher totally fails to see
the direct relation between the methods used by Lenin and Trotsky
in 1921 and those other methods, perfected by Stalin and later used
against the Old Bolsheviks themselves during the notorious Moscow trials of 1936, 1937 and 1938.

In Victor Serge's *Memoirs of a Revolutionary* there is a chapter
devoted to Kronstadt.[8] Serge's writings are particularly interesting
in that he was in Leningrad in 1921 and supported what the Bolsheviks were doing, albeit reluctantly. He did not however resort to
the slanders and misrepresentations of other leading Party members. His comments throw light on the almost schizophrenic frame
of mind of the rank and file of the Party at that time. For different reasons neither the Trotskyists nor the anarchists have forgiven
Serge his attempts to reconcile what was best in their respective
doctrines: the concern with reality and the concern with principle.

Easily available and worthwhile *anarchist* writings on the subject (in English) are virtually non-existent, despite the fact that

---

6. For an interesting account of the growth of the Factory Committees Movement -
and of the opposition to them of the Bolsheviks at the First All-Russian Trade Union
Convention (January 1918), see Maximov's *The Guillotine at Work* (Chicago, 1940).

7. At the Ninth Party Congress (March 1920) Lenin introduced a resolution to the
effect that the task of the unions was to explain the need for a "maximum curtailment
of administrative collegia and the gradual introduction of individual management in
units directly engaged in production" (Robert V. Daniels, *The Conscience of the Revolution*
(Cambridge, Mass., 1960), p. 124).

8. Serge's writings on this matter were first brought to the attention of readers in the
UK in 1961 (*Solidarity*, I, 7). This text was later reprinted as a pamphlet.

many anarchists consider this area relevant to their ideas. Emma Goldman's *Living My Life* and Berkman's *The Bolshevik Myth* contain some vivid but highly subjective pages about the Kronstadt rebellion. *The Kronstadt Revolt* by Anton Ciliga (produced as a pamphlet in 1942) is an excellent short account which squarely faces up to some of the fundamental issues. It has been unavailable for years. Voline's account, on the other hand, is too simplistic. Complex phenomena like the Kronstadt revolt cannot be meaningfully interpreted by loaded generalizations like "as Marxists, authoritarians and statists, the Bolsheviks could not permit any freedom or independent action of the masses." (Many have argued that there are strong Blanquist and even Bakuninist strands in Bolshevism, and that it is precisely these departures from Marxism that are at the root of Bolshevism's "elitist" ideology and practice.) Voline even reproaches the Kronstadt rebels with "speaking of power (the power of the Soviets) instead of getting rid of the word and of the idea altogether ..." The practical struggle however was not against "words" or even "ideas." It was a physical struggle against their concrete incarnation in history (in the form of bourgeois institutions). It is a symptom of anarchist muddle-headedness on this score that they can both reproach the Bolsheviks with dissolving the Constituent Assembly ... and the Kronstadt rebels for proclaiming that they stood for soviet power![9] The "Soviet anarchists" clearly perceived what was at stake— even if many of their successors fail to. They fought to defend the deepest conquest of October—soviet power—against *all* its usurpers, including the Bolsheviks.

Our own contribution to the fiftieth anniversary celebrations will not consist in the usual panegyrics to the achievements of Russian rocketry. Nor will we chant paeans to Russian pig-iron statistics. Industrial expansion may be the prerequisite for a fuller, better life for all but is in no way synonymous with such a life, unless *all* social

---

9. See Nicolas Walter's article in *Freedom* (October 28, 1967) entitled "October 1917: No Revolution at All."

relations have been revolutionized. We are more concerned at the social costs of Russian achievements.

Some perceived what these costs would be at a very early stage. We are interested in bringing their prophetic warnings to a far wider audience. The final massacre at Kronstadt took place on March 18, 1921, exactly fifty years after the slaughter of the Communards by Thiers and Calliffet. The facts about the Commune are well known. But fifty years after the Russian Revolution we still have to seek basic information about Kronstadt. The facts are not easy to obtain. They lie buried under the mountains of calumny and distortion heaped on them by Stalinists and Trotskyists alike.

The publication of this pamphlet in English, at this particular time, is part of this endeavour. Ida Mett's book *La Commune de Cronstadt* was first published in 1938. It was republished in France ten years later but has been unobtainable for several years. In 1962 and 1963 certain parts of it were translated into English and appeared in *Solidarity* (II, 6 to 11). We now have pleasure in bringing to English-speaking readers a slightly abridged version of the book as a whole, which contains material hitherto unavailable in Britain.

Apart from various texts published in Kronstadt itself in March 1921, Ida Mett's book contains Petrichenko's open letter of 1926, addressed to the British Communist Party. Petrichenko was the President of the Kronstadt Provisional Revolutionary Committee. His letter refers to discussions in the Political Bureau of the CPGB on the subject of Kronstadt, discussions which seem to have accepted that there was no extraneous intervention during the uprising. (Members of the CP and others might seek further enlightenment on the matter from King Street, whose archives on the matter should make interesting reading.)

Ida Mett writes from an anarchist viewpoint. Her writings however represent what is best in the revolutionary tradition of "class struggle" anarchism. She thinks in terms of a collective, proletarian solution to the problems of capitalism. The rejection of the class struggle, the anti-intellectualism, the preoccupation with transcendental morality and with personal salvation that characterize so many of the anarchists of today should not for a minute detract "Marxists" from paying serious attention to what she writes. We do not necessarily endorse all her judgments and have—in footnotes—corrected one or two minor factual inaccuracies in her text. Some of her generalizations seem to us too sweeping and some of her analyses of the bureaucratic phenomenon too simple to be of real use. But as a chronicle of what took place before, during and after Kronstadt, her account remains unsurpassed.

Her text throws interesting light on the attitude to the Kronstadt uprising shown at the time by various Russian political tendencies (anarchists, Mensheviks, Left and Right S.R.s, Bolsheviks, etc.). Some whose approach to politics is superficial in the extreme (and for whom a smear or a slogan is a substitute for real understanding) will point accusingly to some of this testimony, to some of these resolutions and manifestos as evidence irrevocably damning the Kronstadt rebels. "Look," they will say, "what the Mensheviks and Right SRs were saying. Look at how they were calling for a return to the Constituent Assembly, and at the same time proclaiming their solidarity with Kronstadt. Isn't this proof positive that Kronstadt was a counter-revolutionary upheaval? You yourselves admit that rogues like Victor Chernov, President elect of the Constituent Assembly, offered to help the Kronstadters? What further evidence is needed?"

We are not afraid of presenting *all* the facts to our readers. Let them judge for themselves. It is our firm conviction that most Trotskyists and Leninists are—and are kept—as ignorant of this period of Russian history as Stalinists are of the period of the Moscow Trials. At best they vaguely sense the presence of skeletons in the cupboard. At worst they vaguely parrot what their leaders tell them, intellectually too lazy or politically too well-conditioned to probe for themselves. Real revolutions are never "pure." They unleash the deepest passions of men. People actively participate or are dragged into the vortex of such movements for a variety of often contradictory reasons. Consciousness and false consciousness are inextricably mixed. A river in full flood inevitably carries a certain amount of rubbish. A revolution in full flood carries a number of political corpses—and may even momentarily give them a semblance of life.

During the Hungarian Revolution of 1956 many were the messages of verbal or moral support for the rebels, emanating from the West, piously preaching the virtues of bourgeois democracy or of free enterprise. The objective of those who spoke in these terms were anything but the institution of a classless society. But their support for the rebels remained purely verbal, particularly when it became clear to them what the real objectives of the revolution were: a fundamental democratization of Hungarian institutions *without* a reversion to private ownership of the means of production.

The backbone of the Hungarian revolution was the network of workers' councils. Their main demands were for workers' management of production and for a government based on the councils. These facts justified the support of revolutionaries throughout the world. Despite the Mindszentys. Despite the Smallholders and Social-Democrats—or their shadows—now trying to jump on to the revolutionary bandwagon. The class criterion is the decisive one.

Similar considerations apply to the Kronstadt rebellion. Its core was the revolutionary sailors. Its main objectives were ones with which no real revolutionary could disagree. That others sought to take advantage of the situation is inevitable—and irrelevant. It is a question of who is calling the tune.

Attitudes to the Kronstadt events, expressed nearly fifty years after the event often provide deep insight into the political thinking of contemporary revolutionaries. They may in fact provide a deeper insight into their conscious or unconscious aims than many a learned discussion about economics, or philosophy, or about other episodes of revolutionary history.

It is a question of one's basic attitude as to what socialism is all about. What are epitomized in the Kronstadt events are some of the most difficult problems of revolutionary strategy and revolutionary ethics: the problems of ends and means, of the relations between Party and masses, in fact of whether a Party is necessary at all.

Can the working class by itself only develop a trade union consciousness."[10] Should it even be allowed, at all times, to go that far?[11]

Or can the working class develop a deeper consciousness and understanding of its interests than can any organization allegedly acting on its behalf? When the Stalinists or Trotskyists speak of Kronstadt as "an essential action against the class enemy," when more "sophisticated" revolutionaries refer to it as a "tragic necessity," one is entitled to pause for a moment. One is entitled to ask how seriously they accept Marx's dictum that "the emancipation of the working class is the task of the working class itself." Do they take this seriously or do they pay mere lip-service to the words? Do they identify socialism with the autonomy (organizational and ideological) of the working class? Or do they see themselves, with their wisdom as to the "historical interests" of others, and with their judgments as to what should be "permitted," as the leadership around which the future elite will crystallize and develop? One is entitled not only to ask ... but also to suggest the answer!

---

10. Lenin proclaimed so explicitly in his *What Is To Be Done?* (1902).

11. In a statement to the tenth Party Congress (1921) Lenin refers to a mere *discussion* on the trade unions as an "absolutely impermissible luxury" which "we" should not have permitted. These remarks speak unwitting volumes on the subject (and incidentally deal decisively with those who seek desperately for an "evolution" in their Lenin).

The Kronstadt Commune

Ida Mett

The Kronstadt Events

"A new White plot ... expected and undoubtedly prepared by the French counter-revolution." *Pravda*, March 3, 1921.

"White generals, you all know it, played a great part in this. This is fully proved." Lenin, report delivered to the 10th Congress of the R.C.P.(B), March 8, 1921, *Selected Works*, vol. IX, p. 98.

"The Bolsheviks denounced the men of Kronstadt as counter-revolutionary mutineers, led by a White general. The denunciation appears to have been groundless." Isaac Deutcher, *The Prophet Armed*, (Oxford University Press, 1954) p. 511.

"No pretence was made that the Kronstadt mutineer were White Guards." Brian Pearce (Historian of the *Socialist Labour Leaque*) in *Labour Review*, vol. V, No. 3.

1. Background to the Kronstadt insurrection

The Kronstadt insurrection broke out three months after the con-clusion of the civil war on the European front.

As the Civil War drew to a victorious end the working masses of Russia were in a state of chronic famine. They were also increas-ingly dominated by a ruthless regime, ruled by a single party. The generation which had made October still remembered the promise of the social revolution and the hopes they had of building a new kind of society.

This generation had comprised a very remarkable section of the working class. It had reluctantly abandoned its demands for equality and for real freedom, believing them to be, if not incompatible with war, at least difficult to achieve under wartime conditions. But once victory was assured, the workers in the towns, the sailors, the Red Army men, and the peasants, all those who had shed their blood during the Civil War, could see no further justification for their hardships and for blind submission to a ferocious discipline. Even if these might have had some reason in wartime, such reasons no longer applied.

While many had been fighting at the front, others—those enjoying dominant positions in the State apparatus—had been consolidating their power and detaching themselves more and more from the workers. The bureaucracy was already assuming alarming proportions. The State machine was in the hands of a single Party, itself more and more permeated by careerist elements. A non Party worker was worth less, on the scale of everyday life, than an ex bourgeois or nobleman, who had belatedly rallied to the Party. Free criticism no longer existed. Any Party member could denounce as 'counter revolutionary' any worker simply defending his class rights and his dignity as a worker.

Industrial and agricultural production were declining rapidly. There were virtually no raw materials for the factories. Machinery was worn and neglected. The main concern of the proletariat was the bitter fight against famine. Thefts from the factories had become a sort of compensation for miserably paid labour. Such thefts continued despite the repeated searches carried out by the Cheka at the factory gates.

Workers who still had connections with the countryside would go there to barter old clothes, matches, or salt in exchange for food. The trains were crammed with such people (the *Mechotchniki*). Despite a thousand difficulties, they would try to bring food to the famished cities. Working class anger would break out repeatedly, as barrages of militia confiscated the paltry loads of flour or potatoes workers would be carrying on their backs to prevent their children from starving.

The peasants were submitted to compulsory requisitions. They were sowing less, despite the danger of famine that now resulted from bad crops. Bad crops had been common. Under ordinary conditions such crops had not automatically had these disastrous effects. The cultivated areas were larger and the peasants would usually set something aside for more difficult times.

The situation preceding the Kronstadt uprising can be summed up as a fantastic discrepancy between promise and achievement. There were harsh economic difficulties. But as important was the fact that the generation in question had not forgotten the meaning of the rights it had struggled for during the Revolution. This was to provide the real psychological background to the uprising.

The Red Navy had problems of its own. Since the Brest Litovsk peace, the Government had undertaken a complete reorganisation of the armed forces on the basis of a rigid discipline, a discipline quite incompatible with the erstwhile principle of election of officers by the men. A whole hierarchical structure had been introduced. This had gradually stifled the democratic tendencies which had prevailed at the onset of the Revolution. For purely technical reasons such a reorganisation had not been possible in the Navy, where revolutionary traditions had strong roots. Most of the naval officers had gone over to the Whites, and the sailors still retained many of the democratic rights they had won in 1917. It had not been possible to completely dismantle their organisations.

This state of affairs was in striking contrast with what pertained in the rest of the armed forces. It could not last. Differences between the rank and file sailors and the higher command of the armed forces steadily increased. With the end of the Civil War in European Russia these differences became explosive.

Discontent was rampant not only among the non-Party sailors. It also affected Communist sailors. Attempts to 'discipline' the Fleet by introducing 'Army customs' met with stiff resistance from 1920 on. Zof, a leading Party member and a member of the Revolutionary War Committee for the Baltic Fleet, was officially denounced by the Communist sailors for his 'dictatorial attitudes.' The enormous gap developing between the rank and file and the leadership was shown up during the elections to the Eighth Congress of Soviets, held in December 1920. At the naval base of Petrograd large numbers of sailors had noisily left the electoral meeting, openly protesting against the dispatch there as official delegates of people from Politotdiel and from Comflot (i.e., from the very organisations monopolising political control of the Navy).

On 15th February 1921, the Second Conference of Communist Sailors of the Baltic Fleet had met. It had assembled 300 delegates who had voted for the following resolutions:

"This Second Conference of Communist Sailors condemns the work of Poubalt (Political Section of the Baltic Fleet).
1. Poubalt has not only separated itself from the masses but also from the active functionaries. It has become transformed into a bureaucratic organ enjoying no authority among the sailors.
2. There is total absence of plan or method in the work of Poubalt. There is also a lack of agreement between its actions and the resolutions adopted at the Ninth Party Congress.
3. Poubalt, having totally detached itself from the Party masses, has destroyed all local initiative. It has transformed all political work into paper work. This has had harmful repercussions on the organisation of the masses in the Fleet. Between June and November last year, 20 per cent of the sailor Party members have left the Party. This can be explained by the wrong methods of the work of Poubalt.
4. The cause is to be found in the very principles of Poubalt's organisation. These principles must be changed in the direction of greater democracy."

Several delegates demanded in their speeches the total abolition of the 'political sections' in the Navy, a demand we will find voiced again in the sailors' resolutions during the Kronstadt uprising. This was the frame of mind in which the famous discussion on the trade union question preceding the Tenth Party Congress took place.

In the documents of the period one can clearly perceive the will of certain Bolshevik leaders (amongst whom Trotsky) not only to ignore the great discontent affecting the workers and all those who had fought in the previous period, but also to apply military methods to the problems of everyday life, particularly to industry and to the trade unions.

In these heated discussions, the sailors of the Baltic Fleet adopted a viewpoint very different from Trotsky's. At the elections to the Tenth Party Congress, the Baltic Fleet voted solidly against its leaders: Trotsky, Peoples Commissar of War (under whose authority the Navy came), and Raskolnikov, Chief of the Baltic Fleet. Trotsky and Raskolnikov were in agreement on the Trade Union question.

The sailors sought to protest against the developing situation by abandoning the Party en masse. According to information released by Sorine, Commissar for Petrograd, 5,000 sailors left the Party in January 1921 alone.

There is no doubt that the discussion taking place within the Party at this time had profound effects on the masses. It overflowed the narrow limits the Party sought to impose on it. It spread to the working class as a whole, to the soldiers and to the sailors. Heated local criticism acted as a general catalyst. The proletariat had reasoned quite logically: if discussion and criticism were permitted to Party members, why should they not be permitted to the masses themselves who had endured all the hardships of the Civil War?

In his speech to the Tenth Congress—published in the Congress Proceedings—Lenin voiced his regret at having 'permitted' such a discussion. 'We have certainly committed an error,' he said, 'in having authorised this debate. Such a discussion was harmful just before the Spring months that would be loaded with such difficulties.'

2. Petrograd on the Eve of Kronstadt

Despite the fact that the population of Petrograd had diminished by two thirds, the winter of 1920–21 proved to be a particularly hard one.

Food in the city had been scarce since February 1917 and the situation had deteriorated from month to month. The town had always relied on food stuffs brought in from other parts of the country. During the Revolution the rural economy was in crisis in many of these regions. The countryside could only feed the capital to a very small extent. The catastrophic condition of the railways made things even worse. The ever increasing antagonisms between town and country created further difficulties everywhere.

To these partly unavoidable factors must be added the bureaucratic degeneration of the administration and the rapacity of the State organs for food supply. Their role in feeding the population was actually a negative one. If the population of Petrograd did not die of hunger during this period, it was above all thanks to its own adaptability and initiative. It got food wherever it could!

Barter was practised on a large scale. There was still some food to be had in the countryside, despite the smaller area under cultivation. The peasant would exchange this produce for the goods he lacked: boots, petrol, salt, matches. The population of the towns would try and get hold of these commodities in any way it could. They alone had real value. It would take them to the countryside. In exchange people would carry back a few pounds of flour or potatoes. As we have mentioned before, the few trains, unheated, would be packed with men carrying bags on their shoulders. En route, the trains would often have to stop because they had run out of fuel. Passengers would get off and cut logs for the boilers.

Market places had officially been abolished. But in nearly all towns there were semi-tolerated illegal markets, where barter was carried out. Such markets existed in Petrograd. Suddenly, in the Summer of 1920, Zinoviev issued a decree forbidding any kind of commercial transaction. The few small shops still open were closed and their doors sealed. However, the State apparatus was in no position to supply the towns. From this moment on, famine could no longer be attenuated by the initiative of the population. It became extreme. In January 1921, according to information published by Petrokommouns (the State Supplies of the town of

Petrograd), workers in metal smelting factories were allocated rations of 800 grams of black bread a day; shock workers in other factories 600 grams; workers with A.V. cards: 400 grams; other workers: 200 grams. Black bread was the staple diet of the Russian people at this time.

But even these official rations were distributed irregularly and in even smaller amounts than those stipulated. Transport workers would receive, at irregular intervals, the equivalent of 700 to 1,000 calories a day. Lodgings were unheated. There was a great shortage of both clothing and footwear. According to official statistics, working class wages in 1920 in Petrograd were only 9 percent of those in 1913.

The population was drifting away from the capital. All who had relatives in the country had rejoined them. The authentic proletariat remained till the end, having the most slender connections with the countryside.

This fact must be emphasised, in order to nail the official lies seeking to attribute the Petrograd strikes that were soon to break out to peasant elements, 'insufficiently steeled in proletarian ideas.' The real situation was the very opposite. A few workers were seeking refuge in the countryside. The bulk remained. There was certainly no exodus of peasants into the starving towns! A few thousand 'Troudarmeitzys' (soldiers of the labour armies), then in Petrograd, did not modify the picture. It was the famous Petrograd proletariat, the proletariat which had played such a leading role in both previous revolutions, that was finally to resort to the classical weapon of the class struggle: the strike.

The first strike broke out at the Troubotchny factory, on 23rd February 1921. On the 24th, the strikers organised a mass demonstration in the street. Zinoviev sent detachments of 'Koursanty' (student officers) against them. The strikers tried to contact the Finnish Barracks. Meanwhile, the strikes were spreading. The Baltisky factory stopped work. Then the Laferma factory and a number of others: the Skorokhod shoe factory, the Admiralteiski factory, the Bormann and Metalischeski plants, and finally, on 28th February, the great Putilov works itself.

The strikers were demanding measures to assist food supplies. Some factories were demanding the re-establishment of
the local markets, freedom to travel within a radius of thirty
miles of the city, and the withdrawal of the militia detachments
holding the road around the town. But side by side with these
economic demands several factories were putting forward more
political demands: freedom of speech and of the Press, the freeing of working class political prisoners. In several big factories,
Party spokesmen were refused a hearing.

Confronted with the misery of the Russian workers who were
seeking an outlet to their intolerable conditions, the servile Party
Committee and Zinoviev, (who according to numerous accounts
was behaving in Petrograd like a real tyrant), could find no better
methods of persuasion than brute force.

Pukhov, 'official' historian of the Kronstadt revolt, wrote that
'decisive class measures were needed to overcome the enemies of
the revolution who were using a non class conscious section of the
proletariat, in order to wrench power from the working class and
its vanguard, the Communist Party.'[1]

On 24th February, the Party leaders set up a special General
Staff, called the Committee of Defence. It was composed of three
people: Lachevitch, Anzelovitch, and Avrov. They were to be supported by a number of technical assistants. In each district of the
town, a similar Committee of Three ('troika') was to be set up,
composed of the local Party organiser, the commander of the Party
battalion of the local territorial brigade and of a Commissar from
the Officers' Training Corps. Similar Committees were organised
in the outlying districts. These were composed of the local Party
organiser, the President of the Executive of the local Soviet and the
military Commissar for the District.

On 24th February the Committee of Defence proclaimed a
state of siege in Petrograd. All circulation on the streets was for-
bidden after 11 PM, as were all meetings and gatherings, both out
of doors and indoors, that had not been specifically permitted by

---

1. Poukhov: *The Kronstadt Rebellion of 1921*. State Publishing House. "Young Guard" edition, 1931. In the series: "Stages of the Civil War."

the Defence Committee. 'All infringements would be dealt with according to military law.' The decree was signed by Avrov (later shot by the Stalinists), Commander of the Petrograd military region, by Lachevitch (who later committed suicide), a member of the War Council, and by Bouline (later shot by the Stalinists), Commander of the fortified Petrograd District.

A general mobilisation of party members was decreed. Special detachments were created, to be sent to "special destinations." At the same time, the militia detachments guarding the roads in and out of the town were withdrawn. Then the strike leaders were arrested.

On 26th February the Kronstadt sailors, naturally interested in all that was going on in Petrograd, sent delegates to find out about the strikes. The delegation visited a number factories. It returned to Kronstadt on the 28th. That same day, the crew of the battleship 'Petropavlovsk,' having discussed the situation, voted the following resolution:[2]

"Having heard the reports of the representatives sent by the General Assembly of the Fleet to find out about the situation in Petrograd, the sailors demand:

1. Immediate new elections to the Soviets. The present Soviets no longer express the wishes of the workers and peasants. The new elections should be by secret ballot, and should be preceded by free electoral propaganda.
2. Freedom of speech and of the press for workers and peasants, for the Anarchists, and for the Left Socialist parties.
3. The right of assembly, and freedom for trade union and peasant organisations.
4. The organisation, at the latest on 10th March 1921, of a Conference of non-Party workers, solders, and sailors of Petrograd, Kronstadt and the Petrograd District.

---

2. This resolution was subsequently endorsed by all the Kronstadt sailors in General Assembly, and by a number of groups of Red Army Guards. It was also endorsed by the whole working population of Kronstadt in General Assembly. It became the political programme of the insurrection. It therefore deserves a careful analysis.

5. The liberation of all political prisoners of the Socialist parties, and of all imprisoned workers and peasants, soldiers, and sailors belonging to working class and peasant organisations.

6. The election of a commission to look into the dossiers of all those detained in prisons and concentration camps.

7. The abolition of all political sections in the armed forces. No political party should have privileges for the propagation of its ideas, or receive State subsidies to this end. In the place of the political sections various cultural groups should be set up, deriving resources from the State

8. The immediate abolition of the militia detachments set up between towns and countryside.

9. The equalisation of rations for all workers, except those engaged in dangerous or unhealthy jobs.

10. The abolition of Party combat detachments in all military groups. The abolition of Party guards in factories and enterprises. If guards are required, they should be nominated, taking into account the views of the workers.

11. The granting to the peasants of freedom of action on their own soil, and of the right to own cattle, provided they look after them themselves and do not employ hired labour.

12. We request that all military units and officer trainee groups associate themselves with this resolution.

13. We demand that the Press give proper publicity to this resolution.

14. We demand the institution of mobile workers' control groups.

15. We demand that handicraft production be authorised provided it does not utilise wage labour."

ANALYSIS OF THE KRONSTADT PROGRAMME

The Kronstadt sailors and the Petrograd strikers knew quite well that Russia's economic status was at the root of the political crisis. Their discontent was caused both by the famine and by the whole evolution of the political situation. The Russian workers were increasingly disillusioned in their greatest hope: the Soviets. Daily they saw the power of a single Party substituting itself for that of the Soviets. A Party, moreover, which was degenerating rapidly through the exercise of absolute power, and which was already riddled with careerists. It was against the monopoly exercised by this Party in all fields of life that the working class sought to react.

Point one of the Kronstadt resolution expressed an idea shared by the best elements of the Russian working class. Totally 'bolshevised' Soviets no longer reflected the wishes of the workers and peasants. Hence the demand for new elections, to be carried out according to the principal of full equality for all working class political tendencies.

Such a regeneration of the Soviets would imply the granting to all working class tendencies of the possibility for expressing themselves freely, without fear of calumny or extermination. Hence, quite naturally, there followed the idea of freedom of expression, of the Press, of Assembly, and of organisation, contained in Point two.

We must stress that by 1921 the class struggle in the countryside had been fought to a virtual standstill. The vast majority of the kulaks had been dispossessed. It is quite wrong to claim that the granting of basic freedoms to the peasants—as demanded in Point three—would have meant restoring political rights to the kulaks. It was only a few years later that the peasants were exhorted to 'enrich themselves'—and this by Bukharin, then an official Party spokesman.

The Kronstadt revolution had the merit of stating things openly and clearly. But it was breaking no new ground. Its main ideas were being discussed everywhere. For having, in one way or another, put forward precisely such ideas, workers and peasants were already filling the prisons and the recently set up concentration camps. The men of Kronstadt did not desert their comrades. Point six of their resolution shows that they intended to look into the whole juridical apparatus. They already had serious doubts as to its objectivity as an organ of their rule. The Kronstadt sailors were thereby showing a spirit of solidarity in the best working class tradition. In July 1917, Kerensky had arrested a deputation of the Baltic Fleet that had come to Petrograd. Kronstadt had immediately sent a further deputation to insist on their release. In 1921, this tradition was being spontaneously renewed.

Points seven and ten of the resolution attacked the political monopoly being exercised by the ruling Party. The Party was using State funds in an exclusive and uncontrolled manner to extend its influence both in the Army and in the police.

Point nine of their resolution demanded equal rations for all workers This destroys Trotsky's accusation of 1938 according to which 'the men of Kronstadt wanted privileges, while the country was hungry.'[3]

Point fourteen clearly raised the question of workers control. Both before and during the October Revolution this demand had provoked a powerful echo among the working class. The Kronstadt sailors understood quite clearly that real control had escaped from the hands of the rank and file. They sought to bring it back. The Bolshevik meanwhile sought to vest all control in the hands of a special Commissariat, the Rabkrin—Workers and Peasants inspection.[4]

Point eleven reflected the demands of the peasants to whom the Kronstadt sailors had remained linked—as had, as a matter of fact, the whole of the Russian proletariat. The basis of this link is to be found in the specific history of Russian industry. Because of feudal backwardness, Russian industry did not find its roots in petty handicraft. In their great majority, the Russian workers came directly from the peasantry. This must be stressed. The Baltic sailors of 1921 were, it is true, closely linked with the peasantry. But neither more so nor less than had been the sailors of 1917.

---

3. The accusation was made in answer to a question put to Trotsky by Wedelin Thomas, a member of the New York Commission of Enquiry into the Moscow Trials.

4. Whom has history vindicated in this matter? Shortly before his second stroke, Lenin was to write (*Pravda*, 28th January, 1923): "Let us speak frankly. The Inspection now enjoys no authority whatsoever. Everybody knows that there is no worse institution than our Inspection." This was said a bare eighteen months after the suppression of Kronstadt. (It is worth pointing out that Stalin had been the chief of the Rabkrin from 1919 till the spring of 1922, when he became General Secretary of the Party. He continued to exercise a strong influence over Rabkrin even after he had formally left it. Lenin, incidentally, had voiced no objection to Stalin's appointment or activities in this post. That only came later. Lenin had in fact defended both Stalin and Rabkrin against some of Trotsky's more far-sighted criticisms—see. I. Deutscher, *The Prophet Unarmed*, pp. 47–48. (Note added in 'Solidarity', Vol. 2, No. 7, p. 27.)

In their resolution, the Kronstadt sailors were taking up once again one of the big demands of October. They were supporting those peasant claims demanding the land and the right to own cattle for those peasants who did not exploit the labour of others. In 1921, moreover, there was another aspect to this particular demand. It was an attempt to solve the food question, which was becoming desperate. Under the system of forced requisition, the population of the towns was literally dying of hunger. Why, incidentally, should the satisfaction of these demands be deemed 'tactically correct' when advocated by Lenin, in March 1921, and 'counter revolutionary' when put forward by the peasants themselves a few weeks earlier?

What was so counter revolutionary about the Kronstadt programme? What could justify the crusade launched by the Party against Kronstadt? A workers and peasants' regime that did not wish to base itself exclusively on lies and terror, had to take account of the peasantry. It need not thereby have lost its revolutionary character. The men of Kronstadt were not alone, moreover, in putting forward such demands in 1921, Makhno's followers were still active in the Ukraine. This revolutionary peasant movement was evolving its own ideas and methods of struggle. The Ukrainian peasantry had played a predominant role in chasing out the feudal hordes. It had earned the right itself to determine the forms of its social life.

Despite Trotsky's categorical and unsubstantiated assertions, the Makhno movement was in no sense whatsoever a kulak movement. Koubanin, the official Bolshevik historian of the Makhno movement, shows statistically, in a book edited by the Party's Historical institute, that the Makhno movement at first appeared and developed most rapidly, in precisely those areas where the peasants were poorest. The Makhno movement was crushed before it had a chance of showing in practice its full creative abilities. The fact that during the Civil War it had been capable of creating its own specific forms of struggle, leads one to guess that it could have been capable of a lot more.

As a matter of fact, in relation to agrarian policy, nothing was to prove more disastrous than the zig zags of the Bolsheviks. In

1931, ten years after Kronstadt, Stalin was to decree his famous 'liquidation of the kulaks.' This resulted in an atrocious famine and in the loss of millions of human lives.

Let us finally consider Point fifteen of the Kronstadt resolution, demanding freedom for handicraft production. This was not a question of principle. For the workers of Kronstadt, handicraft production was to compensate for an industrial production that had fallen to nought. Through this demand they were seeking a way out of their intolerable economic plight.

3. Mass meetings and Bolshevik slanders

MASS MEETINGS

The Kronstadt Soviet was due to be renewed on 2nd March.

A meeting of the First and Second Battleship Sections had been planned for 1st March. The notification had been published in the official journal of the city of Kronstadt. The speakers were to include Kalinin, President of the All Russian Executive of Soviets, and Kouzmin, political commissar to the Baltic Fleet. When Kalinin arrived, he was received with music and flags. All military honours were accorded him.

Sixteen thousand people attended the meeting. Party member Vassiliev, president of the local soviet, took the chair. The delegates who had visited Petrograd the previous day gave their reports. The resolution adopted on 28th February by the crew of the battleship 'Petropavlovsk' was distributed. Kalinin and Kouzmin opposed the resolution. They proclaimed that 'Kronstadt did not represent the whole of Russia.'

Nevertheless, the mass assembly adopted the Petropavlovsk resolution. In fact only two people voted against it: Kalinin and Kouzmin!

The mass assembly decided to send a delegation of 30 workers to Petrograd to study the situation on the spot. It was also decided to invite delegates from Petrograd to visit Kronstadt, so that they would get to know what the sailors were really thinking. A further mass meeting was planned for the following day, grouping delegates from ships' crews, from the Red Army groups, from State institutions, from the dockyards and factories, and from the trade unions, to decide on the procedure of new elections to the local soviet. At the end of the meeting, Kalinin was allowed to regain Petrograd in all safety.

The following day, 2nd March, the delegates' meeting took place in the House of Culture. According to the official Kronstadt 'Izvestia,' the appointment of delegates had taken place properly. The delegates all insisted that the elections be carried out in a loyal and correct manner. Kouzmin and Vassiliev spoke first. Kouzmin stated that the Party would not relinquish power without a fight. Their speeches were so aggressive and provocative that the assembly ordered them to leave the meeting and put them under arrest. Other Party members were, however, allowed to speak at length during the debate.

The meeting of delegates endorsed by an overwhelming majority the Petropavlovsk resolution. It then got down to examining in detail the question of elections to the new soviet. These elections were to 'prepare the peaceful reconstruction of the Soviet regime.' The work was constantly interrupted by rumours, spreading through the assembly, to the effect that the Party was preparing to disperse the meeting by force. The situation was extremely tense.

THE PROVISIONAL COMMITTEE

Because of the threatening speeches of the representatives of the State power—Kouzmin and Vassiliev—and fearing retaliation, the assembly decided to form a Provisional Revolutionary Committee, to which it entrusted the administration of the town and the fortress. The Committee held its first session aboard the 'Petropavlovsk,' the Battle ship in which Kouzmin and Vassiliev were being detained.

The leading body of the assembly of delegates all became members of the Provisional Revolutionary Committee. They were:

- Petritchenko, chief quartermaster of the battleship 'Petropavlovsk,'
- Yakovenko, liaison telephonist to the Kronstadt section,
- Ossossov, boiler man in the battleship 'Sebastopol,'
- Arkhipov, chief engineer,
- Perepelkin, electrician in the battleship 'Sebastopol,'
- Patrouchev, chief electrician in the 'Petropavlovsk,'
- Koupolov, head male nurse,
- Verchinin, sailor in the 'Sebastopol,'
- Toukin, worker in the 'Electrotechnical' factory,
- Romanenko, docks maintenance worker,
- Orechin, headmaster of the Third labour School,
- Valk, sawmill worker,
- Pavlov, worker in a marine mining shop,
- Boikev, head of the building section of the Kronstadt fortress,
- Kilgast, harbour pilot.

The majority of the members of the Provisional Revolutionary Committee were sailors with a long service. This contradicts the official version of the Kronstadt events, which seeks to attribute the leadership of the revolt to elements recently joining the Navy and having nothing in common with the heroic sailors of 1917–1919.

The first proclamation of the Provisional Revolutionary Committee stated: 'We are concerned to avoid bloodshed. Our aim is to create through the joint efforts of town and fortress the proper conditions for regular and honest elections to the new soviet.'

Later that day, under the leadership of the Provisional Revolutionary Committee, the inhabitants of Kronstadt occupied all strategic points in the town, taking over the State establishments, the Staff Headquarters, and the telephone and wireless buildings. Committees were elected in all battleships and regiments. At about 9:00 p.m., most of the forts and most detachments of the Red Army had rallied. Delegates coming from Oranienbaum had also declared their support for the Provisional Revolutionary Committee. That same day the 'Izvestia' print-shops were occupied.

On the morrow, 3rd March, the men of Kronstadt published the first issue of the *Izvestia of the Provisional Revolutionary Committee*.[5] In it one read: 'The Communist Party, master of the State, has detached itself from the masses. It has shown itself incapable of getting the country out of its mess. Countless incidents have recently occurred in Petrograd and Moscow which show clearly that the Party has lost the confidence of the working masses. The Party is ignoring working class demands because it believes that these demands are the result of counter revolutionary activity. In this the Party is making a profound mistake.'

Bolshevik Slanders

Meanwhile, Moscow Radio was broadcasting as follows:
'Struggle against the White Guard Plot.' And, 'Just like other White Guard insurrections, the mutiny of ex General Kozlovsky and the crew of the battle ship "Petropavlovsk" has been organised by Entente spies. This is clear from the fact that the French paper *Le Monde* published the following message from Helsingfors two weeks before the revolt of General Kozlovsky: "We are informed from Petrograd that as the result of the recent Kronstadt revolt, the Bolshevik military authorities have taken a whole series of measures to isolate the town and to prevent the soldiers and sailors of Kronstadt from entering Petrograd."'

'It is therefore clear that the Kronstadt revolt is being led from Paris. The French counter espionage is mixed up in the whole affair. History is repeating itself. The Socialist Revolutionaries, who have their headquarters in Paris, are preparing the ground for an insurrection against the Soviet power. The ground prepared, their real master, the Tsarist general appeared. The history of Koltchak, installing his power in the wake of that of the Socialist Revolutionaries, is being repeated.' (Radio Stanzia Moskva and Radio Vestnik Rosta Moskva, 3rd. March 1921.)

The two antagonists saw the facts differently. Their outlooks were poles apart.

---

5. The entire life of this short lived journal was reprinted as an appendix to a book *Pravda o Kronshtadte*, (The Truth about Kronstadt), published in Prague, in 1921.

The call issued by Moscow's Radio was obviously coming from the Politbureau's top leaders. It had Lenin's approval, who must have been fully aware of what was happening at Kronstadt. Even assuming that he had to rely on Zinoviev for information, whom he knew to be cowardly and liable to panic, it is difficult to believe that Lenin misunderstood the real state of affairs. On 2nd March, Kronstadt had sent an official delegation to see him. It would have been enough to cross question it in order to ascertain the true situation.

Lenin, Trotsky, and the whole Party leadership knew quite well that this was no mere 'generals' revolt.' Why then invent this legend about General Kozlovsky, leader of the mutiny? The answer lies in the Bolshevik outlook, an outlook at times so blind that it could not see that lies were as likely to prove nefarious as to prove helpful. The legend of General Kozlovsky opened the path to another legend: that of the Wrangel officer allegedly conspiring with Trotsky in 1928–29. It in fact opened the path to the massive lying of the whole Stalin era.

Anyway, who was this General Kozlovsky, denounced by the official radio as the leader of the insurrection? He was an artillery general, and had been one of the first to defect to the Bolsheviks. He seemed devoid of any capacity as a leader. At the time of the insurrection he happened to be in command of the artillery at Kronstadt. The communist commander of the fortress had defected. Kozlovsky, according to the rules prevailing in the fortress, had to replace him. He, in fact, refused, claiming that as the fortress was now under the jurisdiction of the Provisional Revolutionary Committee, the old rules no longer applied. Kozlovsky remained, it is true, in Kronstadt, but only as an artillery specialist. Moreover, after the fall of Kronstadt, in certain interviews granted to the Finnish press, Kozlovsky accused the sailors of having wasted precious time on issues other than the defence of the fortress. He explained this in terms of their reluctance to resort to bloodshed. Later, other officers of the garrison were also to accuse the sailors of military incompetence, and of complete lack of confidence in their technical advisers. Kozlovsky was the only general to have been present at Kronstadt. This was enough for the Government to make use of his name.

The men of Kronstadt did, up to a point, make use of the military know-how of certain officers in the fortress at the time. Some of these officers may have given the men advice out of sheer hostility to the Bolsheviks. But in their attack on Kronstadt, the Government forces were also making use of ex Tsarist officers. On the one side there were Kozlovsky, Salomianov, and Arkannihov; On the other, ex Tsarist officers and specialists of the old regime, such as Toukhatchevsky. Kamenev, and Avrov. On neither side were these officers an independent force.

4. Effects on the Party Rank and File

On 2nd March, the Kronstadt sailors, aware of their rights, their duties and the moral authority vested in them by their revolutionary past, attempted to set the soviets on a better path. They saw how distorted they had become through the dictatorship of a single party.

On 7th March, the Central Government launched its military onslaught against Kronstadt.

What had happened between these two dates?

In Kronstadt, the Provisional Revolutionary Committee, enlarged during a mass meeting by the co-option of five new members, had started to reorganise social life in both town and fortress. It decided to arm the workers of Kronstadt to ensure the internal protection of the town. It decreed the compulsory re-election, within three days, of the leading trade union committees and of the Congress of Trade Unions, in which bodies it wished to vest considerable powers.

Rank and file members of the Communist Party were showing their confidence in the Provisional Revolutionary Committee by a mass desertion from the Party. A number of them formed a Provisional Party Bureau which issued the following appeal:

'Give no credence to the absurd rumours spread by provocateurs seeking bloodshed according to which responsible Party comrades are being shot or to rumours alleging that the Party is preparing an attack against Kronstadt. This is an absurd lie, spread by agents of the Entente, seeking to overthrow the power of the Soviets.

The Provisional Party Bureau considers re-elections to the Kronstadt Soviet to be indispensable. It calls on all its supporters to take part in these elections.

The Provisional Party Bureau calls on all its supporters to remain at their posts and to create no obstacles to the measures taken by the Provisional Revolutionary Committee. Long live the power of the Soviets! Long live international working class unity!

Signed (on behalf of the Provisional Party Bureau of Kronstadt): Iline (ex commissar for supplies), Pervouchin (ex President of the local Executive Committee), Kabanov (ex President of the Regional Trade Union Bureau).'

The Stalinist historian Poukhov referring to this appeal, declared that 'it can only be considered a treasonable act and an opportunist step towards an agreement with the leaders of the insurrection, who are obviously playing a counter revolutionary role".'[6] Poukhov admits that this document had 'a certain effect' on the rank and file of the Party. According to him, 780 Party members in Kronstadt left the Party at this time!

Some of those resigning from the Party sent letters to the Kronstadt 'Izvestia,' giving reasons for their action. The teacher Denissov wrote:

'I openly declare to the Provisional Revolutionary Committee that as from gunfire directed at Kronstadt, I no longer consider myself a member of the Party. I support the call issued by the workers of Kronstadt. All power to the Soviets, not to the Party!'

A military group assigned to the special company dealing with discipline also issued a declaration:

'We, the undersigned, joined the Party believing it to express the wishes of the working masses. In fact the Party has proved itself an executioner of workers and peasants. This is revealed quite clearly

---

6. Poukhov: *The Kronstadt Rebellion of 1921*, in series "Stages of the Civil War," p. 95. "Young Guard" edition. 1931; State Publishing House. Moscow.

by recent events in Petrograd. These events show up the face of the Party leaders. The recent broadcasts from Moscow show clearly that the Party leaders are prepared to resort to any means in order to retain power.

We ask that henceforth, we no longer be considered Party members. We rally to the call issued by the Kronstadt garrison in its resolution of 2nd. March. We invite other comrades who have become aware of the error of their ways, publicly to recognise the fact.

Signed:
Gutman, Yefimov, Koudriatzev, Andreev. ('Izvestia' of the Provisional Revolutionary Committee, 7th. March 1921).'

The Communist Party members in the 'Rif' fort published the following resolution:

'During the last three years, many greedy careerists have flocked to our Party. This has given rise to bureaucracy and has gravely hampered the struggle for economic reconstruction.

Our Party has always faced up to the problem of the struggle against the enemies of the proletariat and of the working masses. We publicly declare that we intend to continue in the future our defence of the rights secured by the working class. We will allow no White Guard to take advantage of this difficult situation confronting the Republic of Soviets. At the first attempt directed against its power we will know how to retaliate.

We fully accept the authority of the Provisional Revolutionary Committee, which is setting itself the objective of creating soviets genuinely representing the proletarian and working masses.

Long live the power of the Soviets, the real defenders of working class rights.

Signed: the Chairman and Secretary of the meeting of Communists in Fort Rif' ('Izvestia' of the Provisional Revolutionary Committee. 7th. March 1921.

Were such declarations forcibly extracted from Party members by the regime of terror directed against Party members allegedly reigning in Kronstadt at the time? Not a shred of evidence has been produced to this effect. *Throughout the whole insurrection not a single imprisoned Communist was shot.* And this despite the fact that among the prisoners were men responsible for the fleet such as Kouzmin and Batys. The vast majority of Communist Party members were in fact left entirely free.

In the 'Izvestia' of the Provisional Revolutionary Committee for 7th March, one can read under the heading 'We are not seeking revenge,' the following note:

'The prolonged oppression to which the Party dictatorship has submitted the workers has provoked a natural indignation among the masses. This has led, in certain places, to boycotts and sackings directed against the relatives of Party members. This must not take place. We are not seeking revenge. We are only defending our interests as workers. We must act cautiously. We must only take action against those who sabotage or those who through lying propaganda seek to prevent a reassertion of working class power and rights.'

In Petrograd, however, humanist ideas of rather a different kind were prevailing. As soon as the arrests of Kouzmin and Vassiliev were learned, the Defence Committee ordered the arrests of the families of all Kronstadt sailors known to be living in Petrograd. A Government plane showered Kronstadt with leaflets saying:

'The Defence Committee announces that it has arrested and imprisoned the families of the sailors as hostages for the safety of communist comrades arrested by the Kronstadt mutineers. We refer specifically to the safety of Fleet Commissar Kouzmin, and Vassiliev, President of the Kronstadt Soviet. If a hair of their heads is touched, the hostages will pay with their lives.' ('Izvestia' of the Provisional Revolutionary Committee, 5th. March 1921).

The Provisional Revolutionary Committee replied with the following radio message:

'In the name of the Kronstadt garrison, the Provisional Revolutionary Committee of Kronstadt insists on the liberation, within

24 hours, of the families of the workers, sailors and red soldiers arrested as hostages by the Petrograd Soviet.

The Kronstadt garrison assures you that in the city of Kronstadt, Party members are entirely free and that their families enjoy absolute immunity. We refuse to follow the example of the Petrograd Soviet. We consider such methods, even when conducted by ferocious hatred, as utterly shameful and degrading.

Signed: Petritchenko, sailor, President of the Provisional Revolutionary Committee; Kilgast, Secretary.'

To refute rumours according to which Party members were being ill-treated, the Provisional Revolutionary Committee set up a special Commission to investigate the cases of the imprisoned communists. In its issue of 4th March, the 'Izvestia' of the Provisional Revolutionary Committee announced that a Party member would be attached to the Commission. It is doubtful if this body ever got to work, as two days later the bombardment of Kronstadt began. The Provisional Revolutionary Committee did, however, receive a Party delegation. It granted it permission to visit the prisoners in the 'Petropavlovsk.' The prisoners had even been allowed to hold meetings among themselves, and to edit a wall newspaper (Zaikovski: 'Kronstadt from 1917 to 1921').

There was no terror in Kronstadt. Under very difficult and tragic circumstances, the 'rebels had done their utmost to apply the basic principles of working class democracy. If many rank and file communists decided to support the Provisional Revolutionary Committee, it was because this body expressed the wishes and aspirations of the working people. In retrospect, this democratic self assertion of Kronstadt may appear surprising. It certainly contrasted with the actions and frame of mind prevailing among the Party leaders in Petrograd and Moscow. They remained blind, deaf and totally lacking in understanding of what Kronstadt and the working masses of the whole of Russia really wanted.

Catastrophe could still have been averted during those tragic days: Why then did the Petrograd Defence Committee use such abusive language? The only conclusion an objective observer can come to is that it was done with the deliberate intention of provoking bloodshed, thereby 'teaching everyone a lesson' as to the need for absolute submission to the central power.

5. Threats, Bribes and Skirmishes

THREATS AND BRIBES
On 5th March, the Petrograd Defence Committee issued a call to the rebels.

'You are being told fairy tales when they tell you that Petrograd is with you or that the Ukraine supports you. These are impertinent lies. The last sailor in Petrograd abandoned you when he learned that you were led by generals like Kozlovskv. Siberia and the Ukraine support the Soviet power. Red Petrograd laughs at the miserable efforts of a handful of White Guards and Socialist Revolutionaries. You are surrounded on all sides. A few hours more will lapse and then you will he compelled to surrender. Kronstadt has neither bread nor fuel. *If you insist, we will shoot you like partridges.*

At the last minute, all those generals, the Kozlovskvs, the Bourksers, and all that riff raff, the Petrichenkos, and the Tourins will flee to Finland, to the White guards. And you, rank and file soldiers and sailors, where will you go then? Don't believe them when they promise to feed you in Finland. Haven't you heard what happened to Wrangel's supporters? They were transported to Constantinople. There they are dying like flies, in their thousands, of hunger and disease. This is the fate that awaits you, unless you immediately take a grip of yourselves. Surrender Immediately! Don't waste a minute. Collect your weapons and come over to us. Disarm and arrest your criminal leaders, and in particular the Tsarist generals. Whoever surrenders immediately will be forgiven. Surrender now.
Signed: The Defence Committee.'

In reply to these threats from Petrograd, the Provisional Revolutionary Committee Issued a final appeal.

'TO ALL, TO ALL, TO ALL.

Comrades, workers, red soldiers and sailors. Here in Kronstadt we know full well how much you and your wives and your children are suffering under the iron rule of the Party. We have overthrown the Party-dominated Soviet. The Provisional Revolutionary Committee is today starting elections to a new Soviet. It will be freely elected, and it will reflect the wishes of the whole working population, and of the garrison—and not just those of a handful of Party members.

Our cause is just. We stand for the power of the Soviets, not for that of the Party. We stand for freely elected representatives of the toiling masses. Deformed Soviets, dominated by the Party, have remained deaf to our pleas. Our appeals have been answered with bullets.

The workers' patience is becoming exhausted. So now they are seeking to pacify you with crumbs. On Zinoviev's orders the militia barrages have been withdrawn. Moscow has allocated ten million gold roubles for the purchase abroad of food stuffs and other articles of first necessity. But we know that the Petrograd proletariat will not be bought over in this way. Over the heads of the Party, we hold out to you the fraternal hand of revolutionary Kronstadt.

Comrades, you are being deceived. And truth is being distorted by the basest of calumnies.

Comrades, don't allow yourselves to be misled.

In Kronstadt, power is in the hands of the sailors, of the red soldiers and of the revolutionary workers. It is not in the hands of white Guards commanded by General Kozlovsky, as Moscow Radio lyingly asserts.

Signed: The Provisional Revolutionary Committee.'

Foreign communists were in Moscow and Petrograd at the time of the revolt. They were in close contact with leading Party circles. They confirmed that the Government had made hasty purchases abroad (even chocolate was bought, which had always been a luxury in Russia). Moscow and Petrograd had suddenly changed their tactics. The Government had a better grasp of psychological war than had the men of Kronstadt. It understood the corrupting influence of white bread on a starving population. It was in vain that Kronstadt asserted that crumbs would not buy the Petrograd proletariat. The Government's methods had undoubted effect, especially when combined with vicious repression directed against the strikers.

Support in Petrograd

Part of the Petrograd proletariat continued to strike during the Kronstadt events. Poukhov, the Party historian, himself admits this. The workers were demanding the liberation of the prisoners. In certain factories, copies of the 'Ivestia' of the Provisional Revolutionary Committee were found plastered on the walls. A lorry even drove through the street of Petrograd scattering leaflets from Kronstadt. In certain enterprises (for instance, the State Printing Works No. 26), the workers refused to adopt a resolution condemning the Kronstadt sailors. At the 'Arsenal' factory, the workers organised a mass meeting on 7th March, (the day the bombardment of Kronstadt began). This meeting adopted a resolution of the mutinous sailors! It elected a commission which was to go from factory to factory, agitating for a general strike.

Strikes were continuing in the biggest factories of Petrograd: Poutilov, Baltisky, Oboukhov, Nievskaia Manoufactura, etc. The authorities sacked the striking workers, transferred the factories to the authority of the local troikas (three men committees), who proceeded to selective rehiring of workers. Other repressive measures were also taken against the strikers.

Strikes were also starting in Moscow, in Nijni Novgorod and In other cities. But here too, the prompt delivery of foodstuffs, combined with calumnies to the effect that Tsarist generals were in command at Kronstadt had succeeded in sowing doubts among the workers.

The Bolsheviks' aim had been achieved. The proletariat of Petrograd and of the other industrial cities was in a state of confusion. The Kronstadt sailors, who had been hoping for the support of the whole of working class Russia, remained isolated, confronting a Government determined to annihilate them, whatever the cost.

FIRST SKIRMISHES

On 6th March, Trotsky addressed an appeal by radio to the Kronstadt garrison:

'The Workers' and Peasants' Government has decided to reassert its authority without delay, both over Kronstadt and over the mutinous battleships, and to put them at the disposal of the Soviet Republic. I therefore order all those who have raised a hand against the Socialist Fatherland, immediately to lay down their weapons. Those who resist will be disarmed and put at the disposal of the Soviet Command. The arrested commissars and other representatives of the Government must be freed immediately. Only those who surrender unconditionally will be able to count on the clemency of the Soviet Republic. I am meanwhile giving orders that everything be prepared to smash the revolt and the rebels by force of arms. The responsibility for the disasters which will effect the civilian population must fall squarely on the heads of the White Guard insurgents.

Signed: Trotsky, President of the Military Revolutionary Council of the Soviet Republic, KAMENEV,[7] Glavkom (Commanding Officer).'

On 8th March, a plane flew over Kronstadt and dropped a bomb. On the following days, Government artillery continued to shell the fortress and neighbouring forts, but met with stiff resistance. Aircraft dropped bombs which provoked such fury among the civilian population that they started firing back. The Provisional Revolutionary Committee had to order the defenders not to waste their ammunition.

By 1921 the Kronstadt garrison had been markedly reduced. Figures issued by the General Staff of the defenders put the number

---

7. This Kamenev was an ex-Tsarist officer, now collaborating with the Soviet Government. He was a different Kamenev from the one shot by the Stalinists in 1936.

at 3,000. Gaps between infantrymen defending the perimeter were at least 32 feet wide. Stocks of ammunition and shells were also limited.

During the afternoon of 3rd March, the Revolutionary Committee had met in conference together with certain military specialists. A Military Defence Committee was set up which prepared a plan to defend the fortress. But when the military advisers proposed an assault in the direction of Oranienbaum (where there were food stocks, at Spassatelnaia), the Provisional Revolutionary Committee refused. It was not putting its faith in the military capacity of the sailors; but in the moral support of the whole of proletarian Russia. Until the first shot had been fired, the men of Kronstadt refused to believe that the Government would militarily attack them. This is no doubt why the Provisional Revolutionary Committee had not set out to prevent the approach of the Red Army by breaking the ice around the foot of the fortress. For much the same reasons, fortified barrages were not set up along the probable line of attack.

Kronstadt was right. Militarily they could not win. At best, they could have held a fortnight. This might have been important, for once the ice had melted, Kronstadt could have become a real fortress, capable of defending itself. Nor must we forget that their human reserves were infinitesimal, compared with the numbers the Red Army could throw into battle.

6. Demoralisation in the Red Army

What was morale like in the Red Army at this time? In an interview given to 'Krasnaia Gazeta,' Dybenko described how all the military units participating in the assault on Kronstadt had to be reorganised.[8] This was an absolute necessity. During the first day of military operations, the Red Army had shown that it did not wish

---

8. Old Bolshevik. President of the Tsentrobalt (Central Committee of the Sailors of the Baltic Fleet) in July 1917. After October Revolution member of the First Soviet of Peoples' Commissars. Together with Antonov Ovseenko and Krylenko was put in charge of Army and Navy.

to fight against the sailors, against the 'bratichki' (little brothers), as they were known at the time. Amongst the advanced workers, the Kronstadt sailors were known as people most devoted to the Revolution. And anyway, the very motives that were driving Kronstadt to revolt, existed among the ranks of the Red Army. Both were hungry and cold, poorly clad and poorly shod and this was no mean burden in the Russian winter, especially when what was asked of them was to march and fight on ice and snow.

During the night of 8th March, when the Red Army attack against Kronstadt started, a terrible snow storm was blowing over the Baltic. Thick fog made the tracks almost invisible. The Red Army soldiers wore long white blouses which hid them well against the snow. This is how Poukhov[9] described morale in Infantry Regiment 561 in an official communiqui. The regiment was approaching Kronstadt from the Oranienbaum side.

'At the beginning of the operation the second battalion had refused to march. With much difficulty and thanks to the presence of communists, it was persuaded to venture on the ice. As soon as it reached the first south battery, a company of the 2nd. battalion surrendered. The officers had to return alone. The regiment stopped. Dawn was breaking. We were without news of the 3rd. battalion, which was advancing towards south batteries 1 and 2. The battalion was marching in file and was being shelled by artillery from the forts. It then spread out and veered to the left of Fort Milioutine, from which red flags were being waved. Having advanced a further short distance, it noticed that the rebels had fitted machine guns on the forts, and were offering them the choice of surrendering or being massacred. Everybody surrendered, except the battalion commissar and three or four soldiers who turned back on their steps."

On 8th. March, Oublanov, Commissar for the Northern Sector, wrote to the Petrograd Party:

'I consider it my revolutionary duty to clarify you as to the state of affairs on the northern sector. It is impossible to send the Army into a second attack on the forts. I have already spoken to Comrades Lachevitch, Avrov and Trotsky about the morale

---

9. Op. cit.

of the Koursantys (cadet officers, deemed most fit for battle). I have to report the following tendencies. The men wish to know the demands of Kronstadt. They want to send delegates to Kronstadt. The number of political commissars in this sector is far from sufficient.'

Army morale was also revealed in the case of the 79th Brigade of the 27th Omsk Division. The Division comprised three regiments. It had shown its fighting capacities in the struggle against Koltchak. On 12th March, the division was brought to the Kronstadt front. The Orchane regiment refused to fight against Kronstadt. The following day, in the two other regiments of the same division, the soldiers organised impromptu meetings where they discussed what attitude to take. Two of the regiments had to be disarmed by force, and the 'revolutionary' tribunal posed heavy sentences.

There were many similar cases. Not only were the soldiers unwilling to fight against their class brothers, but they were not prepared to fight on the ice in the month of March. Units had been brought in from other regions of the country, where by mid March the ice was melting already. They had little confidence in the solidity of the Baltic ice. Those who had taken part in the first assault, had seen that the shells from Kronstadt were opening up enormous holes in its surface, in which the unfortunate Government troops were being engulfed. These were hardly encouraging scenes. All this contributed to the failure of the first assaults against Kronstadt.

REORGANISATION

The regiments to be used in the final assault against Kronstadt were thoroughly reorganised. Groups that had shown any sympathy towards Kronstadt were disarmed and transferred to other units. Some were severely punished by the Revolutionary Tribunal. Party members were mobilised and allocated to various battalions for purposes of propaganda and for reporting back on unsure elements.

Between 8th and 15th of March, while the cannons exchanged fire over the ice at Kronstadt, the Tenth Party Congress was held in Moscow. The Congress despatched 300 delegates to the front, among them Vorochilov, Boubnov, Zatousky, Roukhimovitch and Piatakov. The 'delegates' were nominated 'political commissars' and appointed to the military section of the Tcheka, or to 'special commissions for the struggle against desertion.' Some just fought in the ranks.

The Revolutionary Tribunals were working overtime. Poukhov describes how 'they would vigorously react to all unhealthy tendencies. Troublemakers and provocateurs were punished according to their deserts.' The sentences would immediately be made known to the soldiers. Some times they would even be published in the papers.

But despite all the propaganda, all the reorganisation, and all the repression, the soldiers retained their doubts. On 14th March, there were further acts of insubordination. Regiment 561, reorganised on 8th March, still refused to march. 'We will not fight against our brothers from the same "stanltsas,"'[10] they proclaimed.

Small groups of Red Army men surrendered to the rebels and started fighting on their side. Witnesses described how some units lost half their men before even entering the line of fire of the insurgents. They were being machined gunned from the rear 'to prevent them surrendering to the rebels.'

Official sources described how issues of the Kronstadt 'Izvestia' were being read with great interest in the Red Army. So were the leaflets distributed by the Kronstadt rebels. Special political commissions were set up to prevent such material from entering the barracks. But this had an opposite effect from the one expected.

Party organisations throughout the country were mobilised. Intensive propaganda was carried out among the troops in the rear. The human and material resources available to the Government were far greater than those available to Kronstadt. Trains were daily bringing new troops to Petrograd. Many were being sent from the Kirghiz and Bachkir lands (i.e., were composed of men as far removed as possible from the 'Kronstadt frame of mind'). As

---

10. Cossack villages. Regiment 560, also composed of Cossacks and Ukrainians, was fighting on the side of Kronstadt.

to the defenders of Kronstadt, their forces were not only diminishing numerically (through losses sustained in fighting), but they were more and more exhausted. Badly clad and half starving, the Kronstadt rebels remained at their guns, almost without relief, for just over a week. At the end of this period, many of them could hardly stand.

7. The Final Assault

Aware of these facts and having taken all necessary measures in relation to organisation, supplies, and improvement in morale Toukhatchevsky, commander of the 7th Army, issued his famous proclamation of 15th March. He ordered that Kronstadt be taken by all out assault in the night of 16th–17th March. Entire regiments of the 7th Army were equipped with hand grenades, white blouses, shears for cutting barbed wire and with small sleighs for carrying machine guns.

Toukhatchevsky's plan was to launch a decisive attack from the south, and then to capture Kronstadt by a massive simultaneous assault from three different directions.

On 16th March, the Southern Group opened its artillery barrage at 14.20 hrs. At 17.00 hrs. the Northern Group also started shelling Kronstadt. The Kronstadt guns answered back. The bombardment lasted four hours. Aircraft then bombed the city, with a view to creating panic among the civilian population. In the evening, the artillery bombardment ceased. The Kronstadt searchlights swept over the ice looking for the invaders.

Towards midnight, the Government troops had taken up their position and started to advance. At 2:45 a.m., the Northern Force had occupied Fort 7, abandoned by the Kronstadt defenders. At 4:30 a.m., Government troops attacked Forts 4 and 6, but suffered very heavy losses from the Kronstadt artillery. At 6:40 a.m., Government officer cadets finally captured Fort 6.

At 5:00 a.m., the Southern Force launched an attack on the forts facing them. The defenders, overwhelmed, fell back towards the city. A fierce and bloody battle then broke out in the streets. Machine guns were used, at very close range. The sailors defended each house, each attic, each shed. In the town itself, they were rein-forced by the workers' militias. The attacking troops were, for a few hours, thrown back towards the forts and suburbs. The sail-ors reoccupied the Mechanical Institute, which had been captured early by the 80th government Brigade.

The street fighting was terrible. Red Army soldiers were losing their officers, Red Army men and defending troops were mixing in indescribable confusion. No one quite knew who was on which side. The civilian population of the town tried to fraternise with the Government troops, despite the shooting. Leaflets of the Pro-visional Revolutionary Committee were still being distributed. To the bitter end the sailors were trying to fraternise.

Throughout 17th. March the fighting raged on. By the evening the Northern Group had occupied most of the forts. Street fight-ing continued throughout the night and well into the following morning. One by one the last forts—Milioutine, Constantine, and Obroutchev—fell. Even after the last one had been occupied, iso-lated groups of defenders were still desperately fighting back with machine guns. Near the Tolbukhin light house, a final group of 150 sailors put up a desperate resistance.

THE BALANCE SHEET

Figures Issued by the Military Health Authorities of the Petrograd District—and relating to the period between 3rd. and 21st. March—spoke of 4,127 wounded and 527 killed. These fig-ures do not include the drowned, or the numerous wounded left to die on the ice.[11] Nor do they include the victims of the Revo-lutionary Tribunals.

We do not even have approximate figures as to the losses on the Kronstadt side. They were enormous, even without the repri-sal massacres that later took place. Perhaps one day the archives of

---

11. So numerous were the latter that the Finnish Foreign Ministry started discussions with Bersine, the Russian ambassador, with a view to joint frontier guard patrols clearing the corpses from the ice. The Finns feared that hundreds of bodies would be washed on to the Finnish shores after the ice had melted.

the Tcheka and of the Revolutionary Tribunals will reveal the full and terrible truth.

This is what Poukhov, 'official' Stalinist historian of the revolt, says on the matter: 'While steps were being taken to re-establish normal life, and as the struggle against rebel remnants was being pursued, the Revolutionary Tribunals of the Petrograd Military District were carrying out their work in many areas ... Severe proletarian justice was being meted out to all traitors to the Cause ... The sentences were given much publicity in the press and played a great educational role.' These quotations from official sources refute Trotskyist lies that 'the fortress was surrounded and captured with insignificant losses.'[12]

In the night of 17th–18th March, part of the Provisional Revolutionary Committee left Kronstadt. Some 8,000 people (some sailors and the most active part of the civilian population), moved towards Finland and permanent exile. When the Red Army—defenders of the 'soviet' power—finally entered Kronstadt, they did not re-establish the Kronstadt soviet. Its functions were taken over by the Political Section of the Secretariat of the new Assistant Commander of the Fortress.

The whole Red Fleet was profoundly reorganised. Thousands of Baltic sailors were sent to serve in the Black Sea, in the Caspian and in Siberian naval stations. According to Poukhov: 'the less reliable elements, those infected with the Kronstadt spirit, were transferred. Many only went reluctantly. This measure contributed to the purification of an unhealthy atmosphere.'

In April, the new Naval Command started an individual check. 'A special commission dismissed 15,000 sailors in "non essential" (i.e., non specialised) categories V, G, and D—as well as sailors not considered reliable from a political point of view.'

After the physical annihilation of Kronstadt, its very spirit had to be eradicated from the Fleet.

---

12. On 10th September 1937, Trotsky wrote in *La Lutte Ouvrière*, 'the legend that would have it that Kronstadt 1921 was a great massacre.'

8. What they said at the time

'Revolts by workers and peasants have shown that their patience has come to an end. The uprising of the workers is near at hand. The time has come to overthrow the bureaucracy... Kronstadt has raised for the first time the banner of the Third Revolution of the toilers... The autocracy has fallen. The Constituent Assembly has departed to the region of the damned. The bureaucracy is crumbling...' Isvestia of the Kronstadt Provisional Revolutionary Committee. Etapy Revoliutsi (Stages of the Revolution), March 12, 1921.

'In the bourgeois newspapers you can read that we brought up Chinese, Kalmuk and other regiments against Yudemitch and Kronstadt. This is, of course, a lie. We brought up our youth. The storming of Kronstadt was indeed symbolic. Kronstadt, as I said, was about to pass into the hands of French and English imperialism.' L. Trotsky. Speech delivered at 2nd Congress of Communist Youth International, July 14, 1921. *The First Five Years of The Communist International* (Pioneer Publishers, 1945), p. 312.

THE ANARCHISTS

Did the Kronstadt sailors put forward their demands and resolutions by themselves? Or were they acting under the influence of political groups, which might have suggested slogans to them? Anarchist influence is often incriminated when this subject is described. How sure can one be of the matter? Among members of the Provisional Revolutionary Committee, as among the Kronstadters in general, there were certainly individuals claiming to be anarchists. But if one bases oneself on documentary evidence, as we have sought to do throughout this study, one must conclude that there was no direct intervention by anarchist groups.

The Menshevik Dan, who was in prison for a while in Petrograd with a group of Kronstadt rebels, tells us in his memoirs that Perepelkin, one of the members of the Provisional Revolutionary Committee, was close to anarchism.[13] He also tells us that the Kron-

---

13. Dan, T: *Two years of roaming (1919–21)* in Russian.

stadt sailors were both disillusioned and fed up with Communist Party policy and that they spoke with hatred about political parties in general. In their eyes, the Mensheviks and the Socialist Revolutionaries were as bad as the Bolsheviks. All were out to seize power and would later betray the people who had vested their confidence in them. According to Dan, the conclusion of the sailors, disappointed with political parties was: 'You are all the same. What we need is anarchism, not a power structure!'

The anarchists of course defend the Kronstadt rebels. It seems likely to us that had any of their organisations really lent a hand in the insurrection the anarchist press would have mentioned the fact. In the anarchist press of the time, however, there is no mention of such help. For instance Yartchouk, an old anarcho-syndicalist[14] who before October had enjoyed considerable authority amongst the population and sailors of Kronstadt, mentions no such anarchist role in his pamphlet devoted to the 1921 uprising,[15] written immediately after the events. We must consider his judgement as fairly conclusive evidence.

At the time of the insurrection the anarchists were already being persecuted all over the country. Isolated libertarians and the few remaining anarchist groupings were undoubtedly 'morally' on the side of the insurgents. This is shown for instance in the following leaflet, addressed to the working class of Petrograd:

'The Kronstadt revolt is a revolution. Day and night you can hear the sound of the cannon. You hesitate to intervene directly against the Government to divert its forces from Kronstadt, although the cause of Kronstadt is your cause... The men of Kronstadt are always in the forefront of rebellion. After the Kronstadt revolt let us see the revolt of Petrograd. And after you, let anarchism prevail.'

Four anarchists then in Petrograd (Emma Goldman, Alexander Berkman, Perkus, and Petrovsky) foresaw a bloody outcome to events. On March 5, they sent the following letter to the Petrograd Council for Labour and Defence:

---

14. In 1926 he became a Communist and returned to Russia.
15. Yartchouk. *The Kronstadt Revolt.* In Russian and Spanish.

'It Is not only impossible but in fact criminal to keep quiet at the present time. Recent developments compel us anarchists to give our opinion on the present situation. The discontent and ferment in the minds of the workers and sailors are the result of circumstances which deserve serious attention from us. Cold and famine have provoked discontent, while the absence of any possibility of discussion or criticism drive the workers and sailors to seek an outlet to this discontent. The fact that a workers' and peasants' government uses force against workers and sailors is even more important. It will create a reactionary impression in the international labour movement and will therefore harm the cause of the social revolution. Bolshevik comrades, think while there is still time. Don't play with fire. You are about to take a decisive step. We propose the following to you: nominate a commission of six, of which two should be anarchists, to go to Kronstadt to solve the differences peacefully. In the present circumstances this is the most rational way of doing things. It will have an international revolutionary significance.'

These anarchists certainly did their duty. But they acted on their own and there is nothing to show that they were organisationally linked with the rebels in any way. Moreover the very fact that they proposed this kind of mediation suggests that they were not in direct contact with the sailors, who had themselves sent a deputation to Petrograd through which it would have been possible to negotiate. And if, in the 'Petropavlovsk' resolution, we find the demand of freedom of speech and freedom of publication for the anarchists, this merely shows that the Kronstadters of 1921 had retained their ideas and traditions of before October.

Before October both Bolsheviks and Anarchists had considerable influence at Kronstadt.[16] In the summer of 1917, at a meeting of the Petrograd Soviet, Trotsky had been able to answer the Menshevik leader Tseretelli:

'Yes, the Kronstadters are anarchists. But during the final stage of the Revolution the reactionaries who are now inciting you to

16. According to the testimony of well-known Bolsheviks such as Flerovski and Raskolnikov.

exterminate Kronstadt will be preparing ropes to hang both you and us. And it will be the Kronstadters who will fight to the last to defend us.'

The anarchists were well-known in Kronstadt as revolutionaries. That is why the rebels, when they spoke of opening the doors of the Soviets to different socialist tendencies, had first thought of the anarchists as well as of the left Socialist Revolutionaries.

The most important of the demands of the Petropavlovsk resolution were those calling for democratic rights for the workers and those peasants not exploiting the labour of others and the demand calling for the abolition of the monopoly of Party influence. These demands were part of the programme of other socialist tendencies, already reduced to illegality. The anarchists agreed with these demands and were not the only ones to be putting them forward.

On the other hand the Kronstadters repeatedly insisted that they were 'for soviet power.' A small minority of Russian libertarians (the 'soviet anarchists') were known to support the idea of close collaboration with the soviets, which were already integrated into the state machine. The Makhnovist movement on the other hand (which was not exclusively anarchist although under the strong personal influence of Makhno, an anarchist since the age of 16) did not speak of 'soviet power' as some thing to be defended. Its slogan was 'free soviets,' i.e. soviets where different political tendencies might coexist, without being vested with state power.

The Kronstadters believed that the trade unions had an important role to play. This idea was by no means an exclusively anarchist one. It was shared by the left Socialist Revolutionaries and by the Workers' Opposition (Kollontai and Chliapnikov) in the Communist Party itself. Later other oppositional communist tendencies (like the Sapronovites) were to espouse it. In short the idea was the hallmark of all those who sought to save the Russian Revolution through proletarian democracy and through an opposition to the one-party monopoly which had started dominating and was now replacing all other tendencies.

We may conclude by saying that anarchism had an influence on the Kronstadt insurrection to the extent that it advocated the idea of proletarian democracy.

THE MENSHEVIKS

The Mensheviks had never carried much weight among the sailors. The number of Menshevik deputies to the Kronstadt Soviet bore no real relation to their influence in the Fleet. The anarchists, who after the second election only had three or four deputies to the Soviet, enjoyed a far greater popularity. This paradoxical situation arose from the lack of organisation among the anarchists and also from the fact that in 1917 the differences between bolshevism and anarchism were hardly perceptible to the masses. Many anarchists at that time saw bolshevism as a kind of Bakouninized Marxism.[17]

The Mensheviks—at least their official faction—although fundamentally hostile to Bolshevism, were not in favour of an armed struggle against the State power. Because of this they were hostile to armed intervention.[18] They tried to play the role of a legal opposition both in the Soviets and in the trade unions. Opposed both to the dictatorship of the proletariat and to the dictatorship of a single party and convinced that a stage of capitalist development still confronted Russia, they felt that armed interventions would only prevent the democratic forces in Russia from establishing themselves. They hoped that once the armed struggle had come to an end the regime would be compelled to follow a course of democratic transformation.

On March 7, 1921, during the Kronstadt insurrection, the underground Petrograd Committee of the Mensheviks published the following leaflet:

'To the workers, red soldiers and Koursantys of Petrograd.

Stop the slaughter! The guns are thundering and the Communists who claim to be a Workers Party are shooting the sailors of Kronstadt.

---

17. This idea was later developed by Hermann Sandomirski, a 'soviet anarchist,' in an article published in the Moscow *Izvestia*, on the occasion of Lenin's death.
18. In fact during Denikin's offensive of 1919 they had told their members to enter the Red Army.

We don't know all the details about what has happened at Kronstadt. But we do know that the Kronstadters have called for free elections to the soviets and for the release of arrested socialists and of arrested non-party workers and soldiers. They have called for the convening, on March 10, of a non-party conference of workers, red soldiers and sailors to discuss the critical situation of Soviet Russia.

A genuine workers' power should have been able to clarify the real causes of the Kronstadt events. It should have discussed things openly with the workers and sailors of Kronstadt, in front of the whole of working class Russia. Instead, the Bolsheviks have proclaimed a state of siege and have machine-gunned the soldiers and sailors.

Comrades, we cannot, we must not just sit and listen to the sound of the guns. Each salvo may destroy dozens of human lives. We must intervene and put an end to this massacre.

Insist that military operations against the sailors and workers of Kronstadt be ended immediately. Insist that the Government start immediate negotiations with Kronstadt, with the participation of Petrograd factory delegates. Elect delegates forthwith to participate in these discussions. Stop the slaughter!'

The Central Committee of the Mensheviks had also published a leaflet. This proclaimed that 'what was necessary was not a policy of violence towards the peasantry but a policy of conciliation towards it. Power should really be in the hands of the working masses. To this end new and free elections to the soviets were essential. What was needed was that Workers' Democracy, much talked about but of which one couldn't see the slightest trace.'

Sozialistitchenski Vestnik, the official organ of Russian Social Democracy (published abroad) assessed the Kronstadt insurrection as follows: 'It is precisely the masses themselves, who until now had supported bolshevism, who have now taken the initiative in a decisive struggle against the present regime.' The paper considered the Kronstadt slogans to be Menshevik ones and added that Mensheviks 'had all the greater right to be pleased about it, in view of the fact that their party had played no role in the insurrection, given the total lack of any Menshevik organisation in the Fleet.'

Martov, the leader of Russian Menshevism was already out of Russia. In an article in *Freiheit*, published on May 1st 1921, he denied that either Mensheviks or Social Revolutionaries had played any part in the insurrection. The initiative, he felt, was coming from the sailors who were breaking with the Communist Party at the organisational level, but not at the level of principles.

Poukhov quotes another leaflet signed by one of the numerous groups of Mensheviks. It said: "Down with the lies of the Counter Revolution! Where are the real counter-revolutionaries? They are the Bolsheviks, the commissars, those who speak of 'soviet power.' Against them the real Revolution is rising up. We must support it. We must come to the rescue of Kronstadt. Our duty is to help Kronstadt. Long live the Revolution. Long live the Constituent Assembly!" The Menshevik Central Committee declined all responsibility for slogans put forward by such dissident groupings.

THE RIGHT S.R.s.

The call for the convening of the Constituent Assembly was the central theme of the propaganda of the Right wing Socialist Revolutionaries. In *Revolutzionaia Rossia*, their Party organ (which in March 1921 was being published abroad) Victor Tchernov, ex-president of the dissolved Constituent Assembly and leader of the Right S.R.s. wrote: 'All those who want to find a way out of the disgusting, bloodstained Bolshevik dictatorship, all those who wish to tread the path of freedom must stand up around Kronstadt and come to its help. The crown of democracy must be the Constituent Assembly".

Now Tchernov was fully aware that in No. 6 of the *Kronstadt Isvestia* the rebel sailors had written 'The workers and peasants will go forward. *They will leave behind them the Utchred-Nika* (pejorative form for the Constituent Assembly) *and its bourgeois regime. They will also leave behind them the Communist Party dictatorship with its tchekas and its State Capitalism*, which has seized the masses by the throat and is threatening to throttle them." When Tchernov discussed these lines of the Kronstadters he attributed them to an ideological survival of past Bolshevik influence.

By personal and political temperament, Tchernov was diametrically opposed to the Mensheviks. With his political friends he launched a passionate appeal to the sailors.

'The Bolsheviks killed the cause of liberty and democracy when they counterpoised, in the popular mind, the idea of soviets to the idea of the Constituent Assembly. Instead of seeing the soviets as a support for the Constituent Assembly, as a powerful link between the Assembly and the country, they raised the soviets against the Assembly and thereby killed both the soviets and the Assembly. This is what you must understand, deceived workers, soldiers, and sailors. Let your slogan "free elections to the soviets" reverberate, as a call to a march from the soviets to the Constituent Assembly.'

Tchernov went even further. From a private ship he sent the following radio message to the Provisional Revolutionary Committee:

'The President of the Constituent Assembly, Victor Tchernov, sends fraternal greetings to the heroic sailor, soldier and worker comrades who, for the third time since 1905, are shaking off the yoke of tyranny. Acting as an intermediary, he proposes, with the help of Russian co-operative organisations now abroad, to send men to ensure the feeding of Kronstadt. Let me know what you need and how much you need. I am prepared to come personally and to place both my forces and my authority at the disposal of the popular revolution. I have confidence in the final victory of the working people. From every corner we are receiving news that the masses are ready and willing to rise in the name of the Constituent Assembly. Don't be trapped into negotiations with the Bolsheviks. They will only enter into such negotiations in order to gain time and to concentrate around Kronstadt those formations of the privileged soviet military corps of which they can be sure. Glory to those who were the first to raise the flag of popular liberation. Down with the despotism of both right and left. Long live liberty and democracy.'

At the same time a second appeal was sent to Kronstadt by special courier, from the 'deputation abroad of the Socialist Revolutionary Party':

'The Party has abstained from any type of putchism. In Russia it has lately put the brakes on the upsurges of popular anger while frequently trying, through the pressure of worker and peasant opinion, to compel the Kremlin dictators to concede to the demands of the people. But now that popular anger has overflowed, now that the flag of popular revolution has been proudly hoisted over Kronstadt, our Party is offering the rebels the help of all the forces it can muster in the struggle for liberty and democracy. The S.R.s are prepared to share your fate and to win or die in your ranks. Let us know how we can help you. Long live the people's revolution. Long live free soviets and the Constituent Assembly!'

To these concrete proposals, Tchernov received, on March 3 1921, the following answer by radio:

'The Provisional Revolutionary Committee of the city of Kronstadt has received the greetings of comrade Tchernov, dispatched from Reval. To all our brothers abroad we express our gratitude for their sympathy. We thank Comrade Tchernov for suggestions but ask him not to come for the time being until the matter has been clarified. For the time being we are noting his proposal.

Signed: Petrichenko President of the
Provisional Revolutionary Committee.'

The Bolsheviks claim that the Provisional Revolutionary Committee consented in principle to Tchernov's arrival. They also claim that Tchernov made his offer to send provisions to Kronstadt conditional on the rebels launching the slogan of the Constituent Assembly. On March 20, 1921 the communist Komarov declared at a meeting of the Petrograd Soviet that the Provisional Revolutionary Committee had asked Tchernov to wait for 12 days during which time the food situation in Kronstadt would have become such that it would be possible to launch the slogan asked for by the S.R.s. Komarov claimed that this information had been obtained in the course of the cross-questioning of Perepelkin a member of the Provisional Revolutionary Committee who had fallen into Bolshevik hands. Perepelkin was even alleged to have said that the President of the Provisional Revolutionary Committee had secretly sent a positive answer to Tchernov.

The sailor Perepelkin was shot and his 'confessions' cannot be verified. But in prison, just before, he had met the Menshevik Dan and had mentioned no such thing to him although during their joint exercise periods Perepelkin had provided Dan with many details concerning the insurrection. One is led to believe that already in 1921, Bolshevik 'justice' knew how to concoct confessions.

In an article published in January 1926, in *Znamia Borby*, organ of the left S.R.s, Petrichenko, President of the Provisional Revolutionary Committee, confirms the answer given to Tchernov by the committee. He explains that the Committee itself could not deal with this question. It proposed to hand the problem over to the newly elected soviet. Petrichenko adds 'I am describing things as they took place in reality and independent of my own political opinion.' As for Tchernov, he denies having posed conditions for the rebels. He claims openly to have supported the slogan of the Constituent Assembly, 'convinced that sooner or later the rebels would have adopted it.'

THE LEFT S.R.s.

In the June 1921 issue of their paper *Znamia* published abroad, this is how the left S.R.s outlined their programme:

'The essential aim of the left (internationalist) S.R. Party is the reconstitution of the soviets and the restoration of genuine Soviet power.... We are aiming at the permanent re-establishment of the violated Constitution of the Soviet Republic, as adopted on June 10, 1918, at the Fifth All-Russian Congress of Soviets.... the peasantry, which is the backbone of the working population in Russia, should have the right to dispose of its fate.... another essential demand is the re-establishment of the self-activity and of the free initiative of the workers in the cities. Intensive labour cannot be demanded of men who are starving and half dead. First they must be fed and to this end it is essential to co-ordinate the interests of workers and peasants.'

The spirit of the *Petropavlovsk* Resolution is undoubtedly very close to that of the left S.R. programme. The left S.R.s, however, deny participation in the insurrection. In the same issue of *Znamia* one of their Moscow correspondents writes: 'At Kronstadt, there wasn't a single responsible representative of left populism. The whole movement developed without our participation. At the onset we were outside of it but it was nevertheless essentially left populist in outlook. Its slogans and its moral objectives are very close to our own.'

In the wish to establish historical truth we will now quote two further authorised testimonies, that of Lenin and that of the sailor Petrichenko, one of the leaders of the insurrection.

LENIN'S VIEWS

In his article 'The Tax in Kind' this is what Lenin has to say about Kronstadt[19]:

'In the spring of 1921, mainly as a result of the failure of the harvest and the dying of cattle, the condition of the peasantry, which was extremely bad already as a consequence of the war and blockade, became very much worse. This resulted in political vacillation which, generally speaking, expresses the very "nature" of the small producer. The most striking expression of this vacillation was the Kronstadt mutiny.... There was very little of anything that was fully formed, clear and definite. We heard nebulous slogans about "liberty," "free trade," "emancipation from serfdom," "Soviets without the Bolsheviks," or new elections to the Soviets, or relief from "party dictatorship," and so on and so forth. Both the Mensheviks and the Socialist-Revolutionaries declared the Kronstadt movement to be "their own."'

---

19. Ida Mett's quotations from Lenin are wrongly attributed to his article on 'The Tax in Kind.' This report was delivered at the 10th Party Congress, on March 15, 1921 (Selected Works, Volume 9, p. 107). In fact the quotations relate to an article on "The Food Tax" (*Selected Works*, Volume 9, pp. 194–198). Ed. *Solidarity*.

Victor Chernov sent a runner to Kronstadt: on the proposal of this runner, the Menshevik Valk, one of the Kronstadt leaders, voted for the 'Constituent.' In a flash, with radio-telegraphic speed, one might say, the White Guards mobilised all their forces 'for Kronstadt.' The White Guard military experts in Kronstadt, a number of experts, and not Kozlovsky alone, drew up a plan for a landing of forces at Oranienbaum, a plan which frightened the vacillating Menshevik-Socialist-Revolutionary non-party masses.

More than fifty Russian White Guard newspapers published abroad are conducting a furious campaign 'for Kronstadt.' The big banks, all the forces of finance capital, are collecting funds to assist Kronstadt. The wise leader of the bourgeoisie and the landlords, the Cadet Milyukov, is patiently explaining to the fool Victor Chernov directly (and to Dan and Rozhkov who are in Petrograd jail for their connection with the Kronstadt Mensheviks, indirectly) that they need be in no hurry with their Constituent, and that they *can and must support the Soviets only without the Bolsheviks.*

Of course, it is easy to be cleverer than conceited fools like Chernov, the hero of petty-bourgeois phrases, or like Martov, the knight of philistine reformism painted to look like 'Marxism.' Properly speaking, the point is not that Milyukov, as an individual, is cleverer, but that because of his class position the party leader of the big bourgeoisie sees, understands the class essence and political interaction of things more clearly than the leaders of the petty bourgeoisie, the Chernovs and Martovs. The bourgeoisie is really a class force which inevitably rules under capitalism, both under a monarchy and in the most democratic republic, and which also inevitably enjoys the support of the world bourgeoisie.

But the petty bourgeoisie. i.e.. all the heroes of the Second International and of the 'Two-and-a-Half' International, cannot, by the very economic nature of the case, be anything else than the expression of class impotence; hence the vacillation, phrases and helplessness....

When in his Berlin Journal Martov declared that Kronstadt not only adopted Menshevik slogans but also proved that an anti-Bolshevik movement was possible which did not entirely serve the interests of the White Guards, the capitalists and the landlords, he served as an example of a conceited philistine Narcissus. He said in effect: 'Let us close our eyes to the fact that all the real White Guards greeted the Kronstadt mutineers and through the banks collected funds in aid of Kronstadt!' Milyukov is right compared with the Chernovs and Martovs, for he proposes real tactics for a real White Guard Force, the force of the capitalists and landlords. He says in effect: 'It does not matter whom we support, even the anarchists, any sort of Soviet government, *as long as* the Bolsheviks are overthrown, *as long as shifting of power* can be brought about! It makes no difference, to the Right or to the Left, to the Mensheviks or to the anarchists, as long as power shifts away from the Bolsheviks.' As for the rest—'we,' the Milyukovs, we shall give the anarchists, the Chernovs and the Martovs a good slapping and kick them out as was done to Chernov and Maisky in Siberia, to the Hungarian Chernovs and Martovs in Hungary, to Kautsky in Germany and Friedrich Adler and Co. in Vienna. The real, practical bourgeoisie fooled hundreds of these philistine Narcissuses: the Mensheviks, Socialist-Revolutionaries and non-party people, and kicked them out scores of times in all revolutions in all countries. This is proved by history. It is corroborated by facts. The Narcissuses will chatter; the Milyukovs and White Guards will act....

The events of the spring of 1921 once again revealed the role of the Socialist-Revolutionaries and Mensheviks: they are helping the vacillating petty-bourgeois element to recoil from the Bolsheviks, to cause a 'shifting of power' for the benefit of the capitalists and landlords. The Mensheviks and Socialist-Revolutionaries have now learnt to disguise themselves as 'non-party.'

PETRICHENKO'S EVIDENCE

We will finally quote the main passages of Petrichenko's evidence, as published in his article in the left S.R. paper *Znamia Borby*, In January 1926:

'I have read the letters exchanged between the left S.R. organisation and the British Communists. In this correspondence the question of the Kronstadt insurrection of 1921 is raised...

As I was the President [of the Provisional Revolutionary Committee] I feel it a moral obligation briefly to throw some light on these events for the benefit of the Political Bureau of the British Communist Party. I know you get your information from Moscow. I also know that this information is one-sided and biased. It wouldn't be a bad thing if you were shown the other side of the coin....

You have yourselves admitted that the Kronstadt insurrection of 1921 was not inspired from the outside. This recognition implies that the patience of the working masses, sailors, red soldiers, workers and peasants had reached its final limit.

Popular anger against the dictatorship of the Communist Party—or rather against its bureaucracy—took the form of an insurrection. This is how precious blood came to be spilt. There was no question of class or caste differences. There were workers on both sides of the barricades. The difference lay in the fact that the men of Kronstadt marched forward consciously and of their own free will, while those who were attacking them had been misled by the Communist Party leaders and some were even acting against their own wishes. I can tell you even more: the Kronstadters didn't enjoy taking up arms and spilling blood!

What happened then to force the Kronstadters to speak the language of guns with the Communist Party bosses, daring to call themselves a "Workers and Peasants Government"?

The Kronstadt sailors had taken an active part in the creation of such a government. They had protected it against all the attacks of the Counter-revolution. They not only protected the gates of Petrograd—the heart of the world revolution—but they also formed military detachments for the innumerable fronts against the White Guards, starting with Kornilov and finishing with Generals Youdienitch and Neklioudov.

You are asked to believe that these same Kronstadters had suddenly become the enemies of the Revolution. The "Workers and Peasants" Government denounced the Kronstadt rebels as agents of the Entente, as French spies, as supporters of the bourgeoisie, as S.R.s, as Mensheviks, etc., etc. It is astounding that the men of Kronstadt should suddenly have become dangerous enemies just when real danger from the generals of the armed counter-revolution had disappeared—just when the rebuilding of the country had to be tackled—just when people were thinking of tasting the fruits of October—just when it was a question of showing the goods in their true colour, of showing one's political baggage (i.e. when it was no longer a question of making promises but of sticking to them). People were beginning to draw up a balance sheet of revolutionary achievements. We hadn't dared dream about this during the Civil War. Yet it is just at this point in time that the men of Kronstadt were found to be enemies. What crime had Kronstadt, therefore, committed against the revolution?

As the Civil War subsided, the Petrograd workers thought it their right to remind the Soviet of that town that the time had come to remember their economic plight and to pass from a war regime to a regime of peace.

The Petrograd Soviet considered this harmless and essential demand to be counter-revolutionary. It not only remained deaf and dumb to these claims but it started resorting to home searches and arrests of workers, declaring them spies and agents of the Entente. These bureaucrats became corrupt during the Civil War at a time when no one dared resist them. They hadn't noticed that the situation had changed.

The workers answered by resorting to strikes. The fury of the Petrograd Soviet then became like the fury of a wild animal. Assisted by Its Opritchniks it kept the workers hungry and exhausted.[20] It held them in an iron grip, driving them to work by all kinds of constraint. The Red soldiers and sailors, despite their sympathy with the workers, didn't dare rise in their defence. But this time the "workers" and "peasants" Government came unstuck about Kronstadt. Somewhat belatedly Kronstadt had learned about the true state of affairs in Petrograd.

---

20. The Opritchniks were the personal guard of Ivan the Terrible and at the same time his higher political police force. During the seven years of their existence (1565–1572) they distinguished themselves by their ferocious activity.

You are therefore right, British comrades, when you say that the Kronstadt revolt was not the result of the activities of any one particular person.

Furthermore I would like you to know more about the alleged support to Kronstadt of counter-revolutionary foreign and Russian organisations! I repeat again that the uprising was not provoked by any political organisation. I doubt they even existed at Kronstadt. The revolt broke out spontaneously. It expressed the wishes of the masses themselves, both the civilian population and the garrison. This is seen in the resolutions adopted and in the composition of the Provisional Revolutionary Committee, where one cannot detect the dominant influence of any anti-soviet party. According to the Kronstadters any thing that happened or was done there was dictated by the circumstances of the moment. The rebels didn't place their faith in anyone. They didn't even place it in the hands of the Provisional Revolutionary Committee or in the hands of the assemblies of delegates, or in the hands of meetings, or anywhere else. There was no question about this. The Provisional Revolutionary Committee never attempted anything in this direction, although it could have done. The Committee's only concern was strictly to implement the wishes of the people. Was that a good thing or a bad thing? I cannot pass judgement.

The truth is that the masses led the Committee and not the other way round. Among us there were no well-known political figures, of the kind who see everything three archines deep and know all that needs to be done, and how to get the most out of every situation.[21] The Kronstadters acted without predetermined plans or programme, feeling their way according to circumstances and within the context of the resolutions they had adopted. We were cut off from the entire world. We didn't know what was going on outside Kronstadt, either in Russia or abroad. Some may possibly have drawn up their own blueprints for our insurrection as usually happens. They were wasting their time. It is fruitless to speculate as to what would have happened if things had evolved differently, for the turn of events itself might have

---

21. Archine = Russian measure of length.

been quite different from what we were anticipating. One thing is certain, the Kronstadters didn't want the initiative to pass out of their hands.

In their publications the Communists accuse us of accepting an offer of food and medicine from the Russian Red Cross, in Finland. We admit we saw nothing wrong in accepting such an offer. Both the Provisional Revolutionary Committee and the assembly of delegates agreed to it. We felt that the Red Cross was a philanthropic organisation, offering us disinterested help that could do us no harm. When we decided to allow the Red Cross delegation to enter Kronstadt we lead them blindfolded to our head-quarters. At our first meeting we informed them that we gratefully accepted their offer of help as coming from a philanthropic organisation, but that we considered ourselves free of any undertakings towards them. We accepted their request to leave a permanent representative in Kronstadt, to watch over the regular distribution to women and children of the rations which they were proposing to send us.

Their representative, a retired naval officer called Vilken, remained in Kronstadt. He was put in a permanently guarded flat and couldn't even step outside without our permission. What danger could this man have represented? All he could see was the resolve of the garrison and of the civilian population of Kronstadt.

Was this the "aid of the international bourgeoisie"? Or did this aid perhaps lie in the fact that Victor Tchernov had sent us his greetings? Was this the "support of both the Russian and international counter-revolution"? Can you really believe that the men of Kronstadt were ready to throw themselves into the embrace of any anti-soviet party? Remember that when the rebels learned that the right wing was beginning to devise plans about their insurrection they didn't hesitate to warn the workers about it. Remember the article of March 6 in the *Kronstadt Isvestia*, entitled "gentlemen or comrades."'

9. Kronstadt: last upsurge of the Soviets

This luxury was really absolutely impermissible. By permitting (sic!) such a discussion (on the trade unions) we undoubtedly made a mistake and failed to see that in this discussion a question came to the forefront which, because of the objective conditions, should not have been in the forefront. —Lenin. Report to 10th Party Congress, March 8, 1921. Selected Works, Vol. IX, p. 90.

What the rebels of Kronstadt demanded was only what Trotsky had promised their elder brothers and what he and the Party had been unable to give. Once again a bitter and hostile echo of his own voice came back to him from the lips of other people, and once again he had to suppressed it. —Isaac Deutscher, *The Prophet Armed*, p. 512–3.

TROTSKY'S ACCUSATIONS

Taking everything into account, what was the Kronstadt uprising? Was it a counter-revolutionary insurrection? Was it a revolt without conscious counter-revolutionary objectives, but which was bound to open the doors to the counter-revolution? Or was it simply an attempt by the working masses to materialise some of the promise of October? Was the revolt inevitable? And was the bloody end to which it came also inevitable? We will conclude by trying to answer these questions.

The accusations made against Kronstadt by the Bolsheviks in 1921 are exactly the same as those mentioned later by the Stalinist historian Poukhov, in his book published in 1931. Trotsky repeated them. The trotskyists still repeat them today.

Trotsky's attitude on this question was however always somewhat embarrassed and awkward. He would issue his accusations by the dropper instead of proclaiming them once and for all. In 1937, when he discussed Kronstadt for the first time in writing (in his books on the Russian Revolution he hardly ever dealt with the subject) he starts by saying that 'The country was hungry, and the Kronstadt sailors were demanding privileges. The mutiny was motivated by their wish for privileged rations.'[22] Such a demand was never put forward by the men of Kronstadt. In his later writings Trotsky, having doubtless taken care to read more on the matter, was to abandon this particular accusation. What remains, however, is that he started his public accusations with a lie.

In an article in the Belgian paper *Lutte Ouvriere* (February 26, 1938) Trotsky wrote:

'From a class point of view, which—no offence to the eclectics—remains the fundamental criterion both in politics and in history, it is extremely important to compare the conduct of Kronstadt with that of Petrograd during these critical days. In Petrograd too the whole leading stratum of the working class had been skimmed off. Famine and cold reigned in the abandoned capital, even more cruelly than in Moscow... The paper of the Kronstadt rebels spoke of barricades in Petrograd, of thousands of people killed.[23] The Press of the whole world was announcing the same thing. In fact the exact opposite took place. The Kronstadt uprising did not attract the workers of Petrograd. It repelled them. The demarcation took place along class lines. The workers immediately felt that the Kronstadt rebels were on the other side of the barricade and they gave their support to the Government.'

Here again Trotsky is saying things which are quite untrue. Earlier on we showed how the wave of strikes had started in Petrograd and how Kronstadt had followed suit. It was against the strikers of Petrograd that the Government had to organise a special General Staff: the Committee of Defence. The repression was first directed against the Petrograd workers and against their demonstrations, by the despatch of armed detachments of Koursantys.[24]

But the workers of Petrograd had no weapons. They could not defend themselves as could the Kronstadt sailors. The military repression directed against Kronstadt certainly intimidated the Petrograd workers. The demarcation did not take place 'along class lines' but according to the respective strengths of the organs

---

22. Bulletin of the Opposition, No. 56–57 (In Russian).
23. It is untrue that the paper of the Kronstadters, the *Kronstadt Izvestia* ever spoke of 'thousands of people killed' in Petrograd.
24. Officer cadets.

of repression. The fact that the workers of Petrograd did not follow those of Kronstadt does not prove that they did not sympathise with them. Nor, at a later date, when the Russian proletariat failed to follow the various 'oppositions' did this prove that they were in agreement with Stalin! In such instances it was a question of the respective strengths of the forces confronting one another.

In the same article Trotsky repeats his points concerning the exhaustion of Kronstadt, from the revolutionary point of view. He claims that, whereas the Kronstadt sailors of 1917 and 1918 were ideologically at a much higher level than the Red Army, the contrary was the case by 1921. This argument is refuted by official Red Army documents. These admit that the frame of mind of Kronstadt had infected large layers of the army.

Trotsky denounces those who attack him over Kronstadt over the belatedness of their strictures. 'The campaign around Kronstadt' he says 'is conducted, in certain places, with unrelenting energy. One might imagine that events took place yesterday and not seventeen years ago.' But seventeen years is a very short period, on any historical scale. We don't accept that to speak of Kronstadt is to 'evoke the days of the Egyptian Pharaohs.' Moreover it appears logical to us to seek some of the roots of the great Russian catastrophe in this striking and symptomatic episode. After all it took place at a time when the repression of the Russian workers was not being perpetrated by some Stalin or other but by the flower of Bolshevism, by Lenin and Trotsky themselves. Seriously to discuss the Kronstadt revolt is therefore not, as Trotsky claims, 'to be interested in discrediting the only genuinely revolutionary tendency, the only tendency never to have reneged its flag, never to have compromised with the enemy, the only tendency to represent the future.'

During the subsequent seventeen years Trotsky shed none of his hostility towards the rebels. Lacking arguments he resorts to gossip. He tells us that 'at Kronstadt, where the garrison was doing nothing and only living on its past, demoralisation had reached important proportions. When the situation became particularly difficult in famished Petrograd, the Political Bureau discussed several times whether to raise an internal loan in Kronstadt, where there still remained old stores of all sorts. But the Petrograd delegates would answer: "They will give us nothing of their own free will. They speculate on cloth, coal, bread, for in Kronstadt all the old scum has raised its head again!'"

This argument concerning 'old stores of all sorts' is in bad faith. One need only recall the ultimatum to the Kronstadters issued by the Petrograd Defence Committee on March 5th (referred to elsewhere): "You will be obliged to surrender. Kronstadt has neither bread nor fuel." What had happened in the meantime to the said old stories?

Further information on this topic comes from the *Kronstadt Ivestia*. It describes the distribution to children of one pound of dried potatoes on presentation of ration vouchers 5 and 6. On March 8th, four litres of oats were distributed to last four days—and on March 9th a quarter of a pound of black biscuit made of flour and dried potato powder. On March 10th the Regional Committee of Metalworkers decided to place at the disposal of the community the horse meat to which its members were entitled. During the insurrection there was also distributed a tin of condensed milk per person, on one occasion some meat preserves, and finally (to children only), half a pound of butter.

That no doubt is what Trotsky refers to as "old stores of all sorts"! According to him these might have been borrowed to alleviate the great Russian famine. We should add that before the insurrection these "stores" were in the hands of communist functionaries and that it was upon these people alone that consent to the proposed "loan" depended. The rank and file sailor, who took part in the insurrection, had no means open to him whereby he could have opposed the loan, even if he had wanted to. So much for the question of "stores"—which in passing shows the worth of some of the accusations used against Kronstadt.

To resort to such arguments in the course of a serious discussion (and consciously to substitute for such a discussion a polemic about the Spanish Revolution) shows up a serious flaw: the absence of valid arguments on the matter among the Bolsheviks (for Trotsky isn't the central figure in the repression of

Kronstadt). Lenin and the Politbureau directed the whole operation. The Workers' Opposition must also shoulder its share of responsibility. According to the personal testimony of foreign Communists residing in Russia at the time, the Workers' Opposition didn't agree with the measures being taken against the rebels. But neither did it dare open its mouth for the defence of Kronstadt. At the 10th Party Congress no one protested at the butchery of the rebels. The worker Lutovinov, a well known member of the Central Executive Committee of the Soviets and one of the leaders of the Workers Opposition, was sent to Berlin in March 1921 on a diplomatic mission (in reality this was a form of political exile). He declared that: 'The news published abroad concerning the Kronstadt events was greatly exaggerated. The Soviet Government is strong enough to finish off the rebels. The slowness of the operation is to be explained by the fact that we wish to spare the population of Kronstadt" (*L'Humanite*. March 18, 1921).[25]

Trotsky uses yet another argument against the rebels: he accuses them of seeking to take advantage of their revolutionary past. This is a most dangerous argument for anyone in opposition. Stalin was to use it against Trotsky and the old Bolshevik. It was only later that Stalin accused them of having been, from the very beginning of the Revolution, the agents of the international bourgeoisie. During the first years of the struggle he conceded that Trotsky had rendered great services to the Revolution but he would add that Trotsky had subsequently passed into the ranks of the counter-revolution. One had to judge a man on what he did now. The example of Mussolini was constantly mentioned.

However, there are many things that Trotsky is unable to explain. He cannot explain how Kronstadt and the whole Red Fleet came to renounce their ideological support for the Government. He cannot explain the frame of mind of the communist elements in the Fleet during the discussions on the Trade Union question. He cannot explain their attitude during the 8th All-Russian Soviet Congress elections or during the Second Communist Conference of the Baltic Fleet, which took place on

---

25. Lutovinov committed suicide in Moscow, in May 1924.

the eve of the insurrection. These are, however, key points around which the discussion should centre. When Trotsky asserts that all those supporting the government were genuinely proletarian and progressive, whereas all others represented the peasant counter-revolution, we have a right to ask of him that he present us with a serious factual analysis in support of his contention. The unfurling of subsequent events showed that the Revolution was being shunted onto a disastrously wrong track. This was first to compromise then to destroy all its social, political, and moral conquests. Did the Kronstadt revolt really represent an attempt to guide the Revolution along new lines? That is the crucial question one has to ask. Other problems should be seen as of secondary importance and flowing from this serious concern.

It is certainly not the smashing of the Kronstadt revolt that put a brake to the course of the Revolution. On the contrary, in our opinion, it was the political methods used against Kronstadt and widely practised throughout Russia which contributed to the setting up, on the ruins of the Social Revolution, of an oligarchic regime which had nothing in common with the original ideas of the Revolution.[26]

THE BOLSHEVIK INTERPRETATIONS

In 1921 the Bolshevik Government claimed that Kronstadt had rebelled according to a preconceived plan. This particular interpretation was based on a note published in certain French newspapers (*Le Matin, L'Echo de Paris*) on February 15th. This note

---

26. In his last book, written in the tragic context of an unequal struggle with his mortal enemy, Trotsky made what was for him a great effort at being objective. This is what he says about Kronstadt: 'The Stalinist school of falsification is not the only one that flourishes today in the field of Russian history. Indeed, it derives a measure of sustenance from certain legends built on ignorance and sentimentalism, such as the lurid tales concerning Kronstadt, Makhno and other episodes of the Revolution. Suffice it to say that what the Soviet Government did reluctantly at Kronstadt was a tragic necessity; naturally the revolutionary government could not have "presented" the fortress that protected Petrograd to the insurgent sailors only because a few dubious Anarchists and S.R.s were sponsoring a handful of reactionary peasants and soldiers in rebellion. Similar considerations were involved in the case of Makhno and other potentially revolutionary elements that were perhaps well-meaning but definitely ill-acting.' *Stalin* by Trotsky. Hollis and Carter (1947), p. 337.

announced the uprising and led to the claim that the uprising was led by the Entente.

This was the argument which enabled Lenin to claim, at the 10th Party Congress:

'The transfer of political power from the hands of the Bolsheviks to a vague conglomeration or alliance of heterogeneous elements who seem to be only a little to the Right of the Bolsheviks, and perhaps even to the "Left" of the Bolsheviks—so indefinite is the sum of political groupings which tried to seize power in Kronstadt. Undoubtedly, at the same time, White generals—you all know it—played a great part in this. This is fully proved. The Paris newspapers reported a mutiny in Kronstadt two weeks before the events in Kronstadt took place.'[27]

The publication of false news about Russia was nothing exceptional. Such news was published before, during, and after the Kronstadt events. It is undeniable that the bourgeoisie throughout the world was hostile to the Russian Revolution and would exaggerate any bad news emanating from that country. The Second Communist Conference of the Baltic Fleet had just voted a resounding resolution, critical of the political leadership of the Fleet. This fact could easily have been exaggerated by the bourgeois press, once again confusing the wishes with reality. To base an accusation on a 'proof' of this kind is inadmissible and immoral.

In 1938 Trotsky himself was to drop this accusation. But in the article we have already mentioned he refers his readers to a study of the Kronstadt rebellion undertaken by an American trotskyst John G. Wright. In an article published in the New International (in February 1938) Mr Wright takes up once again the claim that the revolt must have been planned before-hand. In view of the fact the press had announced it on February 15th. He says: 'the connection between Kronstadt and the counterrevolution can be established not only out of the mouths of the enemies of Bolshevism but also on the basis of irrefutable facts.' What irrefutable facts? Again, quotations from the bourgeois press (Le Matin, Vossische Zeitung, The Times) giving false news before and during the insurrection.

---

27. Lenin. *Selected Works*. Lawrence and Wishart (1937). Volume 9, p. 97.

It is interesting that these arguments were not much used at the time, during the battle itself, but only years later. If, at the time the Bolshevik Government had proof of these alleged contacts between Kronstadt and the counter-revolutionaries why did it not try the rebels publicly? Why did it not show the working masses of Russia the 'real' reasons for the uprising? If this wasn't done it was because no such proof existed.

We are also told that if the New Economic policy had been introduced in time the insurrection would have been avoided. But as we have just shown the uprising did not take place according to a preconceived plan. No one knew that it was necessarily going to take place. We have no theory as to the exact timing and development of popular movements and it is quite possible that under economic and political conditions different from those prevailing in the spring of 1921 the insurrection might never have taken place. On the other hand the uprising might have occurred in a different form, or in a different place, for instance in Nijni Novgorod where an important strike movement took place, coinciding with the great strike wave in Petrograd. The particular conditions relating to the Fleet and to Kronstadt's revolutionary past certainly had an effect, but one can't be certain just exactly how significant this effect was. Much the same applies to the statement that 'if the N.E.P. had been introduced a few months earlier there would have been no Kronstadt revolt.'

The N.E.P. was admittedly proclaimed at the same time as the rebels were being massacred. But it doesn't follow in any way that the N.E.P. corresponded to the demands put forward by the sailors. In the *Kronstadt Isvestia* of March 14th we find a characteristic passage on this subject. The rebels proclaimed that 'Kronstadt is not asking for freedom of trade but for genuine power to the Soviets.' The Petrograd strikers were also demanding the reopening of the markets and the abolition of the road blocks set up by the militia. But they too were stating that freedom of trade by itself would not solve their problems.

Insofar as the N.E.P. replaced the forced requisition of foodstuffs by the tax in kind and insofar as it re-established internal trade it certainly satisfied some of the demands of the men of Kronstadt and of the striking Petrograd workers. With the N.E.P. rationing and arbitrary seizures ceased. Petty owners were able to sell their goods on the open markets, lessening the effects on the great famine. The N.E.P. appeared to be first and foremost a safety measure.

But the N.E.P. unleashed the capitalist elements in the country just at a time when the one party dictatorship was leaving the proletariat and working peasants without means of defence against these capitalist forces. 'The class exerting the dictatorship is in fact deprived of the most elementary political rights' proclaimed the Worker's Truth, an oppositional communist group in 1922. The Worker's Group, another oppositional tendency, characterised the situation as follows: 'The working class is totally deprived of rights, the trade unions being a blind instrument in the hands of the functionaries.'

This was certainly not what the Kronstadt rebels were asking for! On the contrary. They were proposing measures which would have restored to the working class and working peasantry their true place in the new regime. The Bolsheviks only implemented the least important demands of the Kronstadt programme (those coming in eleventh place in the resolution of the rebels!). They totally ignored the basic demand, the demand for workers' democracy!

This demand, put forward in the Petropavlovsky resolution was neither utopian nor dangerous. We here take issue with Victor Serge. In *Revolution Proletarienne* (of September 10th, 1937) Serge stated that 'while the sailors were engaged in mortal combat, they put forward a demand which, at that particular moment, was extremely dangerous—although quite genuine and sincerely revolutionary: the demand for freely elected soviets... they wished to unleash a cleansing tornado but in practice they could only have opened the doors to the peasant counterrevolution, of which the Whites and foreign intervention would have taken advantage... Insurgent Kronstadt was not counterrevolutionary, but its victory would inevitably have led to the counterrevolution.' Contrary to Serge's assertion we believe that the political demands of the sailors were full of a deep political wisdom. They were not derived from any abstract theory but from a profound awareness of the conditions of Russian life. They were in no way counterrevolutionary.

ROSA LUXEMBOURG'S VIEWS

It is worth recalling what Rosa Luxemburg, a political personality respected throughout the world as a great socialist militant, had written about the lack of democracy in the leadership of the Russian Revolution, as early as 1918.

'It is an incontestable fact,' she wrote, 'that the rule of the broad, popular masses is inconceivable without unlimited freedom of the press, without absolute freedom of meeting and of association... the gigantic tasks which the Bolsheviks have tackled with courage and resolution require the most intensive political education of the masses and accumulation of experience which is impossible without political freedom. Freedom restricted to those who support the Government or to Party members only, however numerous they may be, is not real freedom. Freedom is always freedom for the one who thinks differently. This is not because of fanaticism for abstract justice but because everything that is instructive, healthy and cleansing in political liberty hinges on this and because political liberty loses its value when freedom becomes a privilege.'

'We have never worshipped at the altar of formal democracy,' she continued. 'We have always distinguished between the social content end the political form of bourgeois democracy. The historical task facing the proletariat after its accession to power is to replace bourgeois democracy by proletarian democracy, not to abolish all democracy... The dictatorship (of the proletariat) consists in the way democracy is applied, not in its abolition. It must be the action of the class and not of a small minority, managing things in the name of the class.... If political life throughout the country is stifled it must fatally follow that life in the soviets themselves will be paralysed. Without general elections, without unlimited freedom of the press and of assembly, without free confrontation of opinions, life will dry up in all public institutions—or it will be only a sham life, where the bureaucracy is the only active element.'

We have dwelt on these quotations to show that Rosa Luxembourg, in her statements about the need for democracy, went much further than the Kronstadt rebels. They restricted their comments about democracy to matters of interest to the proletariat and to the working peasantry. Moreover Rosa Luxemburg formulated her criticisms of the Russian Revolution in 1918, in a period of full civil war, whereas the Petropavlovsk resolution was voted at a time when the armed struggle had virtually come to an end.

Would anyone dare accuse Rosa, on the basis of her criticisms, of having been in collusion with the international bourgeoisie? Why then are the demands of the Kronstadt sailors denounced as 'dangerous' and as inevitably leading to the counterrevolution? Has not the subsequent evolution of events amply vindicated both the Kronstadt rebels and Rosa Luxemburg? Was Rosa Luxemburg not right when she asserted that the task of the working class was to exercise working class power and not the dictatorship of a party or of a clique? For Rosa Luxemburg working class power was defined as 'the achievement in a contest of the widest discussion, of the most active and unlimited participation of the popular masses in an unrestricted democracy.'

A third Soviet Revolution

When putting forward their democratic demands, the Kronstadt rebels had probably never heard of the writings of Rosa Luxemburg. What they had heard of, however, was the first Constitution of the Soviet Republic, voted on July 10, 1918, by the 5th All Russian Congress of Soviets. Article 13, 14, 15 and 16 of the Constitution assured all workers of certain democratic rights (freedom of worship, freedom of assembly, freedom of union, freedom of the press). These articles sought to prevent the allocation of special privileges to any specific group or Party (articles 22 and 23).

The same Constitution proclaimed that no worker could be deprived of the right to vote or of the right to stand as a candidate, provided he satisfied the conditions stipulated in articles 64 and 65, that is to say provided he did not exploit the labour of others or live off income other than that which he had earned.

The central demand of the Kronstadt insurrection—all power to the Soviets (and not to the Party)—was in fact based on an article of the Constitution. This proclaimed that all central and local power would henceforth be precisely in the hands of the soviets! From the very beginning this Constitution was violated by the Bolsheviks—or rather its provisions were never put into effect. It is worth recalling that Rosa Luxemburg's criticisms were formulated a few months after the vote of this new constitution charter. When in 1921 the sailors were to insist on a genuine application of the rights they had acquired in 1918 they were called 'counterrevolutionaries' and denounced as 'agents of the international bourgeoisie.' Sixteen years later Victor Serge was to say that the demands of the rebels would necessarily have led to the counterrevolution. This shows how deep-going were Bolshevik attitudes concerning the dangers of democracy.

The basic laws of the Soviet Republic constitute a juridical summary of the ideology of the October Revolution. By the end of the Civil War these ideas had been pushed so far back that a third revolution would have been necessary to reinstate them and have them applied in everyday life. This is what the Kronstadt rebels meant when they spoke of the Third Revolution. In the *Kronstadt Isvestia* of March 8 they wrote: 'At Kronstadt the foundation stone has been laid of the Third Revolution. This will break the final chains which still bind the working masses and wall open up new paths of socialist creation.'

We do not know if it would have been possible to save the conquests of October by democratic methods. We do not know if the economic situation of the country and its markedly peasant character were really suitable for the first attempt at building socialism. These problems should be discussed. But the task of those seeking truth is to proclaim the facts without embellishments. It is not good enough to take a superciliously scientific air to explain away historical phenomena.

When Trotsky sought to explain the development of the bureaucracy which had strangled all real life in the institutions of the Soviet State he found no difficulty in outlining his conception.

In *The Revolution Betrayed* he states that one of the important causes was the fact that demobilised Red Army officers had come to occupy leading positions in the local soviets and had introduced military methods into them—at a time when the proletariat was exhausted following the prolonged revolutionary upheaval. This apperarently led to the birth of the bureaucracy. Trotsky omits to recall how he himself sought to introduce precisely these methods into the trade unions. Was it to save the proletariat further fatigue? And if the proletariat was that exhausted how come it was still capable of waging virtually total general strikes in the largest and most heavily industrialised cities? And if the Party was still really the driving force of the social revolution how come it did not help the proletariat in the struggle against the nascent, but already powerful, bureaucracy—instead of shooting the workers down, at a time when their energy had been sapped by three years of imperialist war followed by three years of civil war.

Why did the Communist Party identify itself with the authoritarian state? The answer is that the Party was no longer revolutionary. It was no longer proletarian. And this is precisely what the men of Kronstadt were blaming the Party for. Their merit is to have said all this in 1921—when it might still have been possible to change the situation—and not to have waited 15 years, by which time the defeat had become irrevocable.

Bureaucracy is almost an hereditary hallmark in Russia. It is as old as the Russian state itself. The Bolsheviks in power not only inherited the Tsarist bureaucracy itself, but its very spirit. Its very atmosphere. They should have realised that as the state enlarged its functions to encompass economic affairs, as it became the owner of all natural wealth and of industry, an immediate danger would arise of the rebirth and rapid development of the bureaucratic frame of mind.

A doctor treating a patient with a bad heredity takes this into account and advises certain precautions. What precautions did the Bolsheviks take to combat the bureaucratic tendencies which were obvious, in the very first years of the Revolution? What methods could they have used other than to allow a powerful democratic draught to blow through the whole atmosphere, and to encourage a rigorous and effective control to be exerted by the working masses?

True enough, some form of control was envisaged. The trouble was that the Commissariat of the Workers and Peasants inspection was to entrust this control to the very same type of bureaucrat whose power it was seeking to thwart. One need not seek far to find the causes of the bureaucratisation. Its roots lay deeply in the Bolshevik concept of the State commanded and controlled by a single Party, itself organised along absolutist and bureaucratic lines. These causes were of course aggravated by Russia's own bureaucratic traditions.

It is wrong to blame the peasantry for the defeat of the Revolution and for its degeneration into a bureaucratic regime. It would be too easy to explain all Russia's difficulties by the agrarian character of her economy. Some people seem to say at one and the same time that the Kronstadt revolt against the bureaucracy was a peasant revolt and that the bureaucracy itself was of peasant origin. With such a concept of the role of the peasantry one may ask how the Bolsheviks dared advocate the idea of the socialist revolution? How did they dare struggle for it in an agrarian country?

Some claim that the Bolsheviks allowed themselves such actions (as the suppression of Kronstadt) in the hope of a forthcoming world revolution, of which they considered themselves the vanguard. But would not a revolution in another country have been influenced by the spirit of the Russian Revolution? When one considers the enormous moral authority of the Russian Revolution throughout the world one may ask oneself whether the deviations of this Revolution would not eventually have left an imprint on other countries. Many historical facts allow such a judgement. One may recognise the impossibility of genuine socialist construction in a single country, yet have doubts as to whether the bureaucratic deformations of the Bolshevik regime would have been straightened out by the winds coming from revolutions in other countries.

The fascist experience in countries like Germany shows that an advanced stage of capitalist development is an insufficient guarantee against the growth of absolutist and autocratic tenden-cies. Although this is not the place to explain the phenomenon, we must note the powerful wave of authoritarianism coming from economically advanced countries and threatening to engulf old ideas and traditions. It is incontestable that Bolshevism is mor-ally related to this absolutist frame of mind. It had in fact set a precedent for subsequent tendencies. No one can be sure that had another revolution occurred elsewhere following the one in Rus-sia, Bolshevism would have democratised itself. It might again have revealed its absolutist features.

Were there not real dangers in the democratic way? Was there no reason to fear reformist influences in the soviets, if democracy had been given free rein? We accept that this was a real danger. But it was no more of a danger than what inevitably followed the uncontrolled dictatorship of a single party, whose General Secre-tary was already Stalin.[28]

We are told that the country was at the end of its tether, that it had lost its ability to resist. True, the country was weary of war. But on the other hand it was full of constructive forces, ardently seeking to learn and to educate themselves. The end of the Civil War saw a surge of workers and peasants towards schools, work-ers' universities and institutes of technical education. Wasn't this yearning the best testimony to the vitality and resistance of these classes? In a country with a very high level of illiteracy, such an edu-cation could greatly have helped the working masses in the genuine exercise of real power.

But by its very essence a dictatorship destroys the creative capacities of a people. Despite the undoubted attempts of the Gov-ernment to educate workers, education soon became the privilege of Party members loyal to the leading faction. From 1921 on, work-ers' faculties and higher educational establishments were purged of their more independent minded elements. This process gained tempo with the development of oppositional tendencies within

---

28. Ida Matt is wrong in implying that Stalin was General Secretary of the Party at the time of the events she is describing. The post of General Secretary—and Stalin's ap-pointment to it (incidentally endorsed by both Lenin and Trotsky)—only took place in 1922. (Ed. *Solidarity*).

the Party. The attempt at a genuine mass education was increasingly compromised. Lenin's wish that every cook should be able to govern the state became less and less likely to be implemented.

The revolutionary conquest could only be deepened through a genuine participation of the masses. Any attempt to substitute an 'elite' for those masses could only be profoundly reactionary.

In 1921 the Russian Revolution stood at the crossroads. The democratic or the dictatorial way, that was the question. By lumping together bourgeois and proletarian democracy the Bolsheviks were in fact condemning both. They sought to build socialism from above, through skillful manoeuvres of the Revolutionary General Staff. While waiting for a world revolution that was not round the corner, they built a state capitalist society, where the working class no longer had the right to make the decisions most intimately concerning it.

Lenin was not alone in perceiving that the Kronstadt rebellion was a challenge to this plan. Both he and the Bolsheviks were fully aware that what was at stake was the monopoly of their Party. Kronstadt might have opened the way to a genuine proletarian democracy, incompatible with the Party's monopoly of power. That is why Lenin preferred to destroy Kronstadt. He chose an ignoble but sure way: the calumny that Kronstadt was allied to the bourgeoisie and to the agrarian counterrevolution.

When Kouzmin, Commissar to the Baltic Fleet, had stated at the Kronstadt meeting of March 2nd that the Bolsheviks would not surrender power without a fight, he was saying the truth. Lenin must have laughed at this Commissar who obviously didn't understand the ABC of Bolshevik morality or tactics. Politically and morally one had to destroy the opponent—not argue with him using real arguments. And destroy its revolutionary opponents is exactly what the Bolshevik government did.

The Kronstadt rebels were a grey, amorphous mass. But such masses occasionally show an incredible level of political awareness. If there had been among them a number of men of 'higher' political understanding the insurrection might well never have taken place, for those men would have understood firstly that the demands of the rebels were in flagrant conflict with the policies of the Kremlin—and secondly that, at that particular moment in time, the government felt itself firmly enough in the saddle to shoot down, without pity or mercy, any tendency daring seriously to oppose its views or plans.

The men of Kronstadt were sincere but naive. Believing in the justness of their cause they did not foresee the tactics of their opponents. They waited for help from the rest of the country, whose demands they knew they were voicing. They lost sight of the fact that the rest of the country was already in the iron grip of a dictatorship which no longer allowed the people the free expression of its wishes and the free choice of its institutions.

The great ideological and political discussion between 'realists' and 'dreamers' between 'scientific socialists' and the 'revolutionary volnitza'[29] was fought out, weapons in hand. It ended, in 1921, with the political and military defeat of the 'dreamers.' But Stalin was to prove to the whole world that this defeat was also the defeat of socialism, over a sixth of the earth's surface.

---

29. 'open conference.'

The Struggle Against Fascism Begins with the Struggle Against Bolshevism

Otto Rühle

I.

Russia must be placed first among the new totalitarian states. It was the first to adopt the new state principle. It went furthest in its application. It was the first to establish a constitutional dictatorship, together with the political and administrative terror system which goes with it. Adopting all the features of the total state, it thus became the model for those other countries which were forced to do away with the democratic state system and to change to dictatorial rule. Russia was the example for fascism.

No accident is here involved, nor a bad joke of history. The duplication of systems here is not apparent but real. Everything points to the fact that we have to deal here with expressions and consequences of identical principles applied to different levels of historical and political development. Whether party "communists" like it or not, the fact remains that the state order and rule in Russia are indistinguishable from those in Italy and Germany. Essentially they are alike. One may speak of a red, black, or brown "soviet state," as well as of red, black, or brown fascism. Though certain ideological differences exist between these countries, ideology is never of primary importance. Ideologies, furthermore, are changeable and such changes do not necessarily reflect the character and the functions of the state apparatus. Furthermore, the fact that private property still exists in Germany and Italy is only a modification of secondary importance. The abolition of private property alone does not guarantee socialism. Private property within capitalism also can be abolished. What actually determines a socialist society is, besides the doing away with private property in the means of production, the control of the workers over the products of their labour and the end of the wage system. Both of these achievements are unfulfilled in Russia, as well as in Italy and Germany. Though some may assume that Russia is one step nearer to socialism than the other countries, it does not follow that its "soviet state" has helped the international proletariat come in any way nearer to its class struggle goals. On the contrary, because Russia calls itself a socialist state, it misleads and deludes the workers of the world. The thinking worker knows what fascism is and fights it, but as regards Russia, he is only too often inclined to accept the myth of its socialistic nature. This delusion hinders a complete and determined break with fascism, because it hinders the principle struggle against the reasons, preconditions, and circumstances which in Russia, as in Germany and Italy, have led to an identical state and governmental system. Thus the Russian myth turns into an ideological weapon of counter-revolution.

It is not possible for men to serve two masters. Neither can a totalitarian state do such a thing. If fascism serves capitalistic and imperialistic interests, it cannot serve the needs of the workers. If, in spite of this, two apparently opposing classes favour the same state system, it is obvious that something must be wrong. One or the other class must be in error. No one should say here that the problem is one merely of form and therefore of no real significance, that, though the political forms are identical, their content may vary widely. This would be self-delusion. For the Marxist such things do not occur; for him form and content fit to each other and they cannot be divorced. Now, if the Soviet State serves as a model for fascism, it must contain structural and functional elements which are also common to fascism. To determine what they are we must go back to the "soviet system" as established by Leninism, which is the application of the principles of bolshevism to the Russian conditions. And if an identity between bolshevism and fascism can be established, then the proletariat cannot at the same time fight fascism and defend the Russian "soviet system." Instead, the struggle against fascism must begin with the struggle against bolshevism.

II.

From the beginning bolshevism was for Lenin a purely Russian phenomenon. During the many years of his political activity, he never attempted to elevate the bolshevik system to forms of struggles in other countries. He was a social democrat who saw in Bebel and Kautsky the genial leaders of the working class, and he ignored the left-wing of the German socialist movement struggling against these heroes of Lenin and against all the other opportunists. Ignoring them, he remained in consistent isolation surrounded by a small group of Russian emigrants, and he continued to stand under Kautsky's sway even when the German "left," under the leadership of Rosa Luxemburg, was already engaged in open struggle against Kautskyism.

Lenin was concerned only with Russia. His goal was the end of the Czarist feudal system and the conquest of the greatest amount of political influence for his social democratic party within the bourgeois society. However, it realized that it could stay in power and drive on the process of socialization only if it could unleash the world revolution of the workers. But its own activity in this respect was quite an unhappy one. By helping to drive the German workers back into the parties, trade unions, and parliament, and by the simultaneous destruction of the German council (soviet) movement, the Bolsheviks lent a hand, to the defeat of the awakening European revolution.

The Bolshevik Party, consisting of professional revolutionists on the one hand and large backward masses on the other, remained isolated. It could not develop a real soviet system within the years of civil war, intervention, economic decline, failing socialization experiments, and the improvised Red Army. Though the soviets, which were developed by the Mensheviks, did not fit into the bolshevistik scheme, it was with their help that the Bolsheviks came to power. With the stabilisation of power and the economic reconstruction process, the Bolshevik Party did not know how to co-ordinate the strange soviet system to their own decisions and activities. Nevertheless, socialism was also the desire of the Bolsheviks, and it needed the world proletariat for its realization.

Lenin thought it essential to win the workers of the world over to the bolshevik methods. It was disturbing that the workers of other countries, despite the great triumph of Bolshevism, showed little inclination to accept for themselves the bolshevik theory and practice, but tended rather in the direction of the council movement, that arose in a number of countries, and especially in Germany.

This council movement Lenin could use no longer in Russia. In other European countries it showed strong tendencies to oppose the bolshevik type of uprisings. Despite Moscow's tremendous propaganda in all countries, the so-called "ultra-lefts," as Lenin himself pointed out, agitated more successfully for revolution on the basis of the council movement, than did all the propagandists sent by the Bolshevik Party. The Communist Party, following Bolshevism, remained a small, hysterical, and noisy group consisting largely of the proletarianized shreds of the bourgeoisie, whereas the council movement gained in real proletarian strength and attracted the best elements of the working class. To cope with this situation, bolshevik propaganda had to be increased; the "ultra-left" had to be attacked; its influence had to be destroyed in favour of Bolshevism.

Since the soviet system had failed in Russia, how could the radical "competition" dare to attempt to prove to the world that what could not be accomplished by Bolshevism in Russia might very well be realized independently of Bolshevism in other places? Against this competition Lenin wrote his pamphlet "Radicalism, an Infantile Disease of Communism," dictated by fear of losing power and by indignation over the success of the heretics. At first this pamphlet appeared with the subheading, "Attempt at a popular exposition of the Marxian strategy and tactic," but later this too ambitious and silly declaration was removed. It was a little too much. This aggressive, crude, and hateful papal bull was real material for any counterrevolutionary. Of all programmatic declarations of Bolshevism it was the most revealing of its real character. It is Bolshevism unmasked. When in 1933 Hitler suppressed all socialist and communist literature in Germany, Lenin's pamphlet was allowed publication and distribution.

As regards the content of the pamphlet, we are not here concerned with what it says in relation to the Russian Revolution, the history of Bolshevism, the polemic between Bolshevism and other streams of the labour movement, or the circumstances allowing for the Bolshevik victory, but solely with the main points by which at the time of the discussion between Lenin and "ultra-leftism," were illustrated the decisive differences between the two opponents.

III.

The Bolshevik Party, originally the Russian social democratic section of the Second International, was built not in Russia but during the emigration. After the London split in 1903, the Bolshevik wing of the Russian social democracy was no more than a small sect. The "masses" behind it existed only in the brain of its leader. However, this small advance guard was a strictly disciplined organization, always ready for militant struggles and continually purged to maintain its integrity. The party was considered the war academy of professional revolutionists. Its outstanding pedagogical requirements were unconditional leader authority, rigid centralism, iron discipline, conformity, militancy, and sacrifice of personality for party interests. What Lenin actually developed was an elite of intellectuals, a centre which, when thrown into the revolution would capture leadership and assume power. There is no use to try to determine logically and abstractly if this kind of preparation for revolution is right or wrong. The problem has to be solved dialectically. Other questions also must be raised: What kind of a revolution was in preparation? What was the goal of the revolution?

Lenin's party worked within the belated bourgeois revolution in Russia to overthrow the feudal regime of Czarism. The more centralized the will of the leading party in such a revolution and the more single-minded, the more success would accompany the process of the formation of the bourgeois state and the more promising would be the position of the proletarian class within the framework of the new state. What, however, may be regarded as a happy solution of revolutionary problems in a bourgeois revolution cannot at the same time be pronounced as a solution for the proletarian revolution. The decisive structural difference between the bourgeois and the new socialist society excludes such an attitude.

According to Lenin's revolutionary method, the leaders appear as the head of the masses. Possessing the proper revolutionary schooling, they are able to understand situations and direct and command the fighting forces. They are professional revolutionists, the generals of the great civilian army. This distinction between head and body, intellectuals and masses, officers, and privates corresponds to the duality of class society, to the bourgeois social order. One class is educated to rule; the other to be ruled. Out of this old class formula resulted Lenin's party concept. His organisation is only a replica of bourgeois reality. His revolution is objectively determined by the forces that create a social order incorporating these class relations, regardless of the subjective goals accompanying this process.

Whoever wants to have a bourgeois order will find in the divorce of leader and masses, the advance guard and working class, the right strategical preparation for revolution. The more intelligent, schooled, and superior is the leadership and the more disciplined and obedient are the masses, the more chances such a revolution will have to succeed. In aspiring to the bourgeois revolution in Russia, Lenin's party was most appropriate to his goal.

When, however, the Russian revolution changed its character, when its proletarian features came more to the fore, Lenin's tactical and strategical methods ceased to be of value. If he succeeded anyway it was not because of his advance guard, but because of the soviet movement which had not at all been incorporated in his revolutionary plans. And when Lenin, after the successful revolution which was made by the soviets, dispensed again with this movement, all that had been proletarian in the Russian Revolution was also dispensed with. The bourgeois character of the Revolution came to the fore again, finding its natural completion in Stalinism.

Despite his great concern with Marxian dialectics, Lenin was not able to see the social historical processes in a dialectical manner. His thinking remained mechanistic, following rigid rules. For him there was only one revolutionary party—his own; only one revolution—the Russian; only one method—the bolshevik. And what had worked in Russia would work also in Germany, France, America, China, and Australia. What was correct for the bourgeois revolution in Russia would be correct also for the proletarian world revolution. The monotonous application of a once discovered formula moved in an ego-centric circle undisturbed by time and circumstances, developmental degrees, cultural standards, ideas, and men. In Lenin came to light with great clarity the rule of the machine age in politics; he was the "technician," the "inventor," of the revolution, the representative of the all-powerful will of the leader. All fundamental characteristics of fascism were in his doctrine, his strategy, his social "planning," and his art with dealing with men. He could not see the deep revolutionary meaning of the rejection of traditional party policies by the left. He could not understand the real importance of the soviet movement for the socialist orientation of society. He never learned to know the prerequisites for the freeing of the workers. Authority, leadership, force, exerted on one side, and organization, cadres, subordination on the other side,—such was his line of reasoning. Discipline and dictatorship are the words which are most frequent in his writings. It is understandable, then, why he could not comprehend nor appreciate the ideas and actions of the "ultra-left," which would not accept his strategy and which demanded what was most obvious and most necessary for the revolutionary struggle for socialism, namely that the workers once and for all take their fate in their own hands.

IV.

To take their destiny in their own hands—this key-word to all questions of socialism—was the real issue in all polemics between the ultra-lefts and the Bolsheviks. The disagreement on the party question was paralleled by the disagreement on trade unionism. The ultra-left was of the opinion that there was no longer a place for revolutionists in trade unions; that it was rather necessary for them to develop their own organizational forms within the factories, the common working places. However, thanks to their unearned authority, the Bolsheviks had been able even in the first weeks of the German revolution to drive the workers back into the capitalistic reactionary trade unions. To fight the ultra-lefts, to denounce them as stupid and as counter-revolutionary, Lenin in his pamphlet once more makes use of his mechanistic formulas. In his arguments against the position of the left he does not refer to German trade unions but to the trade union experiences of the Bolsheviks in Russia. That in their early beginnings trade unions were of great importance for the proletarian class struggle is a generally accepted fact. The trade unions in Russia were young and they justified Lenin's enthusiasm. However, the situation was different in other parts of the world. Useful and progressive in their beginnings, the trade unions in the older capitalistic countries had turned into obstacles in the way of the liberation of the workers. They had turned into instruments of counterrevolution, and the German left drew its conclusions from this changed situation.

Lenin himself could not help declaring that in the course of time there had developed a layer of a "strictly trade-unionist, imperialistic orientated, arrogant, vain, sterile, egotistical, petty-bourgeois, bribed, and demoralised aristocracy of labour." This guild of corruption, this gangster leadership, today rules the world trade union movement and lives on the back of the workers. It was of this trade union movement that the ultra-left was speaking when it demanded that the workers should desert it. Lenin, however, demagogically answered by pointing to the young trade union movement in Russia which did not as yet share the character of the long established unions in other countries. Employing a specific experience at a given period and under particular circumstance, he thought it possible to draw from it conclusions of world-wide application. The revolutionist, he argued, must always be where the masses are. But in reality where are the masses? In trade union offices? At membership meetings? At the secret meetings of the leadership with the capitalistic representatives? No, the masses are in the factories, in their working places; and there it is necessary to effect their co-operation and strengthen their solidarity. The factory organization, the council system, is the real organisation of the revolution, which must replace all parties and trade unions.

In factory organizations there is no room for professional leadership, no divorce of leaders from followers, no caste distinction between intellectuals and the rank and file, no ground for egotism, competition, demoralization, corruption, sterility, and philistinism. Here the workers must take their lot in their own hands.

But Lenin thought otherwise. He wanted to preserve the unions; to change them from within; to remove the social democratic officials and replace them with bolshevik officials; to replace a bad with a good bureaucracy. The bad one grows in a social democracy; the good one in Bolshevism.

Twenty years of experience meanwhile have demonstrated the idiocy of such a concept. Following Lenin's advice, the Communists have tried all and sundry methods to reform trade unions. The result was nil. The attempt to form their own trade unions was likewise nil. The competition between social democratic and bolshevik trade union work was a competition in corruption. The revolutionary energies of the workers were exhausted in this very process. Instead of concentrating upon the struggle against fascism, the workers were engaged in a senseless and resultless experimentation in the interest of diverse bureaucracies. The masses lost confidence in themselves and in "their" organizations. They felt themselves cheated and betrayed. The methods of fascism, to dictate each step of the workers, to hinder the awakening of self-initiative, to sabotage all beginnings of class-consciousness, to demoralise the masses through innumerable defeats and to make them impotent—all these methods had already been developed in the twenty years of work in the trade unions in accordance with bolshevik principles. The victory of fascism was such an easy one because the labour leaders in trade unions and parties had prepared for them the human material capable of being fitted into the fascistic scheme of things.

V.

On the question of parliamentarianism, too, Lenin appears in the role of the defender of a decayed political institution which had become a hindrance for further political development and a danger to the proletarian emancipation. The ultra-lefts fought parliamentarianism in all its forms. They refused to participate in elections and did not respect parliamentary decisions. Lenin, however, put much effort into parliamentary activities and attached much importance to them. The ultra-left declared parliamentarianism historically passé even as a tribune for agitation, and saw in it no more than a continuous source of political corruption for both parliamentarian and workers. It dulled the revolutionary awareness and consistency of the masses by creating illusions of legalistic reforms, and on critical occasions the parliament turned into a weapon of counter revolution. It had to be destroyed, or, where nothing else was possible, sabotaged. The parliamentary tradition, still playing a part in proletarian consciousness, was to be fought.

To achieve the opposite effect, Lenin operated with the trick of making a distinction between the historically and politically passé institutions. Certainly, he argued, parliamentarianism was historically obsolete, but this was not the case politically, and one would have to reckon with it. One would have to participate because it still played a part politically.

What an argument! Capitalism, too, is only historically and not politically obsolete. According to Lenin's logic, it is then not possible to fight capitalism in a revolutionary manner. Rather a compromise would have to be found. Opportunism, bargaining, political horse-trading,—that would be the consequence of Lenin's tactic. The monarchy, too, is only historically but not politically surpassed. According to Lenin, the workers would have no right to do away with it but would be obliged to find a compromise solution. The same story would be true as regards the church, also only historically but not politically antedated. Furthermore, the people belong in great masses to the church. As a revolutionist, Lenin pointed out, that one had to be where the masses are. Consistency would force him to say "Enter the Church; it is your revolutionary duty!" Finally, there is fascism. One day, too, fascism will be historically antedated but politically still in existence. What is then to be done? To accept the fact and to make a compromise with fascism. According to Lenin's reasoning, a pact between Stalin and Hitler would only illustrate that Stalin actually is the best disciple of Lenin. And it will not at all be surprising if in the near future the bolshevist agents will hail the pact between Moscow and Berlin as the only real revolutionary tactic.

Lenin's position on the question of parliamentarianism is only an additional illustration of his incapacity to understand the essential needs and characteristics of the proletarian revolution. His revolution is entirely bourgeois; it is a struggle for the majority, for governmental positions, for a hold upon the law machine. He actually thought it of importance to gain as many votes as possible at election campaigns, to have a strong bolshevik fraction in the parliaments, to help determine form and content of legislation, to take part in political rule. He did not notice at all that today parliamentarianism is a mere bluff, an empty make-believe, and that the real power of bourgeois society rests in entirely different places; that despite all possible parliamentary defeats the bourgeoisie would still have at hand sufficient means to assert its will and interest in non-parliamentary fields. Lenin did not see the demoralising effects parliamentarism had upon the masses, he did not notice the poisoning of public morals through parliamentary corruption. Bribed, bought, and cowed, parliamentary politicians were fearful for their income. There was a time in prefascist Germany when the reactionists in parliament were able to pass any desired law merely by threatening to bring about the dissolution of parliament. There was nothing more terrible to the parliamentary politicians than such a threat which implied the end of their easy incomes. To avoid such an end, they would say yes to anything. And how is it today in Germany, in Russia, in Italy? The parliamentary helots are without opinions, without will, and are nothing more than willing servants of their fascist masters.

There can be no question that parliamentarianism is entirely degenerated and corrupt. But, why didn't the proletariat stop this deterioration of a political instrument which had once been used for their purposes? To end parliamentarism by one heroic revolutionary act would have been far more useful and educational for the proletarian consciousness than the miserable theatre in which parliamentarism has ended in the fascistic society. But such an attitude was entirely foreign to Lenin, as it is foreign today to Stalin. Lenin was not concerned with the freedom of the workers from their mental and physical slavery; he was not bothered by the false consciousness of the masses and their human self-alienation. The whole problem to him was nothing more nor less than a problem of power. Like a bourgeois, he thought in terms of gains and losses, more or less, credit and debit; and all his business-like computations deal only with external things: membership figures, number of votes, seats in parliaments, control positions. His materialism is a bourgeois materialism, dealing with mechanisms, not with human beings. He is not really able to think in socio-historical terms. Parliament to him is parliament; an abstract concept in a vacuum, holding equal meaning in all nations, at all times. Certainly he acknowledges that parliament passes through different stages, and he points this out in his discussions, but he does not use his own knowledge in his theory and practice. In his pro-parliamentarian polemics he hides behind the early capitalist parliaments in the ascending stage of capitalism, in order not to run out of arguments. And if he attacks the old parliaments, it is from the vantage point of the young and long outmoded. In short, he decides that politics is the art of the possible. However, politics for the workers is the art of revolution.

VI.

It remains to deal with Lenin's position on the question of compromises. During the World War the German Social Democracy
sold out to the bourgeoisie. Nevertheless, much against its will,
it inherited the German revolution. This was made possible to a
large extent by the help of Russia, which did its share in killing
off the German council movement. The power which had fallen
into the lap of Social Democracy was used for nothing. The Social
Democracy simply renewed its old class collaboration policy, satisfied with sharing power over the workers with the bourgeoisie
in the reconstruction period of capitalism. The German radical
workers countered this betrayal with this slogan, "No compromise
with the counter revolution." Here was a concrete case, a specific
situation, demanding a clear decision. Lenin, unable to recognize
the real issues at stake, made from this concrete specific question
a general problem. With the air of a general and the infallibility of
a cardinal, he tried to persuade the ultra-lefts that compromises
with political opponents under all conditions are a revolutionary
duty. If today one reads those passages in Lenin's pamphlet dealing
with compromises, one is inclined to compare Lenin's remarks in
1920 with Stalin's present policy of compromises. There is not one
deadly sin of bolshevik theory which did not become bolshevistic
reality under Lenin.

According to Lenin, the ultra-lefts should have been willing
to sign the Treaty of Versailles. However, the Communist Party,
still in accordance with Lenin, made a compromise and protested
against the Versailles Treaty in collaboration with the Hitlerites.
The "National Bolshevism" propagandized in 1919 in Germany by
the left-winger Lauffenberg was in Lenin's opinion "an absurdity
crying to heaven." But Radek and the Communist Party—again in
accordance with Lenin's principle—concluded a compromise with
German Nationalism, and protested against the occupation of the
Ruhr basin and celebrated the national hero Schlageter. The League
of Nations was, in Lenin's own words, "a band of capitalist robbers and bandits," whom the workers could only fight to the bitter

end. However, Stalin—in accordance with Lenin's tactics—made a compromise with these very same bandits, and the USSR entered the League. The concept "folk" or "People" is in Lenin's opinion a criminal concession to the counter-revolutionary ideology of the petty bourgeoisie. This did not hinder the Leninists, Stalin and Dimitrov, from making a compromise with the petty bourgeoisie in order to launch the freakish "Peoples Front" movement. For Lenin, imperialism was the greatest enemy of the world proletariat, and against it all forces had to be mobilized. But Stalin, again in true Leninistic fashion, is quite busy with cooking up an alliance with Hitler's imperialism. Is it necessary to offer more examples? Historical experience teaches that all compromises between revolution and counter-revolution can serve only the latter. They lead only to the bankruptcy of the revolutionary movement. All policy of compromise is a policy of bankruptcy. What began as a mere compromise with the German Social Democracy found its end in Hitler. What Lenin justified as a necessary compromise found its end in Stalin. In diagnosing revolutionary non-compromise as "An Infantile Disease of Communism," Lenin was suffering from the old age disease of opportunism, of pseudo-communism.

VII.

If one looks with critical eyes at the picture of bolshevism provided by Lenin's pamphlet, the following main points may be recognized as characteristics of bolshevism:

1. Bolshevism is a nationalistic doctrine. Originally and essentially conceived to solve a national problem, it was later elevated to a theory and practice of international scope and to a general doctrine. Its nationalistic character comes to light also in its position on the struggle for national independence of suppressed nations.

2. Bolshevism is an authoritarian system. The peak of the social pyramid is the most important and determining point. Authority

is realized in the all-powerful person. In the leader myth the bourgeois personality ideal celebrates its highest triumphs.

3. Organizationally, Bolshevism is highly centralistic. The central committee has responsibility for all initiative, leadership, instruction, commands. As in the bourgeois state, the leading members of the organization play the role of the bourgeoisie; the sole role of the workers is to obey orders.

4. Bolshevism represents a militant power policy. Exclusively interested in political power, it is no different from the forms of rule in the traditional bourgeois sense. Even in the organization proper there is no self-determination by the members. The army serves the party as the great example of organization.

5. Bolshevism is dictatorship. Working with brute force and terroristic measures, it directs all its functions toward the suppression of all non-bolshevik institutions and opinions. Its "dictatorship of the proletariat" is the dictatorship of a bureaucracy or a single person.

6. Bolshevism is a mechanistic method. It aspires to the automatic co-ordination, the technically secured conformity, and the most efficient totalitarianism as a goal of social order. The centralistically "planned" economy consciously confuses technical-organizational problems with socio-economic questions.

7. The social structure of Bolshevism is of a bourgeois nature. It does not abolish the wage system and refuses proletarian self-determination over the products of labour. It remains therewith fundamentally within the class frame of the bourgeois social order. Capitalism is perpetuated.

8. Bolshevism is a revolutionary element only in the frame of the bourgeois revolution. Unable to realize the soviet system, it is thereby unable to transform essentially the structure of bourgeois society and its economy. It establishes not socialism but state capitalism.

9. Bolshevism is not a bridge leading eventually into the socialist society. Without the soviet system, without the total radical revolution of men and things, it cannot fulfil the most essential of all socialistic demands, which is to end the capitalist human-self-alienation. It represents the last stage of bourgeois society and not the first step towards a new society.

These nine points represent an unbridgeable opposition between bolshevism and socialism. They demonstrate with all necessary clarity the bourgeois character of the bolshevist movement and its close relationship to fascism. Nationalism, authoritarianism, centralism, leader dictatorship, power policies, terror-rule, mechanistic dynamics, inability to socialize—all these essential characteristics of fascism were and are existing in bolshevism. Fascism is merely a copy of bolshevism. For this reason the struggle against the one must begin with the struggle against the other.

My Disillusionment in Russia
–Afterword

EMMA GOLDMAN

I

Non-Bolshevik Socialist critics of the Russian failure contend that the Revolution could not have succeeded in Russia because industrial conditions had not reached the necessary climax in that country. They point to Marx, who taught that a social revolution is possible only in countries with a highly developed industrial system and its attendant social antagonisms. They therefore claim that the Russian Revolution could not be a social revolution, and that historically it had to evolve along constitutional, democratic lines, complemented by a growing industry, in order to ripen the country economically for the basic change.

This orthodox Marxian view leaves an important factor out of consideration—a factor perhaps more vital to the possibility and success of a social revolution than even the industrial element. That is the psychology of the masses at a given period. Why is there, for instance, no social revolution in the United States, France, or even in Germany? Surely these countries have reached the industrial development set by Marx as the culminating stage. The truth is that industrial development and sharp social contrasts are of themselves by no means sufficient to give birth to a new society or to call forth a social revolution. The necessary social consciousness, the required mass psychology is missing in such countries as the United States and the others mentioned. That explains why no social revolution has taken place there.

In this regard Russia had the advantage of other more industrialized and "civilized" lands. It is true that Russia was not as advanced industrially as her Western neighbours. But the Russian mass psychology, inspired and intensified by the February Revolution, was ripening at so fast a pace that within a few months the people were ready for such ultra-revolutionary slogans as "All power to the Soviets" and "The land to the peasants, the factories to the workers."

The significance of these slogans should not be underestimated. Expressing in a large degree the instinctive and semi-conscious will of the people, they yet signified the complete social, economic, and industrial reorganization of Russia. What country in Europe or America is prepared to interpret such revolutionary mottoes into life? Yet in Russia, in the months of June and July, 1917, these slogans became popular and were enthusiastically and actively taken up, in the form of direct action, by the bulk of the industrial and agrarian population of more than 150 millions. That was sufficient proof of the "ripeness" of the Russian people for the social revolution.

As to economic "preparedness" in the Marxian sense, it must not be forgotten that Russia is preëminently an agrarian country. Marx's dictum presupposes the industrialization of the peasant and farmer population in every highly developed society, as a step toward social fitness for revolution. But events in Russia, in 1917, demonstrated that revolution does not await this process of industrialization and-what is more important-cannot be made to wait. The Russian peasants began to expropriate the landlords and the workers took possession of the factories without taking cognizance of Marxian dicta. This popular action, by virtue of its own logic, ushered in the social revolution in Russia, upsetting all Marxian calculations. The psychology of the Slav proved stronger than social-democratic theories.

That psychology involved the passionate yearning for liberty nurtured by a century of revolutionary agitation among all classes of society. The Russian people had fortunately remained politically unsophisticated and untouched by the corruption and confusion created among the proletariat of other countries by "democratic" liberty and self-government. The Russian remained, in this sense, natural and simple, unfamiliar with the subtleties of politics, of parliamentary trickery, and legal makeshifts. On the other hand, his primitive sense of justice and right was strong and vital, without the disintegrating finesse of pseudo-civilization. He knew what he wanted and he did not wait for "historic inevitability" to bring it to him: he employed direct action. The Revolution to him was a fact of life, not a mere theory for discussion.

Thus the social revolution took place in Russia in spite of the industrial backwardness of the country. But to make the Revolution was not enough. It was necessary for it to advance and broaden, to develop into economic and social reconstruction. That phase of the Revolution necessitated fullest play of personal initiative and collective effort. The development and success of the Revolution depended on the broadest exercise of the creative genius of the people, on the coöperation of the intellectual and manual proletariat. Common interest is the *leit motif* of all revolutionary endeavour, especially on its constructive side. This spirit of mutual purpose and solidarity swept Russia with a mighty wave in the first days of the October-November Revolution. Inherent in that enthusiasm were forces that could have moved mountains if intelligently guided by exclusive consideration for the well-being of the whole people. The medium for such effective guidance was on hand: the labour organizations and the coöperatives with which Russia was covered as with a network of bridges combining the city with the country; the Soviets which sprang into being responsive to the needs of the Russian people; and, finally, the intelligentsia whose traditions for a century expressed heroic devotion to the cause of Russia's emancipation.

But such a development was by no means within the programme of the Bolsheviki. For several months following October they suffered the popular forces to manifest themselves, the people carrying the Revolution into ever-widening channels. But as soon as the Communist Party felt itself sufficiently strong in the government saddle, it began to limit the scope of popular activity. All the succeeding acts of the Bolsheviki, all their following policies, changes of policies, their compromises and retreats, their methods of suppression and persecution, their terrorism and extermination of all other political views-all were but the *means to an end:* the retaining of the State power in the hands of the Communist Party. Indeed, the Bolsheviki themselves (in Russia) made no secret of it. The Communist Party, they contended, is the advance guard of the proletariat, and the dictatorship must rest in its hands. Alas, the Bolsheviki reckoned without their host—without the peasantry, whom neither the *razvyoriska*, the Tcheka, nor the wholesale shooting could persuade to support the Bolshevik régime. The peasantry became the rock upon which the best-laid plans and schemes of Lenin were wrecked. But Lenin, a nimble acrobat, was skilled in performing within the narrowest margin. The new economic policy was introduced just in time to ward off the disaster which was slowly but surely overtaking the whole Communist edifice.

II

The "new economic policy" came as a surprise and a shock to most Communists. They saw in it a reversal of everything that their Party had been proclaiming—a reversal of Communism itself. In protest some of the oldest members of the Party, men who had faced danger and persecution under the old régime while Lenin and Trotsky lived abroad in safety, left the Communist Party embittered and disappointed. The leaders then declared a lockout. They ordered the clearing of the Party ranks of all "doubtful" elements. Everybody suspected of an independent attitude and those who did not accept the new economic policy as the last word in revolutionary wisdom were expelled. Among them were Communists who for years had rendered most devoted service. Some of them, hurt to the quick by the unjust and brutal procedure, and shaken to their depths by the collapse of what they held most high, even resorted to suicide. But the smooth sailing of Lenin's new gospel had to be assured, the gospel of the sanctity of private property and the freedom of cutthroat competition erected upon the ruins of four years of revolution.

However, Communist indignation over the new economic policy merely indicated the confusion of mind on the part of Lenin's opponents. What else but mental confusion could approve of the numerous acrobatic political stunts of Lenin and yet grow indignant at the final somersault, its logical culmination? The trouble with the devout Communists was that they clung to the Immaculate Conception of the Communist State which by the aid of the Revolution was to redeem the world. But most of the leading Communists never entertained such a delusion. Least of all Lenin.

During my first interview I received the impression that he was a shrewd politician who knew exactly what he was about and that he would stop at nothing to achieve his ends. After hearing him speak on several occasions and reading his works I became convinced that Lenin had very little concern in the Revolution and that Communism to him was a very remote thing. The centralized political State was Lenin's deity, to which everything else was to be sacrificed. Someone said that Lenin would sacrifice the Revolution to save Russia. Lenin's policies, however, have proven that he was willing to sacrifice both the Revolution and the country, or at least part of the latter, in order to realize his political scheme with what was left of Russia.

Lenin was the most pliable politician in history. He could be an ultra-revolutionary, a compromiser and conservative at the same time. When like a mighty wave the cry swept over Russia, "All power to the Soviets!" Lenin swam with the tide. When the peasants took possession of the land and the workers of the factories, Lenin not only approved of those direct methods but went further. He issued the famous motto, "Rob the robbers," a slogan which served to confuse the minds of the people and caused untold injury to revolutionary idealism. Never before did any real revolutionist interpret social expropriation as the transfer of wealth from one set of individuals to another. Yet that was exactly what Lenin's slogan meant. The indiscriminate and irresponsible raids, the accumulation of the wealth of the former bourgeoisie by the new Soviet bureaucracy, the chicanery practised toward those whose only crime was their former status, were all the results of Lenin's "Rob the robbers" policy. The whole subsequent history of the Revolution is a kaleidoscope of Lenin's compromises and betrayal of his own slogans.

Bolshevik acts and methods since the October days may seem to contradict the new economic policy. But in reality they are links in the chain which was to forge the all-powerful, centralized Government with State Capitalism as its economic expression. Lenin possessed clarity of vision and an iron will. He knew how to make his comrades in Russia and outside of it believe that his scheme was true Socialism and his methods the revolution. No wonder that Lenin felt such contempt for his flock, which he never hesitated to fling into their faces. "Only fools can believe that Communism is possible in Russia now," was Lenin's reply to the opponents of the new economic policy.

As a matter of fact, Lenin was right. True Communism was never attempted in Russia, unless one considers thirty-three categories of pay, different food rations, privileges to some and indifference to the great mass as Communism.

In the early period of the Revolution it was comparatively easy for the Communist Party to possess itself of power. All the revolutionary elements, carried away by the ultra-revolutionary promises of the Bolsheviki, helped the latter to power. Once in possession of the State the Communists began their process of elimination. All the political parties and groups which refused to submit to the new dictatorship had to go. First the Anarchists and Left Social Revolutionists, then the Mensheviki and other opponents from the Right, and finally everybody who dared aspire to an opinion of his own. Similar was the fate of all independent organizations. They were either subordinated to the needs of the new State or destroyed altogether, as were the Soviets, the trade unions and the coöperatives— three great factors for the realization of the hopes of the Revolution.

The Soviets first manifested themselves in the revolution of 1905. They played an important part during that brief but significant period. Though the revolution was crushed, the Soviet idea remained rooted in the minds and hearts of the Russian masses. At the first dawn which illuminated Russia in February, 1917, the Soviets revived again and came into bloom in a very short time. To the people the Soviets by no means represented a curtailment of the spirit of the Revolution. On the contrary, the Revolution was to find its highest, freest practical expression through the Soviets. That was why the Soviets so spontaneously and rapidly spread throughout Russia. The Bolsheviki realized the significance of the popular trend and joined the cry. But once in control of the Government the Communists saw that the Soviets threatened the supremacy of the State. At the same time they could not destroy them arbitrarily without undermining their own prestige at home and abroad as the sponsors of the Soviet system. They began to shear them gradually of their powers and finally to subordinate them to their own needs.

The Russian trade unions were much more amenable to emasculation. Numerically and in point of revolutionary fibre they were still in their childhood. By declaring adherence to the trade unions obligatory the Russian labour organizations gained in physical stature, but mentally they remained in the infant stage. The Communist State became the wet nurse of the trade unions. In return, the organizations served as the flunkeys of the State. "A school for Communism," said Lenin in the famous controversy on the functions of the trade unions. Quite right. But an antiquated school where the spirit of the child is fettered and crushed. Nowhere in the world are labour organizations as subservient to the will and the dictates of the State as they are in Bolshevik Russia.

The fate of the coöperatives is too well known to require elucidation. The coöperatives were the most essential link between the city and the country. Their value to the Revolution as a popular and successful medium of exchange and distribution and to the reconstruction of Russia was incalculable. The Bolsheviki transformed them into cogs of the Government machine and thereby destroyed their usefulness and efficiency.

III

It is now clear why the Russian Revolution, as conducted by the Communist Party, was a failure. The political power of the Party, organized and centralized in the State, sought to maintain itself by all means at hand. The central authorities attempted to force the activities of the people into forms corresponding with the purposes of the Party. The sole aim of the latter was to strengthen the State and monopolize all economical, political, and social acitivities— even all cultural manifestations. The Revolution had an entirely different object, and in its very character it was the negation of authority and centralization. It strove to open ever-larger fields for proletarian expression and to multiply the phases of individual and collective effort. The aims and tendencies of the Revolution were diametrically opposed to those of the ruling political party.

Just as diametrically opposed were the *methods* of the Revolution and of the State. Those of the former were inspired by the spirit of the Revolution itself: that is to say, by emancipation from all oppressive and limiting forces; in short; by *libertarian principles*. The methods of the State, on the contrary—of the Bolshevik State as of every government—were based on *coercion*, which in the course of things necessarily developed into systematic violence, oppression, and terrorism. Thus two opposing tendencies struggled for supremacy: the Bolshevik State against the Revolution. That struggle was a life-and-death struggle. The two tendencies, contradictory in aims and methods, could not work harmoniously: the triumph of the State meant the defeat of the Revolution.

It would be an error to assume that the failure of the Revolution was due entirely to the character of the Bolsheviki. Fundamentally, it was the result of the principles and methods of Bolshevism. It was the authoritarian spirit and principles of the State which stifled the libertarian and liberating aspirations. Were any other political party in control of the government in Russia the result would have been essentially the same. It is not so much the Bolsheviki who killed the Russian Revolution as the Bolshevik idea. It was Marxism, however modified; in short, fanatical governmentalism. Only this understanding of the underlying forces that crushed the Revolution can present the true lesson of that world-stirring event. The Russian Revolution reflects on a small scale the century-old struggle of the libertarian principle against the authoritarian. For what is progress if not the more general acceptance of the principles of liberty as against those of coercion? The Russian Revolution was a libertarian step defeated by the Bolshevik State, by the temporary victory of the reactionary, the governmental idea.

That victory was due to a number of causes. Most of them have already been dealt with in the preceding chapters. The main cause, however, was not the industrial backwardness of Russia, as claimed by many writers on the subject. That cause was cultural which, though giving the Russian people certain advantages over their more sophisticated neighbours, also had some fatal disadvantages. The Russian was "culturally backward" in the sense of being unspoiled by political and parliamentary corruption. On the other hand, that very condition involved, inexperience in the political game and a naive faith in the miraculous power of the party that talked the loudest and made the most promises. This faith in the power of government served to enslave the Russian people to the Communist Party even before the great masses realized that the yoke had been put around their necks.

The libertarian principle was strong in the initial days of the Revolution, the need for free expression all-absorbing. But when the first wave of enthusiasm receded into the ebb of everyday prosaic life, a firm conviction was needed to keep the fires of liberty burning. There was only a comparative handful in the great vastness of Russia to keep those fires lit—the Anarchists, whose number was small and whose efforts, absolutely suppressed under the Tsar, had had no time to bear fruit. The Russian people, to some extent instinctive Anarchists, were yet too unfamiliar with true libertarian principles and methods to apply them effectively to life. Most of the Russian Anarchists themselves were unfortunately still in the meshes of limited group activities and of individualistic endeavour as against the more important social and collective efforts. The Anarchists, the future unbiased historian will admit, have played a very important rôle in the Russian Revolution—a rôle far more significant and fruitful than their comparatively small number would have led one to expect. Yet honesty and sincerity compel me to state that their work would have been of infinitely greater practical value had they been better organized and equipped to guide the released energies of the people toward the reorganization of life on a libertarian foundation.

But the failure of the Anarchists in the Russian Revolution— in the sense just indicated—does by no means argue the defeat of the libertarian idea. On the contrary, the Russian Revolution has demonstrated beyond doubt that the State idea, State Socialism, in all its manifestations (economic, political, social, educational) is entirely and hopelessly bankrupt. Never before in all history has authority, government, the State, proved so inherently static, reactionary, and even counter-revolutionary in effect. In short, the very antithesis of revolution.

It remains true, as it has through all progress, that only the libertarian spirit and method can bring man a step further in his eternal striving for the better, finer, and freer life. Applied to the great social upheavals known as revolutions, this tendency is as potent as in the ordinary evolutionary process. The authoritarian method has been a failure all through history and now it has again failed in the Russian Revolution. So far human ingenuity has discovered no other principle except the libertarian, for man has indeed uttered the highest wisdom when he said that liberty is the mother of order, not its daughter. All political tenets and parties notwithstanding, no revolution can be truly and permanently successful unless it puts its emphatic veto upon all tyranny and centralization, and determinedly strives to make the revolution a real revaluation of all economic, social, and cultural values. Not mere substitution of one political party for another in the control of the Government, not the masking of autocracy by proletarian slogans, not the dictatorship of a new class over an old one, not political scene shifting of any kind, but the complete reversal of all these authoritarian principles will alone serve the revolution.

In the economic field this transformation must be in the hands of the industrial masses: the latter have the choice between an industrial State and anarcho-syndicalism. In the case of the former the menace to the constructive development of the new social structure would be as great as from the political State. It would become a dead weight upon the growth of the new forms of life.

For that very reason syndicalism (or industrialism) alone is not, as its exponents claim, sufficient unto itself. It is only when the libertarian spirit permeates the economic organizations of the workers that the manifold creative energies of the people can manifest themselves and the revolution be safeguarded and defended. Only free initiative and popular participation in the affairs of the revolution can prevent the terrible blunders committed in Russia. For instance, with fuel only a hundred versts [about sixty-six miles] from Petrograd there would have been no necessity for that city to suffer from cold had the workers' economic organizations of Petrograd been free to exercise their initiative for the common good. The peasants of the Ukraina would not have been hampered in the cultivation of their land had they had access to the farm implements stacked up in the warehouses of Kharkov and other industrial centres awaiting orders from Moscow for their distribution. These are characteristic examples of Bolshevik governmentalism and centralization, which should serve as a warning to the workers of Europe and America of the destructive effects of Statism.

The industrial power of the masses, expressed through their libertarian associations—Anarcho-syndicalism—is alone able to organize successfully the economic life and carry on production. On the other hand, the coöperatives, working in harmony with the industrial bodies, serve as the distributing and exchange media between city and country, and at the same time link in fraternal bond the industrial and agrarian masses. A common tie of mutual service and aid is created which is the strongest bulwark of the revolution-far more effective then compulsory labour, the Red Army, or terrorism. In that way alone can revolution act as a leaven to quicken the development of new social forms and inspire the masses to greater achievements.

But libertarian industrial organizations and the coöperatives are not the only media in the interplay of the complex phases of social life. There are the cultural forces which, though closely related to the economic activities, have yet their own functions to perform. In Russia the Communist State became the sole arbiter of all the needs of the social body. The result, as already described, was complete cultural stagnation and the paralysis of all creative endeavour. If such a débâcle is to be avoided in the future, the cultural forces, while remaining rooted in the economic soil, must yet retain independent scope and freedom of expression. Not adherence to the dominant political party but devotion to the revolution, knowledge, ability, and—above all—the creative impulse should be the criterion of fitness for cultural work. In Russia this was made impossible almost from the beginning of the October Revolution, by the violent separation of the intelligentsia and the masses. It is true that the original offender in this case was the intelligentsia, especially the technical intelligentsia, which in Russia tenaciously clung—as it does in other countries—to the coat-tails of the bourgeoisie. This element, unable to comprehend the significance of revolutionary events, strove to stem the tide by wholesale sabotage. But in Russia there was also another kind of intelligentsia—one with a glorious revolutionary past of a hundred years. That part of the intelligentsia kept faith with the people, though it could not unreservedly accept the new dictatorship. The fatal error of the Bolsheviki was that they made no distinction between the two elements. They met sabotage with wholesale terror against the intelligentsia as a class, and inaugurated a campaign of hatred more intensive than the persecution of the bourgeoisie itself—a method which created an abyss between the intelligentsia and the proletariat and reared a barrier against constructive work.

Lenin was the first to realize that criminal blunder. He pointed out that it was a grave error to lead the workers to believe that they could build up the industries and engage in cultural work without the aid and coöperation of the intelligentsia. The proletariat had neither the knowledge nor the training for the task, and the intelligentsia had to be restored in the direction of the industrial life. But the recognition of one error never safeguarded Lenin and his Party from immediately committing another. The technical intelligentsia was called back on terms which added disintegration to the antagonism against the régime.

While the workers continued to starve, engineers, industrial experts, and technicians received high salaries, special privileges, and the best rations. They became the pampered employees of the State and the new slave drivers of the masses. The latter, fed for years on the fallacious teachings that muscle alone is necessary for a successful revolution and that only physical labour is productive, and incited by the campaign of hatred which stamped every intellectual a counter-revolutionist and speculator, could not make peace with those they had been taught to scorn and distrust.

Unfortunately Russia is not the only country where this proletarian attitude against the intelligentsia prevails. Everywhere political demagogues play upon the ignorance of the masses, teach them that education and culture are bourgeois prejudices, that the workers can do without them, and that they alone are able to rebuild society. The Russian Revolution has made it very clear that both brain and muscle are indispensable to the work of social regeneration. Intellectual and physical labour are as closely related in the social body as brain and hand in the human organism. One cannot function without the other.

It is true that most intellectuals consider themselves a class apart from and superior to the workers, but social conditions everywhere are fast demolishing the high pedestal of the intelligentsia. They are made to see that they, too, are proletarians, even more dependent upon the economic master than the manual worker. Unlike the physicial proletarian, who can pick up his tools and tramp the world in search of a change from a galling situation, the intellectual proletarians have their roots more firmly in their particular social environment and cannot so easily change their occupation or mode of living. It is therefore of utmost importance to bring home to the workers the rapid proletarization of the intellectuals and the common tie thus created between them. If the Western world is to profit by the lessons of Russia, the demagogic flattery of the masses and blind antagonism toward the intelligentsia must cease. That does not mean, however, that the toilers should depend entirely upon the intellectual element. On the contrary, the masses must begin right now to prepare and equip themselves for the great task the revolution will put upon them. They should acquire the knowledge and technical skill necessary for managing and directing the intricate mechanism of the industrial and social structure of their respective countries. But even at best the workers will need the coöperation of the professional and cultural elements. Similarly the latter must realize that their true interests are identical with those of the masses. Once the two social forces learn to blend into one harmonious whole, the tragic aspects of the Russian Revolution would to a great extent be eliminated. No one would be shot because he "once acquired an education." The scientist, the engineer, the specialist, the investigator, the educator, and the creative artist, as well as the carpenter, machinist, and the rest, are all part and parcel of the collective force which is to shape the revolution into the great architect of the new social edifice. Not hatred, but unity; not antagonism, but fellowship; not shooting, but sympathy—that is the lesson of the great Russian débâcle for the intelligentsia as well as the workers. All must learn the value of mutual aid and libertarian coöperation. Yet each must be able to remain independent in his own sphere and in harmony with the best he can yield to society. Only in that way will productive labour and educational and cultural endeavour express themselves in ever newer and richer forms. That is to me the all-embracing and vital moral taught by the Russian Revolution.

IV

In the previous pages I have tried to point out why Bolshevik principles, methods, and tactics failed, and that similar principles and methods applied in any other country, even of the highest industrial development, must also fail. I have further shown that it is not only Bolshevism that failed, but Marxism itself. That is to say, the STATE IDEA, the *authoritarian principle*, has been proven bankrupt by the experience of the Russian Revolution. If I were to sum up my whole argument in one sentence I should say: The inherent tendency of the State is to concentrate, to narrow, and monopolize all social activities; the nature of revolution is, on the contrary, to grow, to broaden, and disseminate itself in ever-wider circles. In other words, the State is institutional and static; revolution is fluent, dynamic. These two tendencies are incompatible and mutually destructive. The State idea killed the Russian Revolution and it must have the same result in all other revolutions, unless the *libertarian idea prevail.*

Yet I go much further. It is not only Bolshevism, Marxism, and Governmentalism which are fatal to revolution as well as to all vital human progress. The main cause of the defeat of the Russian Revolution lies much deeper. It is to be found in the whole Socialist conception of revolution itself.

The dominant, almost general, idea of revolution—particularly the Socialist idea—is that revolution is a violent change of social conditions through which one social class, the working class, becomes dominant over another class, the capitalist class. It is the conception of a purely physical change, and as such it involves only political scene shifting and institutional rearrangements. Bourgeois dictatorship is replaced by the "dictatorship of the proletariat"—or by that of its "advance guard," the Communist Party; Lenin takes the seat of the Romanovs, the Imperial Cabinet is rechristened Soviet of People's Commissars, Trotsky is appointed Minister of War, and a labourer becomes the Military Governor General of Moscow. That is, in essence, the Bolshevik conception of revolution, as translated into actual practice. And with a few minor alterations it is also the idea of revolution held by all other Socialist parties.

This conception is inherently and fatally false. Revolution is indeed a violent process. But if it is to result only in a change of dictatorship, in a shifting of names and political personalities, then it is hardly worth while. It is surely not worth all the struggle and sacrifice, the stupendous loss in human life and cultural values that result from every revolution. If such a revolution were even to bring greater social well being (which has not been the case in Russia) then it would also not be worth the terrific price paid: mere improvement can be brought about without bloody revolution. It is not palliatives or reforms that are the real aim and purpose of revolution, as I conceive it.

In my opinion—a thousandfold strengthened by the Russian experience—the great mission of revolution, of the SOCIAL REVOLUTION, is a *fundamental transvaluation of values*. A transvaluation not only of social, but also of human' values. The latter are even preëminent, for they are the basis of all social values. Our institutions and conditions rest upon deep-seated ideas. To change those conditions and at the same time leave the underlying ideas and values intact means only a superficial transformation, one that cannot be permanent or bring real betterment. It is a change of form only, not of substance, as so tragically proven by Russia.

It is at once the great failure and the great tragedy of the Russian Revolution that it attempted (in the leadership of the ruling political party) to change only institutions and conditions while ignoring entirely the human and social values involved in the Revolution. Worse yet, in its mad passion for power, the Communist State even sought to strengthen and deepen the very ideas and conceptions which the Revolution had come to destroy. It supported and encouraged all the worst anti-social qualities and systematically destroyed the already awakened conception of the new revolutionary values. The sense of justice and equality, the love of liberty and of human brotherhood-these fundamentals of the real regeneration of society-the Communist State suppressed to the point of extermination. Man's instinctive sense of equity was branded as weak sentimentality; human dignity and liberty became a bourgeois superstition; the sanctity of life, which is the very essence of social reconstruction, was condemned as an-revolutionary, almost counter-revolutionary. This fearful perversion of fundamental values bore within itself the seed of destruction. With the conception that the Revolution was only a means of securing political power, it was inevitable that all revolutionary values should be subordinated to the needs of the Socialist State; indeed, exploited to further the security of the newly acquired governmental power. "Reasons of State," masked as the "interests of the Revolution and of the People," became the sole criterion of action, even of feeling. Violence, the tragic inevitability of revolutionary upheavals, became an established custom, a habit. and was presently enthroned as the most powerful and "ideal" institution. Did not Zinoviev himself canonize Dzerzhinsky, the head of the bloody Tcheka, as the "saint of the Revolution"? Were not the greatest public honours paid by the State to Uritsky, the founder and sadistic chief of the Petrograd Tcheka?

This perversion of the ethical values soon crystallized into the all-dominating slogan of the Communist Party: THE END JUSTIFIES ALL MEANS. Similarly in the past the Inquisition and the Jesuits adopted this motto and subordinated to it all morality. It avenged itself upon the Jesuits as it did upon the Russian Revolution. In the wake of this slogan followed lying, deceit, hypocrisy and treachery, murder, open and secret. It should be of utmost interest to students of social psychology that two movements as widely separated in time and ideas as Jesuitism and Bolshevism *reached exactly similar results* in the evolution of the principle that the end justifies all means. The historic parallel, almost entirely ignored so far, contains a most important lesson for all comingrevolutions and for the whole future of mankind.

There is no greater fallacy than the belief that aims and purposes are one thing, while methods and tactics are another. This conception is a potent menace to social regeneration. All human experience teaches that methods and means cannot be separated from the ultimate aim. The means employed become, through individual habit and social practice, part and parcel of the final purpose; they influence it, modify it, and presently the aims and means become identical. From the day of my arrival in Russia I felt it, at first vaguely, then ever more consciously and clearly. The great and inspiring aims of the Revolution became so clouded with and obscured by the methods used by the ruling political power that it was hard to distinguish what was temporary means and what final purpose. Psychologically and socially the means necessarily influence and alter the aims. The whole history of man is continuous proof of the maxim that to divest one's methods of ethical concepts means to sink into the depths of utter demoralization. In that lies the real tragedy of the Bolshevik philosophy as applied to the Russian Revolution. May this lesson not be in vain.

No revolution can ever succeed as a factor of liberation unless the MEANS used to further it be identical in spirit and tendency with the PURPOSES to be achieved. Revolution is the nega-tion of the existing, a violent protest against man's inhumanity to man with all the thousand and one slaveries it involves. It is the destroyer of dominant values upon which a complex system of injustice, oppression, and wrong has been built up by ignorance and brutality. It is the herald of NEW VALUES, ushering in a transformation of the basic relations of man to man, and of man to society. It is not a mere reformer, patching up some social evils; not a mere changer of forms and institutions; not only a re-distributor of social well-being. It is all that, yet more, much more. It is, first and foremost, the TRANSVALUATOR, the bearer of *new* values. It is the great TEACHER of the NEW ETHICS, inspiring man with a new concept of life and its manifestations in social relation-ships. It is the mental and spiritual regenerator.

Its first ethical precept is the identity of means used and aims sought. The ultimate end of all revolutionary social change is to establish the sanctity of human life, the dignity of man, the right of every human being to liberty and well being. Unless this be the essential aim of revolution, violent social changes would have no justification. For *external* social alterations can be, and have been, accomplished by the normal processes of evolution. Revolution, on the contrary, signifies not mere *external* change, but *internal*, basic, fundamental change. That internal change of concepts and ideas, permeating ever-larger social strata, finally culminates in the vio-lent upheaval known as revolution. Shall that climax reverse the process of transvaluation, turn against it, betray it? That is what happened in Russia. On the contrary, the revolution itself must quicken and further the process of which it is the cumulative expression; its main mission is to inspire it, to carry it to greater heights, give it fullest scope for expression. Only thus is revolution true to itself.

Applied in practice it means that the period of the actual rev-olution, the so-called transitory stage, must be the introduction, the prelude to the new social conditions. It is the threshold to the

NEW LIFE, the new HOUSE OF MAN AND HUMANITY. As such it must be of the spirit of the new life, harmonious with the construction of the new edifice.

To-day is the parent of to-morrow. The present casts its shadow far into the future. That is the law of life, individual and social. Revolution that divests itself of ethical values thereby lays the foundation of injustice, deceit, and oppression for the future society. The *means* used to *prepare* the future become its *cornerstone*. Witness the tragic condition of Russia. The methods of State centralization have paralysed individual initiative and effort; the tyranny of the dictatorship has cowed the people into slavish submission and all but extinguished the fires of liberty; organized terrorism has depraved and brutalized the masses and stifled every idealistic aspiration; institutionalized murder has cheapened human life, and all sense of the dignity of man and the value of life has been eliminated; coercion at every step has made effort bitter, labour a punishment, has turned the whole of existence into a scheme of mutual deceit, and has revived the lowest and most brutal instincts of man. A sorry heritage to begin a new life of freedom and brotherhood.

It cannot be sufficiently emphasized that revolution is in vain unless inspired by its ultimate ideal. Revolutionary methods must be in tune with revolutionary aims. The means used to further the revolution must harmonize with its purposes. In short, the ethical values which the revolution is to establish in the new society must be *initiated* with the revolutionary activities of the so-called transitional period. The latter can serve as a real and dependable bridge to the better life only if built of the same material as the life to be achieved. Revolution is the mirror of the coming day; it is the child that is to be the Man of To-morrow.

Cries In The Wilderness: Alexander Berkman and Russian Prisoner Aid

Barry Pateman

"Not even a miserable piece of stone is dedicated to their memory for fear of rippling a placid existence." —Francesc Torres[1]

You can get tired of anniversaries. As you get older there are more and more of them, rolling towards you like a never ending freight train carrying commentary after commentary as the skeleton of each event is enthusiastically picked over to justify the positions and ideas that groups and individuals now hold. I am not interested in doing that for October 1917 (or for any other anniversary come to think of it). I rather think peoples lives and experiences are important in themselves and don't need to be filleted to fit some contemporary idea or abandoned because they don't appear relevant. Their lives might insist we ask questions, though. Even if the answers are difficult.

For Alexander Berkman the Russian events of October 1917, seen from America, appeared to be the hope of the world. The fourteen years of imprisonment he had endured between 1892 and 1906 in the most brutal of conditions, the countless struggles against the viciousness of capitalism that he took part in, and those long evenings arguing about the possibility and nature of revolutionary change all seemed suddenly to have had a purpose.[2] Russia was his birthplace and also home to those heroes and heroines of *Narodnaya Volya* and the other combatant units of the Russian revolutionary tradition that had so influenced him as a young man. He had sensed that the February revolution in Russia had not gone

---

1. Foreword to Antonio Tellez, *The Anarchist Resistance to Franco* (London: Kate Sharpley Library, 1991).
2. For Berkman's prison experiences see the new edition of *Prison Memoirs of an Anarchist* (Chico and Edinburgh: AK Press, 2016).

far enough but felt that all the efforts and sacrifices of these revolutionary forebears had finally come to fruition in the events of
October 1917. In the October 1917 edition of the New York based
anarchist journal *Mother Earth* he described the Bolsheviks as "the
true revolutionists." He would go on to describe his first day on
Soviet soil in January 1920 as "the most sublime day of my life."
Such positive feelings did not last. Bitter and disillusioned by his
two years in Bolshevik Russia he had ended his book *The Bolshevik*[3]
with the line: "The Bolshevik Myth must be destroyed." He presented readers with a harrowing assessment of life in Russia: "The
Revolution is dead; its spirit cries in the wilderness."

The purpose of this piece is not to fully discuss the causes of
this disillusionment, the trajectory of which you can easily trace
in *The Bolshevik Myth*. Some points do need a little explanation and
context, however. Bitterly opposed to World War One and, in particular, to America's recent involvement in the conflict, Berkman
had been imprisoned in Atlanta Federal Penitentiary in America from February 8, 1918 on charges of violating the Espionage
Act and "conspiracy to interfere with the draft." Sentenced along
with Emma Goldman to two years imprisonment, both were also
recommended for deportation to Russia at the end of their sentences. They were shipped from America on the 21st of December
1919 and after a long journey arrived in Soviet Russia on January 20th, 1920. The isolation of Berkman and Goldman while in
prison make it hard for us to be clear what they actually knew and
understood about the situation in Russia. The events around their
hurried deportation did not give them much time to ponder and
reflect on Russian realities even when they were released. We do
know that rumors of tensions between anarchists and Bolsheviks
were circulating within the New York anarchist milieu, but there
was also considerable sympathy within anarchist circles as to what
Revolutionary Russia was, apparently, trying to do. The situation
wasn't helped by the fact that Saul Yanovsky, editor of the Yiddish
anarchist paper *Freie Arbeiter Stimme,* was one of the most prominent

---

3. Alexander Berkman, *The Bolshevik Myth (Diary 1920–1922)* (New York: Boni and Liv-
eright, 1925).

critics of the Bolsheviks. Yanovsky's relationship with Berkman and Goldman had always been fractious and his support for America's entry into World War One certainly hadn't helped matters.

It is unlikely, then, that Berkman had a clear perception of the relationship between anarchists and Bolsheviks in Russia before he and the other deportees sailed out of New York on that cold December morning. By all accounts he was excited and happy and certainly less bothered about leaving America than Emma Goldman was. One newspaper describes the sombrero wearing Berkman as being the center of a "merry group" on the day of deportation.[4] The group played banjos, and sang the *Internationale*. He probably did not know that on April 12, 1918, Moscow's Anarchist Club and 25 other anarchist centers had been attacked by the Bolsheviks. In the fighting 12 Chekists had been killed, around 40 anarchists killed or wounded, and hundreds taken prisoner. Nor, perhaps did he know, that on April 13, 1918 the anarchist press had been suppressed. He may have heard that in November 1918 all attendees at the All-Russian Conference of Anarcho-Syndicalists in Moscow were arrested. He may also have heard that the "Underground" Anarchists, together with some Left Socialist Revolutionaries had bombed the headquarters of the Moscow Committee of the Communist Party in September of 1919 in retaliation for the execution of seven Makhnovists by the Cheka in Kharkov on June 17, 1919. A plenary meeting of the Party was taking place and twelve were killed and many more wounded. He had certainly heard of Nestor Makhno and his comrades and their remarkable attempts to build libertarian communism whilst fighting both Bolshevik and counterrevolutionary armies.

He would arrive in Russia, then, at a time of Bolshevik repression against anarchists. He also arrived at a time when the anarchist movement was riven with internal arguments, often regarding the relationship between anarchism and Bolshevism. Alliances inside the anarchist movement were complicated and unclear and therefore difficult for outsiders to understand. His account of these

---

4. "Army Transport Under Secret Orders," *Fort Wayne Journal Gazette*, December 22, 1919.

experiences is chronicled in *The Bolshevik Myth*, ending with the defeat of the Kronstadt rebels and his departure from Russia into a life of permanent exile. What isn't clear to the modern reader is the tremendous damage that his time in Russia had done to his revolutionary optimism as well as his sense of himself. We have to remember that his time in prison had left a permanent mark on Berkman.[5] Primarily it had made him prone to depression and the events around the Kronstadt Rebellion had a profound effect on him. Those slaughtered rebels had, alongside other comrades in Russia, stood with him, Warren Billings, and Tom Mooney in 1917 by protesting against Mooney's planned execution and the attempt to extradite Berkman from New York to California to stand trial for the Preparedness Day bombing of July 22nd 1916 in San Francisco.[6] All he could do was listen to the Communist guns destroying his comrades. He, Goldman and the other anarchists in Petrograd were helpless to intervene, to stop anything, to make any kind of difference at all. Even his isolation cell in prison had not destroyed his self worth as much as had his helplessness over the deaths at Kronstadt. In a letter to a comrade, the New York anarchist Michael Cohn, in October 1922, Berkman described himself as "disheartened, discouraged, almost desperate."[7]

One of his first acts when he came out of Russia was to pen the article "Bolsheviks Shooting Anarchists" with Emma Goldman that first appeared in the London anarchist paper *Freedom* in January 1922. With its call to arms: "Make haste for the blood of our comrades is flowing in Russia" it had a profound effect in the anarchist world. Of course pessimistic rumors were rife before its publication. Comrades had traveled to Russia and no word had come back from them—or comrades had returned from there with worrying stories of repression. Here, though, were two respected

5. One can see evidence of his depression both in *Prison Memoirs* and in his 1911 diary published in the 2016 edition of his *Prison Memoirs*.
6. For a detailed account of the Preparedness Day bombing see Richard H. Frost. *The Mooney Case* (Stanford: Stanford University Press, 1968). Interesting new details about the bombing have come to light in Paul Avrich and Karen Avrich. *Sasha and Emma* (Cambridge, Mass: The Belknap Press of Harvard University, 2012).
7. Letter from Alexander Berkman to Michael Cohn, October 10, 1922, Alexander Berkman Papers, International Institute of Social History, Amsterdam.

anarchists, with years of sacrifice and devotion to the cause, stating quite clearly, on their return from Russia, that the Bolsheviks were not our allies but our enemies. It became an iconic document. Even then, some anarchists found it hard to believe, and it shocked many others even though they thought it could be true.

Berkman did what he could to let people know about the Bolshevik state. He found public speaking difficult so writing became, more than ever, his primary form of communication. Based in Berlin he wrote his pamphlet *The Russian Tragedy* between January 5th and 10th 1922, in a kind of white heat, and finished his pamphlet *The Kronstadt Rebellion*, later that year. In 1923 he also translated the pamphlet *The Russian Revolution and the Communist Party*, written by four Moscow anarchists. Together the pamphlets constituted what he referred to as his Russian Revolution series. Others were planned but did not materialize. He also spent the year helping Emma Goldman with what would become her book *My Disillusionment In Russia* (which was not her title!) published in 1923.[8] In early January 1923 he began work on *The Bolshevik Myth*.

Alongside all of this writing Berkman still searched for things to do, things that could ease his feeling of helplessness as well as challenge the conception of revolution that was reflected in Bolshevik Russia. Gradually he gained some sense of what was possible for him. In his introduction to *The Bolshevik Myth* he wrote: "The inner life of revolution, which is its sole meaning, has almost entirely been neglected by writers on the Russian revolution." Of course the book is about *his* inner life but such an approach helped him focus on the experiences of the individual victims of Bolshevism. If he was disheartened and desperate as a result of his experiences then the "inner life" of others must be similar. Physically he was free; other comrades were not. The state of repression in Russia was so intense, so suffocating that just to tell an individual story, to send provisions to a prisoner, to discover one person's fate were acts not just of solidarity but of affirmation of their lives, their ideas, and their experiences with Bolshevism. The

---

8. Emma Goldman, *My Disillusionment in Russia* (New York: Doubleday, 1923). Her title, changed by the publisher, was *My Two Years In Russia*.

revolution was not just about economic structures but people and their experiences.

From early 1921 all sorts of international anarchist groupings and organizations had sprung up to publicize the cases of anarchist prisoners in Russia. The Anarchist Black Cross was operating as well as it could within Russia but by 1925 many of its members had been arrested and prisoner support became more and more a clandestine activity. American anarchists had formed the International Aid Federation and were attempting to offer material and political support to anarchists both in Russia and Spain. The London-based group for the Relief of Russian Anarchists published the Yiddish newspaper *Hilsruf.* Three of its contributors—Berkman, Mark Mratchny, and Rudolf Rocker would go on to play important roles in Russian prisoner aid. Things came to an organizational head with the publication of the article "In Russia's Prisons" in the January 1923 *Freedom.* The article urged militants to challenge Communist Party members whenever they could—Anarchists must insist that all the imprisoned and deported/exiled be released and "that an end be put to the absurd system of terrorism now inflicted on the workers." The article was signed by the Union of Maximalist Socialist Revolutionaries, the Anarcho-Syndicalist Committee of Russian Defense appointed by the recently formed International Workingmen's Association (IWMA), The Group of Anarchist refugees in Russia (represented by the anarchist Voline) and Representatives Committee for Aid to Anarchists Imprisoned in Russia (represented by Berkman).

The article ended by asking that all correspondence be sent to the anarchist publisher Franz Kater in Berlin on behalf of the Committee for Aid to Imprisoned Revolutionists and it was that group that in October 1923 published the first issue of the *Bulletin of the Joint Committee For the Defense of Revolutionists Imprisoned in Russia.*[9] Berkman played a large role in the appearance of the *Bulletin,* translating material from Russian into English, including an article by I.

---

9. For a published run of the Russian prisoner support *Bulletins* mentioned in this piece readers are urged to read *The Tragic Procession: Alexander Berkman and Russian Prisoner Aid* (London/Oakland: Kate Sharpley Library/Alexander Berkman Social Club, 2010).

N. Steinberg on the situation of imprisoned Left Socialist Revolutionaries in prions and exile. The *Bulletin* would be published from "time to time" with the aim of "supplying the world with information concerning the situation of the revolutionists in Russia."[10] It set the style for future issues with details of anarchists and other revolutionists who had been recently arrested or exiled, together with calls for money to keep the *Bulletin* going and provide funds and supplies for imprisoned comrades. Behind the scenes we can imagine the time taken to retrieve scraps of information, listening to recently arrived Russian refugees and attempts to distinguish between rumor and fact as arrests continued unabated.

Berkman was a sound choice for involvement in this type of work. It was work that played to some of his strengths. He was multi-lingual and able to translate Russian into German or English and was diligent and thorough in wading through all the paperwork that a project like this engendered. Just as importantly he also had a "name"—one that transcended the splits and tensions inside Russian anarchism, and indeed American and European anarchism as well. Essentially he was an honest broker who was seen by most anarchists as a person of his word. His life spoke for his dedication to the anarchist ideal and was thought of with respect by some beyond the left; people he would try to use to publicize the situation of imprisoned revolutionists in Russia.

Yet problems arose soon after the publication of the first issue. That issue had been incorporated into a one-off journal, *Behind The Bars* (January 1924) published in New York by the Anarchist Red Cross. The approach to prisoners taken by the *Bulletin* appeared to cause tension in some New York anarchist circles that were worried about the amount of work that the Bulletin was doing for non-anarchist prisoners. As a result of this concern a letter was sent to Berkman, probably by the New York Branch of the ARC, suggesting that prisoner support work in Russia that was being carried out by the group around the *Bulletin* should concentrate only on looking after imprisoned anarchists. The writers certainly

---

10. *Bulletin Of The Joint Committee For The Defense Of Revolutionists Imprisoned In Russia* No 1, October 1923 page 1.

had history on their side. The Anarchist Red Cross in the United States had been formed in 1907 because, despite anarchists raising funds for political prisoners in Russia (including anarchist prisoners), money appeared to go only to the Social Democrat prisoners there through the various Social Democratic Russian prisoner support groups. To some anarchists in 1923, it seemed history might be repeating itself and Berkman, of all people, was encouraging this to happen. To other anarchists all types of Socialism and Marxism had been tainted by Bolshevik practice. Why support any of them? Berkman replied rather tersely to the letter a month later, arguing that supplying bread to Maria Spiridonovna (who was a Left Socialist Revolutionary) should be just as imperative as to aid Aron Baron (who was an anarchist).[11] If the people in the Anarchist Red Cross were asserting that they could not work with imprisoned Left Socialist Revolutionaries he himself would find it impossible to work with some of the imprisoned anarchists who he thought were "worse than crazy." He would still support these anarchists in any way he could, however. He suggested that being a revolutionist was the primary criteria to receive prisoner support. How he defined "revolutionist" would change and morph slightly at different periods of his life, but basically he identified revolutionists as those who used decisive action to bring about a wholesale revolutionary change. For him, the Left Socialist Revolutionaries were revolutionists even if he disagreed with them politically. Moreover, he felt that political tendencies mattered far less in prison than outside when it came to matters such as food or mutual aid. Consequently the *Bulletin* would later publicize the cases of imprisoned Social Democrats and Socialist Zionists.

The publishing schedule of "from time to time" was reasonably adhered to. The next issue came out in October–November 1924 with more news of hunger strikes and prison life. Berkman had spent much of that year collating as much information as he could about imprisoned and exiled Russian left wing revolutionists, passing the information on to Roger Baldwin, Director of the

---

11. Letter from Alexander Berkman to Lily Sarnov, July 22, 1924, Alexander Berkman Papers.

American Civil Liberties Union, whom Berkman had known in America.[12] This information, essentially documentary in nature, was published for the International Committee for Political Prisoners by the New York publisher Albert and Charles Boni in 1925 as *Letters From Russian Prisons* and published in England by C.W Daniel Co the same year. Baldwin was nominally editor of the project that Berkman had collated. Berkman obviously realized that the International Committee had more influence and could be far more effective in publicizing what was happening in Russia than the anarchists could. Together with Grigori Maksimov's *The Guillotine At Work*, this volume remains essential reading for evidence of Bolshevik repression.[13] We should add that, according to Boris Yelensky in his account of the Anarchist Red Cross, Berkman suggested Maksimov's magisterial work to the Chicago Prisoner Aid group in a 1935 letter.[14]

By December 1926 the Bulletin was under the wing of the International Working Men's Association and became *The Bulletin of the Relief Fund of the International Working Men's Association for Anarchists and Anarcho-Syndicalists Imprisoned in Russia*. More anarchists became involved in its collation and it advertised itself as now being based in Paris and Berlin. The *Bulletin* had also attempted to widen its readership with issues published in English, French, Spanish, and Russian. The odd issue was also published in Dutch and Esperanto. No matter it's new title, the *Bulletin* still provided readers with details of prisoners who were not anarchists. The December 1926 issue, for instance, carried an appeal from Kharkov prison signed by anarchists, a Left Socialist Revolutionary, Socialist Zionists, and a member of the Socialist Youth. In October 1925 Berkman had, with some difficulty, moved to Paris and continued to help edit the *Bulletin* from there. This was a role he continued until May 1930 when he was deported to Belgium for "conducting

---

12. Baldwin knew Berkman through his acquaintanceship with Emma Goldman who Baldwin had first heard speak in 1908.
13. G.P. Maximoff, *The Guillotine at Work: Twenty years of Terror in Russia* (Chicago: Chicago Section of the Alexander Berkman Fund, 1940).
14. Boris Yelensky, *In The Struggle For Equality: The Story of the Anarchist Red Cross* (Chicago: A. Berkman Aid Fund, 1958), 63.

anarchist propaganda." He managed to return but faced further expulsion battles in November 1930 and July 1931. He had to publicly withdraw from this and other projects but privately he dealt with the English correspondence for the Committee and continued to help with the accounts until his death on June 28th 1936. After Berkman's death his anarchist comrades in America recognized his work on behalf of Russian prisoners. The Chicago Aid Group (a strong financial supporter of the Bulletin and its work) renamed itself the Alexander Berkman Aid Fund.[15] After the defeat of the Spanish Revolution in 1939 the Alexander Berkman Aid Fund provided help to Spanish anarchist refugees in France and elsewhere.

His work for Russian prisoner aid was, by any standards, remarkable. I think it's very easy to underestimate what Berkman and his comrades were up against. We need to remember that those who tried to help Russian prisoners were a very small group indeed. It meant facing up to very unpleasant realities. The anarchist movement was, to quote Emma Goldman, everywhere "shot to pieces"[16] and Soviet Russia had the overwhelming sympathy of many on the left. Even if some were bothered and concerned by what they heard or sensed about the reality of life under Bolshevism they always gave Russia the benefit of the doubt. Consider this extract from a 1922 letter to an anarchist from Andrés Nin, Spanish Marxist, later leader of the POUM (Partido Obrero de Unificación Marxista/ Workers' Party of Marxist Unification) in the Spanish Revolution and murdered by the NKVD (People's Commissariat for Internal Affairs) in 1937:

> Were there errors, injustices? Who doubts that? But who would be able to avoid them? Are we all faultless? Anything but! And we have not had a revolution.[17]

---

15. Ibid., 66.
16. Letter from Emma Goldman to Alexander Berkman October 1924, Alexander Berkman Papers, International Institute for Social History, Amsterdam.
17. Letter from Andrés Nin to Mauro Bajatierra, September 1922. Found in Reiner Tosstorff, "The Syndicalists and the Bolshevik Revolution," *Socialist History*, No. 37 (2010).

Give it time. Don't provide bad publicity. Don't push the baby when it is starting to walk. Perhaps many of the people in prison *were* counter revolutionary. Mistakes will be made. Not to accept the reality of the situation makes one a traitor to the revolution. Such genuinely felt attitudes, articulated by so many people, some whom were former allies, only emphasized the emotional and political isolation felt by Berkman and his comrades. Being pre-scient can be a lonely business.

This isolation was compounded by the nature of the work that had to be done. It certainly wasn't glamorous or eye-catching. We can imagine Berkman sitting at his desk in Berlin or Paris sur-rounded by paper: letters, memos, scraps smuggled in from Rus-sia that had gone through countless hands. Reading it all. Making endless lists, trying to find patterns, and trying to make sense of any patterns he found. Stopping occasionally as he becomes aware of the growing and smothering oppression that has so profession-ally taken over the revolution. Sitting and trying to remember the faces of comrades he knew and wondering if they are still alive. Besides all this bureaucratic work decisions had to be made. How can we gain access to progressive labor forces and encourage them to publicize the situation of prisoners in Russia? Just which, of all the deserving cases, should we prioritize for help? If we mention the names of some prisoners are we putting their families in dan-ger? The questions were exhausting and relentless, the answers were not easy and optimism was hard to find.

Also relentless was the constant struggle for funding. Food and medical parcels needed to be sent. Prisoners' families needed to be supported whether inside or outside of Russia. The Bulletin needed to be produced, as did leaflets and brochures about a spe-cific person or group of prisoners as well as articles for whatever paper would publish them. Berkman wrote circular after circular asking for money, "who deserves our efforts more than those brave men and women who are persecuted for their loyalty to an ideal?" he writes in one, going on to stress that no-one on the Relief Fund committee receives any money for what they do. All money goes to the relief of prisoners. It did and the Bulletin regularly published detailed accounts of donations and expenditure. Berkman lived on what money he could earn from his translation work and the odd handout from American comrades.

Of course there is added poignancy for us in the knowledge that very few of the people whose names appear in the Bulletin ever returned to their homes. Contact with prisoners, exiles, and their families became far less regular as the years rolled on. In his book *In The Struggle For Equality*, Yelensky writes these chilling words "Finally, in 1939, every contact with our comrades in Russia was broken, and our work for the political prisoners in that country came to an end."[18]

So there we have it. Anarchists and radicals of many persuasions lost in the camps, the prisons, and isolated villages of Russia. Starving, alone, and casually executed. Many have just simply disappeared from memory. Repressed, isolated and under surveillance for decades. If you weren't shot for active resistance or simple opposition you might starve to death. Some may have remained anarchist out of sheer stubbornness. We know that others tried to keep up connections, waiting for the next revolution. Many just disappeared from history.

I suggested at the beginning of this essay that the lives and experiences of the people Berkman and his comrades were trying to aid might lead us to ask questions. I'd suggest that the most important one is pretty obvious. What are we to do with all this knowledge, these names that Berkman called "The Tragic Procession," name after name of comrades exiled, imprisoned or just disappeared?[19] How are we to process them? Are we to see them as belonging to the past—a sad story but that was then and this is now? Should we compliment Berkman and the others on their work on Russian prisoner support ninety years ago and move on?

I have to say it is tempting. Sometimes history can weigh you down and getting rid of that weight is an attractive idea. The trouble with that approach is we shouldn't want to let this history go!

---

18. Boris Yelensky, *The Struggle for Equality*, 65.
19. *Bulletin Of The Joint Committee For The Defense Of Revolutionaries Imprisoned In Russia*, March–April 1925, 1.

The work that Berkman and the others carried out sadly remains unfinished. We only know fragments of what happened to these comrades, if we know anything at all. The group carrying out research for the website "Anarchists in the Gulag (and prison and exile)" are carrying on the work begun by Berkman and his comrades all those years ago.[20] Fine scholars like Malcolm Archibald at Black Cat Press[21] and Nick Heath[22] are busy working in the field. Exciting work by Russian and Ukrainian historians has been carried out for some time and slowly some of their work is becoming available to English readers.[23] They are all still picking up tattered pieces of paper with indecipherable scrawl on them and bringing people back to life. What type of movement, what type of fighters for a world of individual freedom and mutual aid would we be if we left undiscovered those who shared similar beliefs but perished in the most desperate and tormented of circumstances?

If finding a name and their individual fate is in itself an affirmation of that person and the philosophy by which they lived their lives, so is it also a condemnation of all those who forced them to suffer so brutally. Surely the emotional and physical torment unleashed on our comrades should make us regularly consider who we can work with now in order to realize our ideal? Berkman, himself, believed that we should support all revolutionists in Bolshevik prisons not just anarchists. He had been a prisoner himself and recognized that political differences count far less in prison than out of it. He was an intelligent man, though, and he must have realized that if the prisoners were ever released it would be near impossible to find a similar unity of purpose outside the prison walls. Simply put, because we have the same enemy does it necessarily mean we should be friends?

20. See the website: gulaganarchists.wordpress.com.

21. Among other works the Press has published excellent works on Russian anarchist history. For their current list go to https://thoughtcrimeink.com/books/publisher/black_cat_press.

22. You can read much of Nick Heath's work on the website Libcom (https://libcom.org). See also Nick Heath. *The Third Revolution? Peasant and Worker Resistance to the Bolshevik Government* (London: Kate Sharpley Library, 2010).

23. We should mention the work of Dmitry Rublev, Viktor Savchenko, Yaroslav Leontiev, Anatoly Shtirbul, the late Igor Podshivalov, Peter Riabov, Vadim Damier, Andrey Fyodorov, and last, but certainly not least, Pavel Talerov.

I think we probably need to try and ask the right questions. I am not convinced that it is sensible asking whether or not there are good Marxists or bad ones; nor if there are good interpretations of Marxism and bad ones. Berkman, himself was asking those questions from 1922 onwards although, as the years passed, he appears to have abandoned them and others took their place. There have been consistent attempts by comrades to find the best in both anarchism and Marxism and create some wonderful bionic radical movement that shares a common history and somehow makes us more potent revolutionaries. Certainly Russian (and other) anarchists and Marxists did some work together before 1917. They shared cells and exile in Tsarist Russia. Perhaps some were friends? Perhaps they, too, looked for the best in each other and their respective ideologies. By 1918 those Marxists and Bolsheviks were sending anarchists to prison, exile, or execution for arguing against Bolshevik ideas. Now we all know this is complicated. Some anarchists weren't imprisoned for a while, some anarchists turned to Bolshevism, others died as anarchists fighting side by side with Bolsheviks, and Bolsheviks slaughtered their own comrades as happily as any other tendency. Sometimes anarchists and Bolsheviks shared common interim goals. And yes, as Berkman argued, some anarchists were a little...strange. Reality is a messy business but constant oppression and death do appear to be a regular theme in how Marxists and their various groupings relate to anarchists. Is it inevitable that we will always be the canary in the mine?

I rather think Berkman understood all this complexity as well as anyone and a little better than most. After all he spent a good few years working with the horror created by Marxist state solutions to the eradication of capitalism. The primary questions that he asked in 1921, and refined throughout the rest of his life were centered around what we understand revolutionary change to be and what it means to "take power." For Berkman these were the central questions we should be asking and, to be honest, I don't think we have truly answered them yet. What we can see in his public writings and letters, from 1922 onwards, is a distinct wariness in his approach to the obsessive self-righteousness of Marxists and their groupings. Taking power for them meant that only they could be right in any assessment of any situation. Only they could decide who was worthy and who wasn't. All their decisions were, of course, based on their correct interpretation of the words of Marx and his acolytes. Once you have got rid of your opposition all that is left is for the various tendencies in your group to turn on each other in search of that seductive revolutionary purity mixed with a twist of political expediency. In all of this the working class and dispossessed became irrelevant—irritants to be shaped and controlled by those who knew best. This assurance of being absolutely right coupled with an unsettling certainty quickly became deadly and nightmarish. Their corrosive effects were clearly on show in Russia from 1918 onwards, where dictatorial behavior was justified by "circumstances." "Circumstances" is a wonderful, convenient idea and, of course, sometimes has to be recognized. After all, circumstances can be irritatingly difficult. Just what "circumstances" necessitated the isolation, exile, and death of so many, however, is a question well worth asking!

If we are looking for friends (and are we that lonely?) we might want to consider how our friends feel about their relationship to power—both personal and political. We may feel we have the answers but how do we, as anarchists, work with the economic and emotional victims of capitalism to create a better world remained, for Berkman, the central question of revolutionary practice. In his pamphlet *The Anti-Climax* (which was essentially the last chapter of *The Bolshevik Myth* that his publishers didn't publish because they thought it an "anti-climax"), Berkman suggested the beginnings of an answer "Not by order of some central authority, but organically from life itself"[24] would social regeneration occur with a firm and secure foundation—a process that he saw as the beginnings of anarchist communism—"a free non-authoritarian communist society."[25]

There are so many books, pamphlets, and papers published about the Russian revolution. In the 1930s the great proletarian

24. Alexander Berkman, *The Anti-Climax: The Concluding Chapter of My Russian Diary "The Bolshevik Myth"* (np; Berlin, 1925), 28.
25. *The Anti-Climax*, 26.

writer Jack Common suggested that Socialism would not be built book by book. Neither will anarchy. It could have been built by the actions of people such as Fanya Baron (executed 1921), Maria Weger (arrested 1921), Vladimir Yegorov (exiled to Siberia after three years of isolation, 1931), M.A. Sednev (arrested 1925), Polya Kurganskaya (died in exile 1929), and thousands like them whose names are still waiting to be discovered, but it wasn't. Even after some of them, and thousands and thousands like them, had helped make February and October 1917 happen, their actions appear to have counted for nothing in Bolshevik minds. We might want to argue that times have changed but we need to also face the fact that the reality of their suffering all those years ago hasn't. Whatever further questions these names and lives force us to consider it's up to us to answer them as truthfully as we can. However many books on Russia we read we shouldn't ever forget who they were. We owe them that.

Bolshevism and Stalinism

PAUL MATTICK

The alleged purpose of Trotsky's biography of Stalin[1] is to show 'how a personality of this sort was formed, and how it came to power by usurpation of the right to such an exceptional role.' The real purpose of the book, however, is to show why Trotsky lost the power position he temporarily occupied and why his rather than Stalin's name should follow Lenin's. Prior to Lenin's death it had always been 'Lenin *and* Trotsky'; Stalin's name had invariably been near or at the end of any list of prominent Bolsheviks. On one occasion Lenin even suggested that he put his own signature second to Trotsky's. In brief, the book helps to explain why Trotsky was of the opinion "that he was the natural successor to Lenin" and in effect is a biography of both Stalin and Trotsky.

All beginnings are small, of course, and the Bolshevism of Lenin and Trotsky differs from present-day Stalinism just as Hitler's brown terror of 1933 differed from the Nazism of World War II. That there is nothing in the arsenal of Stalinism that cannot also be found in that of Lenin and Trotsky is attested to by the earlier writings of Trotsky himself.[2] For example Trotsky, like Stalin, introduced *compulsory labour service* as a 'socialist principle.' He, too, was convinced 'that not one serious socialist will begin to deny to the Labour State the right to lay its hands upon the worker who refuses to execute his labour power.' It was Trotsky who hurried to stress the 'socialistic character' of inequality, for, as he said, 'those workers who do more for the general interest than others receive the right to a greater quantity of the social product than the lazy,

---

1. *Stalin. An appraisal of the man and his influence.* Edited and translated from the Russian by Charles Malamuth. The first seven chapters and the appendix, that is, the bulk of the book, Trotsky wrote and revised himself. The last four chapters, consisting of notes, excerpts, documents and other raw materials, have been edited.
2. See for instance, L. Trotsky's "Dictatorship vs. Democracy," New York, 1922; particularly from page 135 to page 150

the careless, and the disorganisers.' It was his opinion that everything must be done to 'assist the development of rivalry in the sphere of production.'

Of course, all this was conceived as the 'socialist principle' of the 'transformation period.' It was dictated by objective difficulties in the way of full socialisation. There was not the desire but the need to strengthen party dictatorship until it led to the abolishment of even those freedoms of activity which, in one fashion or another, had been granted by the bourgeois state. However, Stalin, too, can offer the excuse of necessity.

In order to find other arguments against Stalinism than his personal dislike for a competitor in intra-party struggles, Trotsky must discover and construct political differences between himself and Stalin, and between Stalin and Lenin in order to support his assertion that without Stalin things would have been different in Russia and elsewhere.

There could not have been any 'theoretic' differences between Lenin and Stalin, as the only theoretical work bearing the name of the latter had been inspired and supervised by Lenin. And if Stalin's 'nature craved' the centralised party machine, it was Lenin who constructed the perfect machine for him, so that on that score, too, no differences could arise. In fact, as long as Lenin was active, Stalin was no trouble to him, however troublesome he may have been to 'The Number Two Bolshevik.'

Still, in order for Trotsky to explain the 'Soviet Thermidor,' there must be a difference between Leninism and Stalinism, provided, of course, there was such a Thermidor. On this point, Trotsky has brought forth various ideas as to when it took place, but in his Stalin biography he ignores the question of time in favour of the simple statement that it had something to do with the 'increasing privileges for the bureaucracy.' However, this only brings us back to the early period of the Bolshevik dictatorship which found Lenin and Trotsky engaged in creating the state bureaucracy and increasing its efficiency by increasing its privileges.

Competitors for Power

The fact that the relentless struggle for position came into the open only after Lenin's death suggests something other than the Soviet Thermidor. It simply indicates that by that time the Bolshevik state was of sufficient strength, or was in a position, to disregard to a certain degree both the Russian masses and the international bourgeoisie. The developing bureaucracy began to feel sure that Russia was theirs for keeps; the fight for the plums of the Revolution entered its more general and more serious stage.

All adversaries in this struggle stressed the need of dictatorship in view of the unsolved internal frictions between 'workers' and 'peasants,' the economic and technological backwardness of the country as a whole, and the constant danger of attack from the outside. But within *this* setting of dictatorship, all sorts of arguments could be raised. The power-struggle within the developing ruling class expressed itself in policy-proposals either for or against the interests of the peasants, either for or against the limitation of factory councils, either for or against an offensive policy on the international front. High-sounding theories were expounded with regard to the estimation of the peasantry, the relationship between bureaucracy and revolution, the question of party generations, etc. and reached their climax in the Trotsky-Stalin controversy on the 'Permanent Revolution' and the theory of 'Socialism in one Country.'

It is quite possible that the debaters believed their own phrases; yet, despite their theoretical differentiations, whenever they acted upon a real situation they all acted alike: In order to suit their own needs, they naturally expressed identical things in different terms. If Trotsky rushes to the front—to all fronts in fact—he merely defends the fatherland. But Stalin 'is attracted by the front, because here for the first time he could work with the most finished of all the administrative machines, the military machine' for which, by the way, Trotsky claims all credit. If Trotsky pleads for discipline, he shows his 'iron hand'; if Stalin does the same, he deals with a 'heavy hand.'

If Trotsky's bloody suppression of the Kronstadt Rebellion was a 'tragic necessity' Stalin's suppression of the Georgian independence movement is in the manner of a 'great-Russian Russifier, riding roughshod over the rights of his own people as a nation.' And *vice versa:* suggestions made by Trotsky are called false and counter-revolutionary by Stalin's henchmen; when carried out under Stalin's auspices, they become additional proof of the great leader's wisdom.

To understand Bolshevism, and in a narrower sense Stalinism, it is not enough to follow the superficial and often silly controversies between Stalinists and Trotskyites. After all, the Russian Revolution embraces more than just the Bolshevik Party. It was not even initiated by organised political groups but by spontaneous reactions of the masses to the breakdown of an already precarious economic system in the wake of military defeat. The February upheavals 'started' with hunger riots in market places, protest strikes in factories, and the spontaneous declaration of solidarity with the rioters on the part of the soldiers. But all spontaneous movements in modern history have been accompanied by organised forces. As soon as the collapse of Czarism was imminent, organisations came to the fore with directives and definite political goals.

If prior to the Revolution Lenin had stressed organisation rather than spontaneity, it was because of the retarded Russian conditions, which gave the spontaneous movements a backward character. Even the politically advanced groups offered only limited programmes. The industrial workers desired capitalistic reforms similar to those enjoyed by the workers in more capitalistically advanced countries. The petty-bourgeoisie and important layers of the capitalist class wanted a Western bourgeois democracy. The peasants desired land in a capitalist agriculture. Though progressive for Czarist Russia, these demands were of the essence of bourgeois revolution.

The new liberalistic February government attempted to continue the war. But it was the conditions of war against which the masses were rebelling. All promised reforms within the Russian setting of that time and within the existing imperialistic power relationships were doomed to remain empty phrases; there was no way of directing the spontaneous movements into those channels desired by the government. In new upsurges the Bolsheviks came into power not by way of a *second revolution* but by a forced change of government. This seizure of power was made easy by the lack of interest that the restless masses were showing in the existing government. The October *coup*, as Lenin said, 'was easier than lifting a feather.' The final victory was 'practically achieved by default ... Not a single regiment rose to defend Russian democracy ... The struggle for supreme power over an empire that comprised one-sixth of the terrestrial globe was decided between amazingly small forces on both sides in the provinces as well as in the two capital cities.'

The Bolsheviks did not try to restore the old conditions in order to reform them, but declared themselves in favour of the *concrete results* of the conceptually backward spontaneous movements: the ending of the war, the workers' control of industry, the expropriation of the ruling classes and the division of land. And so they stayed in power.

The pre-revolutionary demands of the Russian masses had been backward for two reasons: they had long been realised in the main capitalist nations, and they could no longer be realised in view of existing world conditions. At a time when the concentration and centralisation process of world capitalism had brought about the decline of bourgeois democracy almost everywhere, it was no longer possible to initiate it afresh in Russia. If *laissez faire* democracy was out of the question, so were all those reforms in capital-labour relations usually related to social legislation and trade-unionism. Capitalist agriculture, too, had passed beyond the breaking up of feudal estates and production for a capitalist market to the industrialisation of agriculture and its consequent incorporation into the concentration process of capital.

The Bolsheviks and Mass Spontaneity

The Bolsheviks did not claim responsibility for the Revolution. They gave full credit to the spontaneous movements. Of course, they underlined the obvious fact that Russia's previous history, which included the Bolshevik Party, had lent some kind of vague revolutionary consciousness to the unorganised masses and they were not backward about asserting that without their leadership the course of the Revolution would have been different and most probably would have led to a counter-revolution. 'Had the Bolsheviks not seized power,' writes Trotsky, 'the world would have had a Russian name for Fascism five years before the March of Rome.'

But counter-revolution attempts on the part of the traditional powers failed not because of any conscious direction of the spontaneous movements, not because of Lenin's 'sharp eyes, which surveyed the situation correctly,' but because of the fact that these movements could not be diverted from their *own* course. If one wants to use the term at all, the 'counter-revolution' possible in the Russia of 1917 was that inherent in the Revolution itself, that is, in the opportunity it offered the Bolsheviks to restore a centrally-directed social order for the perpetuation of the capitalistic divorce of the workers from the means of production and the consequent restoration of Russia as a competing imperialist power.

During the revolution, the interests of the rebelling masses and of the Bolsheviks merged to a remarkable degree. Beyond the temporary merger, there also existed a deep unity between the socialising concepts of the Bolsheviks and the *consequences* of the spontaneous movements. Too 'backward' for socialism but also too 'advanced' for liberal capitalism, the Revolution could end only in that consistent form of capitalism which the Bolsheviks considered a pre-condition of socialism, namely, State-capitalism.

By identifying themselves with the spontaneous movement they could not control, the Bolsheviks gained control over this movement as soon as it had spent itself in the realisation of its immediate goals. There were many such goals differently reached in different territories. Various layers of the peasantry satisfied, or failed to satisfy, divergent needs and desires. Their interests, however, had no real connection with those of the proletariat. The working class itself was split into various groups with a variety of specific needs and general plans. The petty-bourgeoisie had still other problems to solve. In brief, there was a spontaneous unity against the conditions of Czarism and war, but there was no unity in regard to immediate goals and future policy. It was not too difficult for the Bolsheviks to utilise this social division for building up their own power, which finally became stronger than the whole of society because it never faced society as a whole.

Like the other groups which asserted themselves within the revolution, the Bolsheviks, too, pressed to gain their particular end: the control of government. This goal reached farther than those aspired to by the others. It involved a never-ending struggle, a continuous winning and re-winning of power positions. Peasant groups settled down after dividing the land, workers returned to the factories as wage labourers, soldiers, unable to roam the countrysides forever, returned to the life of peasant and worker, but for the Bolsheviks the struggle only really began with the success of the Revolution. Like all governments, the Bolshevik regime involves submission of all existing social layers to its authority. Slowly centralising all power and control into their hands, the Bolsheviks were soon able to dictate policy. Once more Russia became thoroughly organised in the interests of a special class—the class of privilege in the emerging system of State-capitalism.

The Party 'Machine'

All this has nothing to do with Stalinism and 'Thermidor' but represents Lenin's and Trotsky's policy from the very day they came to power. Reporting to the Sixth Congress of Soviets in 1918, Trotsky complained that 'Not all Soviet workers have understood that our administration has been centralised and that all orders issued from above must be final. ... We shall be pitiless with those Soviet workers who have not yet understood; we will remove them, cast them out of our ranks, pull them up with repressions.' Trotsky now claims that these words were aimed at Stalin who did not co-ordinate his war-activity properly and we are willing to believe him. But how much more directly must they have been aimed at all those who were not even 'second-rate' but had no rating at all in the Soviet hierarchy. There already existed, as Trotsky relates, 'a sharp cleavage between the classes in motion and the interests of the party machines. Even the Bolshevik Party cadres, who enjoyed the benefit of exceptional revolutionary training were definitely inclined to disregard the masses and to identify their own special interests with the interests of the machine on the very day after the monarchy was overthrown.'

Trotsky holds, of course, that the dangers implied in this situation were averted by Lenin's vigilance and by objective conditions which made the 'masses more revolutionary than the Party, and the Party more revolutionary than *its* machine.' But the machine was headed by Lenin. Even before the Revolution, Trotsky points out, the Central Committee of the Party 'functioned almost regularly and was entirely in the hands of Lenin.' And even more so after the Revolution. In the spring of 1918 the 'ideal of "democratic centralism" suffered further reverses, for in effect the power within both the government and the Party became concentrated in the hands of Lenin and the immediate retinue of Bolshevik leaders who did not openly disagree with him and carried out his wishes.' As the bureaucracy made headway nevertheless, the emerging Stalinist machine must have been the result of an oversight on the part of Lenin.

To distinguish between the ruler of the machine and the machine on the one hand, and between the machine and the masses on the other implies that only the masses and its top-leader were truly revolutionary, and that both Lenin and the revolutionary masses were later betrayed by Stalin's machine which, so to speak, made itself independent. Although Trotsky needs such distinctions to satisfy his own political interests, they have no basis in fact. Until his death—disregarding occasional remarks against the dangers of bureaucratisation, which for the Bolsheviks are the equivalent of the bourgeois politicians' occasional crusades for a balanced budget—Lenin never once came out against the Bolshevik Party machine and its leadership, that is, against himself. Whatever policy was decided upon received Lenin's blessing as long as he was at the helm of the machine; and he died holding that position.

Lenin's 'democratic' notions are legendary. Of course state-capitalism under Lenin was different from state-capitalism under Stalin because the dictatorial powers of the latter were greater—thanks to Lenin's attempt to build up his own. That Lenin's rule was less terroristic than Stalin's is debatable. Like Stalin, Lenin catalogued *all* his victims under the heading 'counter-revolutionary.' Without comparing the statistics of those tortured and killed under both regimes, we will admit that the Bolshevik regime under Lenin and Trotsky was not strong enough to carry through such Stalinist measures as enforced collectivisation and slave-labour camps as a main economic and political policy. It was not design but weakness which forced Lenin and Trotsky to the so called *New Economic Policy*, that is, to concessions to private property interests and to a greater lip-service to 'democracy.'

Bolshevik 'toleration' of such non-Bolshevik organisations as the Social Revolutionists in the early phase of Lenin's rule did not spring, as Trotsky asserts, from Lenin's 'democratic' inclinations but from inability to destroy all non-Bolshevik organisations at once. The totalitarian features of Lenin's Bolshevism were accumulating at the same rate at which its control and police power grew. That they were forced upon the Bolsheviks by the 'counter-revolutionary' activity of all non-Bolshevik labour organisations, as Trotsky maintains, can not of course explain their further increase after the crushing of the various nonconformist organisations. Neither could it explain Lenin's insistence upon the enforcement of totalitarian principle in the extra-Russian organisations of the Communist International.

Trotsky, Apologist for Stalinism

Unable to blame non-Bolshevik organisations entirely for Lenin's dictatorship, Trotsky tells 'those theoreticians who attempt to prove that the present totalitarian regime of the U.S.S.R. is due ...

to the ugly nature of Bolshevism itself,' that they forget the years of Civil War, 'which laid an indelible impress on the Soviet Government by virtue of the fact that very many of the administrators, a considerable layer of them, had become accustomed to command and demanded unconditional submission to their orders.' Stalin, too, he continues, 'was moulded by the environment and circumstances of the Civil War, along with the entire group that later helped him to establish his personal dictatorship.' The Civil War, however, was initiated by the international bourgeoisie. And thus the ugly sides of Bolshevism under Lenin, as well as under Stalin, find their chief and final cause in capitalism's enmity to Bolshevism which, if it is a monster, is only a reluctant monster, killing and torturing in mere self-defence.

And so, if only in a roundabout way, Trotsky's Bolshevism, despite its saturation with hatred for Stalin, leads in the end merely to a defence of Stalinism as the only possible self-defence for Trotsky. This explains the superficiality of the ideological differences between Stalinism and Trotskyism. The impossibility of attacking Stalin without attacking Lenin helps to explain, furthermore, Trotsky's great difficulties as an oppositionist. Trotsky's own past and theories preclude on his part the initiation of a movement to the *left* of Stalinism and condemned 'Trotskyism' to remain a mere collecting agency for unsuccessful Bolsheviks. As such it could maintain itself outside of Russia because of the ceaseless competitive struggles for power and positions within the so-called 'communist' world-movement. But it could not achieve significance for it had nothing to offer but the replacement of one set of politicians by another. The Trotskyist defence of Russia in the Second World War was consistent with all the previous policies of this, Stalin's most bitter, but also most loyal, opposition.

Trotsky's defence of Stalinism does not exhaust itself with showing how the Civil War transformed the Bolsheviks from servants into masters of the working class. He points to the more important fact that it is the 'bureaucracy's law of life and death to guard the nationalisation of the means of production and of the land.' This means that 'in spite of the most monstrous bureaucratic distortions, the class basis of the U.S.S.R. remains proletarian.' For a while —we notice—Stalin had Trotsky worried. In 1921, Lenin had been disturbed by the question as to whether the *New Economic Policy* was merely a 'tactic' or an 'evolution.' Because the NEP released private-capitalistic tendencies, Trotsky saw in the growing Stalinist bureaucracy 'nothing else than the first stage of bourgeois restoration.' But his worries were unfounded; 'the struggle against equality and the establishment of very deep social differentiations has so far been unable to eliminate the socialist consciousness of the masses or the nationalisation of the means of production and the land, which were the basic social conquests of the revolution.' Stalin, of course, had nothing to do with this, for 'the Russian Thermidor would have undoubtedly opened a new era of bourgeois rule, if that rule had not proved obsolete throughout the world.'

The Result: State Capitalism

With this last statement of Trotsky's we approach the essence of the matter under discussion. We have said before that the *concrete* results of the revolution of 1917 were neither socialistic nor bourgeois but state-capitalistic. It was Trotsky's belief that Stalin would destroy the state-capitalist nature of the economy in favour of a bourgeois economy. This was to be the Thermidor. The decay of bourgeois economy all over the world prevented Stalin from bringing this about. All he could do was to introduce the ugly features of his personal dictatorship into that society which had been brought into existence by Lenin and Trotsky. In this way, and despite the fact that Stalin still occupies the Kremlin, Trotskyism has triumphed over Stalinism.

It all depends on an equation of state-capitalism with socialism. And although some of Trotsky's disciples have recently found it impossible to continue making the equation, Trotsky was bound to it, for it is the beginning and the end of Leninism and, in a wider sense, of the whole of the social-democratic world-movement of which Leninism was only the more realistic part. Realistic, that is,

269

with regard to Russia. What was, and still is, understood by this movement under 'workers' state is governmental rule by the party; what is meant by 'socialism' is the nationalisation of the means of production. By adding control over the economy to the political control of the government the totalitarian rule over all of society emerges in full. The government secures its totalitarian rule by way of the party, which maintains the social hierarchy and is itself a hierarchical institution.

This idea of 'socialism' is now in the process of becoming discredited, but only because of the experience of Russia and similar if less extensive experiences in other countries. Prior to 1914, what was meant by the seizure of power, either peacefully or violently, was the seizure of the government machinery, replacing a given set of administrators and law-makers with another set. Economically, the 'anarchy' of the capitalistic market was to be replaced by a planned production under the control of the state. As the socialist state would by definition be a 'just' state, being itself controlled by the masses by way of the democratic processes, there was no reason to expect that its decisions would run counter to socialistic ideals. This theory was sufficient to organise parts of the working class into more or less powerful parties.

The theory of socialism boiled down to the demand for centralised economic planning in the interest of all. The centralisation process, inherent in capital-accumulation itself, was regarded as a *socialistic* tendency. The growing influence of 'labour' within the state-machinery was hailed as a step in the direction of socialism. But actually the centralisation process of capital indicated something else than its self-transformation into social property. It was identical with the destruction of *laissez faire* economy and therewith with the end of the traditional business-cycle as the regulator of the economy. With the beginning of the twentieth century the character of capitalism changed. From that time on it found itself under permanent crisis conditions which could not be resolved, by the 'automatic' workings of the market. Monopolistic regulations, state-interferences, national policies shifted the burden of the crisis to the capitalistically under-privileged in the world-economy.

All 'economic' policy became imperialistic policy, culminating twice in world-wide conflagrations.

In this situation, to reconstruct a broken-down political and economic system meant to adapt it to these new conditions. The Bolshevik theory of socialisation fitted this need in an admirable way. In order to restore the national power of Russia it was necessary to do in a radical fashion what in the Western nations had been merely an evolutionary process. Even then it would take time to close the gap between the Russian economy and that of the Western powers. Meanwhile the ideology of the socialist movement served well as protection. The socialist origin of Bolshevism made it particularly fitted for the state-capitalist reconstruction of Russia. Its organisational principles, which had turned the party into a well-functioning institution, would re-establish order in the country as well.

The Bolsheviks of course were convinced that what they were building in Russia was, if not socialism, at least the next best thing to socialism, for they were completing the process which in the Western nations was still only the main *trend* of development. They had abolished the market-economy and had expropriated the bourgeoisie; they also had gained complete control over the government. For the Russian workers, however, nothing had changed; they were merely faced by another set of bosses, politicians and indoctrinators. Their position equalled the workers' position in all capitalist countries during times of war. State-capitalism is a war-economy, and all extra-Russian economic systems transformed themselves into war-economies, into state-capitalistic systems fitted to the imperialistic needs of modern capitalism. Other nations did not copy all the innovations of Russian state-capitalism but only those best suited to their specific needs. The Second World War led to the further unfolding of state-capitalism on a world wide scale. The peculiarities of the various nations and their special situations within the world-power frame provided a great variety of developmental processes towards state-capitalism.

The fact that state-capitalism and fascism did not, and do not grow everywhere in a uniform manner provided Trotsky with the argument of the basic difference between Bolshevism, fascism and capitalism plain and simple. This argument necessarily stresses superficialities of social development. In all essential aspects all three of these systems are identical and represent only various stages of the same development—a development which aims at manipulating the mass of the population by dictatorial governments in a more or less authoritarian fashion, in order to secure the government and the privileged social layers which support it and to enable those governments to participate in the international economy of today by preparing for war, waging war, and profiting by war.

Trotsky could not permit himself to recognise in Bolshevism one aspect of the world-wide trend towards a 'fascist' world economy. As late as 1940 he held the view that Bolshevism prevented the rise of Fascism in the Russia of 1917. It should have long since been clear, however, that all that Lenin and Trotsky prevented in Russia was the use of a non-Marxian ideology for the 'fascist' reconstruction of Russia. Because the Marxian ideology of Bolshevism merely served state-capitalistic ends, it, too, has been discredited. From any view that goes beyond the capitalist system of exploitation, Stalinism and Trotskyism are both relics of the past.

The Role of Bolshevik Ideology in the Birth of the Bureaucracy*

CORNELIUS CASTORIADIS

[1. The Significance of the Russian Revolution]

We are happy to present to our readers the first translation into French of Alexandra Kollontai's pamphlet *The Workers' Opposition in Russia*. This pamphlet was published in Moscow at the beginning of 1921, during the violent controversy that preceded the

* Originally published as "Le Rôle de l'idéologie bolchevique dans la naissance de la bureaucratie (Introduction à l'*Opposition ouvrière* d'Alexandra Kollontaï)," *Socialisme ou Barbarie*, 35 (January 1964). Reprinted in *L'Expérience du mouvement ouvrier*, vol. 2, *Prolétariat et organisation* (Paris: Union Générale d'Éditions, 1974), pp. 385–416, with three additional lettered notes omitted here. [Translator/Editor (hereafter: T/E): We have made extensive use of Maurice Brinton's translation, *From Bolshevism to the Bureaucracy* (*Solidarity Pamphlet*, 24 [no date], 18 pp.). Brinton, whose added subtitles we retain here within brackets, notes that "the present pamphlet was later translated into Italian (under the title "Dal Bolscevismo all Burocrazia") and published in 1968 by the Quademi della Rivoluzione dei Consigli (V. C. Rolando 8/8, Ge-Sampierdarenda). Later in the same year, it was also translated into Swedish (under the title "Bosjevism, Byrakrati!") and published by Libertad (Allmana vage 6, 41460 Göteborg)." Castoriadis's article introduced the next text in the same *Socialisme ou Barbarie* issue: Alexandra Kollontai's "L'Opposition ouvriere," a French translation of the original English-language translation of her work. In Brinton's introduction to his Solidarity translation of Castoriadis's article, he states that this "first English translation" of Kollontai's *The Workers Opposition in Russia* "had appeared (between April 22 and August 19, 1921) in successive issues of Sylvia Pankhurst's *Workers Dreadnought*." Solidarity had already reprinted this 1921 English translation in 1962, and it appeared in 1973 as *The Workers' Opposition* from the League for Economic Democracy (San Pedro, CA). A new paperback edition, *The Workers Opposition in the Russian Communist Party: The Fight for Workers Democracy in the Soviet Union*, was published by Red and Black Publishers (St. Petersburg, FL, 2009). Of note, too, is Brinton's own groundbreaking 1970 Solidarity book, *The Bolsheviks and Workers' Control, 1917 to 1921; The State and Counter-Revolution*. Black and Red (Detroit) reprinted this pamphlet in 1972 and again in 1975. It also appeared in *For Workers' Power: The Selected Writings of Maurice Brinton*, ed. David

Tenth Congress of the Bolshevik Party. This Congress was to close discussion forever on this controversy as well as on all the others.

People have not finished talking about the Russian Revolution, its problems, its degeneration, and about the regime it ultimately produced. And how could one? Of all the revolts of the working class, the Russian Revolution was the only victorious one. And of all the working class's failures, it was the most thoroughgoing and the most revealing.

The crushing of the Paris Commune in 1871 and of the Budapest uprising in 1956 teaches us that insurgent workers encounter immensely difficult organizational and political problems, that an insurrection can find itself isolated, that the ruling classes will not hesitate to employ any kind of violence or barbarian savagery when their power is at stake. The Russian Revolution, however, obliges us to reflect not only on the conditions for a proletarian victory but also on the content and the possible fate of such a victory, on its consolidation and development, on the seeds of a failure whose import infinitely surpasses the victory of the troops of the Versaillese, of Franco's army, or of Khrushchev's tanks.

Since it crushed the White armies and yet succumbed to a bureaucracy it had itself generated, the Russian Revolution puts us face to face with problems of a different nature from those involving a study of the tactics and methods of an armed insurrection or a correct analysis of the relation of forces at a given moment. It obliges us to reflect on the nature of the power of laboring people and on what we mean by socialism. Culminating in a regime in which economic concentration, the totalitarian power of the rulers [*des dirigeants*], and the exploitation of the laboring population have been pushed to the limit, and producing to an extreme degree the centralization of capital and

Goodway (Oakland, CA: AK Press, 2004) and was republished by On Our Own Authority! (Atlanta, GA) in 2012.]

its fusion with the State, in its outcome this revolution presents us with what has been and in certain respects still remains the most highly developed and the "purest" form of a modern exploitative society.

Embodying Marxism for the first time in history—only to make us see immediately in this incarnation a monstrous disfiguration of it—the Russian Revolution allows us to understand more about Marxism than what Marxism itself has been able to help us to understand about the Revolution. The regime the Revolution produced has become the touchstone for all current ideas, not only those of classical Marxism, of course, but just as much those of the bourgeois ideologies. This regime has proved the ruination of Marxism through its very realization and has proved the triumph of the deepest layers of these other ideologies through its very refutations of them. Even as this regime has expanded to embrace a third of the globe, has been challenged by workers' revolts against it [since the mid-1950s], has attempted to reform itself, and has now split into two opposing poles, the Russian and the Chinese, it has not ceased to raise questions of the most pressing importance and to act as the clearest as well as the most enigmatic indicator of world history. The world we live in, reflect in, and act in was launched on its present course by the workers and Bolsheviks of Petrograd in October 1917.

[2. The Main Questions]

Among the innumerable questions raised by the fate of the Russian Revolution, two form the poles around which we may organize all the others.

The first question is, What kind of society was produced by the degeneration of the revolution? (What are the nature and the dynamic of this regime? What is the Russian bureaucracy? What is its relation to capitalism and to the proletariat? What is its place in history? What are its present problems?) This question has already been discussed on several occasions in *Socialisme ou Barbarie*,[1] and will be again.[2]

The second question is, How can a workers' revolution give birth to a bureaucracy, and how did this occur in Russia? We have examined this question in its theoretical form,[3] but so far we have said little from the concrete historical point of view.

Indeed, there is an almost insurmountable obstacle to a close study of this particularly obscure period extending from October 1917 to March 1921, during which the fate of the revolution was played out. The question of most concern to us is, in effect, the following: To what extent did the Russian workers try to take upon themselves the direction of society, the management of production, the regulation of the economy, and the orientation of political life? What was their conscious awareness of these problems, the character of their autonomous activity? What was their attitude toward the Bolshevik Party, toward the nascent bureaucracy? Now, we should point out that it is not workers who write history. It is always *the others*. And these others, whoever they may be, have a historical existence only insofar as the

---

1. See, among other articles, P[ierre] Chaulieu [Cornelius Castoriadis], "Les rapports de production en Russie" (*Socialisme ou Barbarie*, 2 [May–June 1949]) and "L'Exploitation de la paysannerie sous le capitalisme bureaucratique" (*Socialisme ou Barbarie*, 4 [July–August 1949]) [T/E: "The Relations of Production in Russia" and "The Exploitation of the Peasantry under Bureaucratic Capitalism" appear in Castoriadis's *Political and Social Writings*, vol. 1, *1946–1955: From the Critique of Bureaucracy to the Positive Content of Socialism*, trans. and ed. David Ames Curtis (Minneapolis: University of Minnesota Press, 1988)], as well as Claude Lefort's "Le Totalitarisme sans Staline" (*Socialisme ou Barbarie*,19 [July 1956]; reprinted in *Éléments d'une critique de la bureaucratie* [Geneva: Droz, 1971], pp. 130–90 [T/E: now available from Gallimard (Paris, 1979), pp. 155–235; abridged translation, "Totalitarianism without Stalin," in *The Political Forms of Modern Society* (Cambridge, Mass.: MIT Press, and Cambridge, England: Polity Press, 1986), pp. 52–88; another abridged translation, also entitled "Totalitarianism without Stalin," appears in *A Socialisme ou Barbarie Anthology: Autonomy, Critique, Revolution in the Age of Bureaucratic Capitalism*, trans. from the French and ed. anonymously as a public service (June 2016): http://www.notbored.org/SouBA.pdf]).

2. We will publish, in our upcoming issues, some articles on the postindustrial Russian economy and society. [T/E: These articles were not published in *Socialisme ou Barbarie*.]

3. Beyond the texts cited in note 1, see Editorial for the first issue of *Socialisme ou Barbarie* (March–April 1949) and P[ierre] Chaulieu, "Sur le contenu du socialisme," *Socialisme ou Barbarie*, 17 (July–September 1955). [T/E: Both this editorial, "Socialism or Barbarism," and the first part of "On the Content of Socialism" appear in the first volume of Castoriadis's *Political and Social Writings*.]

masses are passive, or active simply to support them, and this is precisely what "the others" will tell us at every opportunity. Most of the time, these others will not even possess eyes to see and ears to hear the gestures and utterances that express people's autonomous activity. In the best of instances, they will sing the praises of this activity so long as it *miraculously* coincides with their own line, but they will radically condemn it, and impute to it the basest motives, as soon as it strays therefrom. Thus Trotsky describes in grandiose terms the anonymous workers of Petrograd moving ahead of the Bolshevik Party or mobilizing themselves during the Civil War, but later on he was to characterize the Kronstadt insurgents as "stool pigeons" and "hirelings of the French High Command." They lack the categories of thought—the brain cells, we might dare say—necessary to understand, or even to record, this activity as it really occurs: to them, an activity that is not instituted, that has neither boss nor program, has no status; it is not even clearly perceivable, except perhaps in the mode of "disorder" and "troubles." The autonomous activity of the masses belongs, by definition, to what is *repressed* in history.

Thus, it is not only that the documentary records most interesting to us during this period are fragmentary, or even that they were and continue to be systematically suppressed by the triumphant bureaucracy. It is that this record of events is infinitely more *selective* and *slanted* than any other historical testimony. The reactionary rage of bourgeois witnesses and the almost equally vicious hostility of the social democrats; the delirious ravings of the anarchists; the official historiography, periodically rewritten to suit the needs of the bureaucracy, and that of the Trotskyist tendency, concerned exclusively with justifying itself after the fact and with hiding its role during the first stages of degeneration—all this "historical evidence" converges on one point: it ignores the signs of the autonomous activity of the masses during this period, or, if necessary, "proves" the a priori impossibility of its very existence.

In this regard, the information contained in Alexandra Kollontai's text is of priceless value. First, because of the direct indications it supplies concerning the attitudes and reactions of Russian workers toward the policy of the Bolshevik Party; second and more important, because it shows that a large portion of the working-class base of the Party was aware of the process of bureaucratization that was taking place, and was taking a stand against it. It is no longer possible, after reading this text, to continue to describe the Russia of 1920 as "just chaos," "a pile of ruins," where the thought of Lenin and the "iron will" of the Bolsheviks were the only elements of order in a country whose proletariat had been pulverized. The workers wanted something, and they showed what they wanted through the Workers' Opposition within the Party and the Petrograd strikes and the Kronstadt revolt outside the Party. Both the intraparty and the extraparty challenges had to be crushed by Lenin and Trotsky for Stalin later to emerge triumphant.

[3. The Traditional "Answers"]

Back to the main question: How could the Russian Revolution have produced a bureaucratic regime? The current answer (first advanced by Trotsky, later taken up by the fellow travelers of Stalinism, and today by Khrushchev's men themselves in order to "explain" the "bureaucratic deformations of the socialist system") is the following: the Revolution took place in a backward country, which in any case could not have built socialism on its own; it found itself isolated by the defeat of the revolution in Europe (and more particularly in Germany between 1919 and 1923); and what is more, the country was completely devastated by the Civil War.

This answer would not deserve a moment's consideration, were it not for the fact that it is widely accepted and that it continues to play a mystificatory role. For it is completely beside the point.

The backwardness, isolation, and devastation of the country—all incontestable facts in themselves—might just as well have explained a pure and simple defeat of the revolution and the restoration of classical capitalism. What we are asking, however, is precisely why there was no pure and simple defeat, why the Revolution overcame its external enemies only to collapse from within, why it "degenerated" precisely in such a way that it led to the power of the bureaucracy.

Trotsky's answer, if we may use a metaphor, is like saying, "This patient developed tuberculosis because he was run down." Feeling run down, however, he might have died instead, contracted some other disease. Why did he contract this *particular* disease? What has to be explained in the degeneration of the Russian Revolution is why it was specifically a *bureaucratic* degeneration. This cannot be done by referring to factors as general as "backwardness" or "isolation." Let us add in passing that this "response" teaches us nothing we could extend beyond the confines of the Russian situation in 1920. The sole conclusion to be drawn from this kind of "analysis" is that revolutionaries should ardently hope that future revolutions break out in more advanced countries, that they should not remain isolated, and that civil wars should not in the least be devastating.

After all, the fact that [since the Second World War] the bureaucratic system of rule has extended its frontiers well beyond the boundaries of Russia, that it has installed similar regimes in countries that in no way can be characterized as backward (such as Czechoslovakia or East Germany), and that industrialization—which has made Russia the second strongest power in the world—has not weakened this bureaucracy at all, shows that all discussion in terms of "backwardness," "isolation," and so forth, is purely and simply anachronistic.

[4. Bureaucracy in the Modern World]

If we wish to understand the emergence of the bureaucracy as an increasingly preponderant managerial stratum in the contemporary world, we are obliged to note at the outset that, paradoxically, it appears at the two opposite poles of social development. On the one hand, it has emerged as the organic product of the maturation process of capitalist society. On the other hand, it appears as the "forced answer" backward countries give to the problem of their own *passage* to the stage of industrialization.

[*A. Modern Capitalist Countries*]

In the first case, the emergence of the bureaucracy offers us no mystery. The concentration of production necessarily leads to the appearance within business firms of a stratum whose function is to take on the collective management of immense economic units. The task to be performed goes qualitatively beyond the capacities of any individual owner. At first in the economic realm, but gradually also in other spheres, the growing role of the State leads both to a quantitative extension of the bureaucratic state apparatus and to a qualitative change in its nature.

At the opposite pole within advanced capitalist societies, the workers' movement degenerates as it becomes bureaucratized, it becomes bureauratized as it becomes integrated into the established order, and it cannot become integrated into this order without becoming bureaucratized. The various technoeconomic, state-political, and "working-class" elements constitutive of the bureaucracy coexist with varying degrees of success. They coexist both with one another and with the more properly "bourgeois" elements of society (owners of the means of production). In any case, as the bureaucracy evolves, the importance of these bureaucratic elements for the management of society constantly increases. In this sense, one can say that the emergence of the bureaucracy corresponds to an "ultimate" phase in the process of capital concentration, that the bureaucracy personifies or embodies capital during this phase, in the same way that the bourgeoisie did during the previous phase.

At least as far as its origins and its social-historical function are concerned, this bureaucracy can be understood in terms of the categories of classical Marxism. (It matters little, in this respect, that today's alleged Marxists, who fall forever short of the possibilities entailed by the very theory they claim as theirs, remain incapable of granting the bureaucracy any kind of sociohistorical status. These so-called Marxists believe that there is no name for this thing in their ideas, and so in practice they deny its existence and speak of capitalism, as if nothing had changed within capitalism for the past century or half century.)

[B. Economically Backward Countries]

In the second case, the bureaucracy emerges, one might say, from the very void found in this type of society. In almost all backward countries, the old ruling strata are clearly incapable of undertaking the industrialization of the country. Foreign capital creates, at "best," merely isolated pockets of modern exploitation, and the late-born national bourgeoisie in such countries has neither the strength nor the courage necessary to undertake this shakeup of the old social structures from top to bottom, as would be required by the process of modernization. Let us add that, because of this very fact, the national proletariat is too weak to play the role assigned to it by the schema of "permanent revolution," that is, it is too weak to eliminate the old ruling strata and to undertake the process of transformation that would lead, in an uninterrupted fashion, from the "bourgeois-democratic" phase through to socialism.

What can happen then? A backward society can stagnate and remain stagnant for a longer or shorter period of time. (This is the situation today in a large number of backward countries, whether or not they have been constituted as States only recently.) But this process of stagnation in fact signifies a relative and sometimes an absolute deterioration of their economic and social situation, as well as a rupture of the old equilibrium built into these societies. Aggravated almost always by apparently "accidental" factors (which in fact recur inevitably and which are amplified to an infinitely greater degree in a society undergoing disintegration), each upset in the balance of these societies turns into a crisis, often colored by some "national" component. This can result in an overt and prolonged national-social struggle (China, Algeria, Cuba, Indochina) or a coup d'état, almost inevitably military in nature (Egypt).

These two examples exhibit immense differences, but they also share a common point.

In the first type of example (China, etc.), the politico-military leadership of the struggle gradually erects itself into an autonomous stratum that manages the "revolution" and, after victory, takes in hand the reconstruction of the country. To this end, it naturally incorporates all those members of the old privileged strata who have rallied to its cause while also selecting certain members of the masses. And as the country industrializes, it constitutes these elements into a hierarchical pyramid that will serve as the skeleton of the new social structure. This industrialization is carried out, of course, according to the classical methods of primitive accumulation. These methods involve intense exploitation of the workers and an even more intense exploitation of the peasantry, who are more or less press-ganged into an industrial army of labor.

In the second example (Egypt, etc.), the state-military bureaucracy, while playing a role of tutelage with regard to the existing privileged strata, does not completely eliminate these strata or the social situation they represent. Also, one can almost always foresee that the country will not be fully transformed and industrialized until there is a further violent convulsion.

In both instances, however, what we discover is that the bureaucracy substitutes or tends to substitute itself for the bourgeoisie as the social stratum that carries out the task of primitive accumulation.

We must note that this bureaucracy has effectively shattered the traditional categories of Marxism. In no way can it be said that this new social stratum has been constituted and has grown within the womb of the preceding society. Nor is it born out of a new mode of production whose development had become incompatible with the maintenance of old forms of economic and social life. It is, on the contrary, the bureaucracy that gives birth to this new mode of production in the societies we are considering. It is not itself born out of the normal functioning of society, but rather out of the inability of this society to function. Almost without metaphor, we can say that it has its origin in the social void: its historical roots plunge wholly into the future.

It obviously makes no sense to say that the Chinese bureaucracy is the product of the country's industrialization when it would be infinitely more reasonable to say that the industrialization of China is the product of the bureaucracy's accession to power. We can only move beyond this antinomy by pointing out that in the present epoch, and short of a revolutionary solution on an international scale, a backward country can industrialize only by becoming bureaucratized.

[C. Russia]

In the case of Russia, one might say that, after the fact, the bureaucracy seems to have fulfilled the "historical function"[4] of the bourgeoisie of earlier times, or of the bureaucracy of a backward country today. Up to a certain point, therefore, the Russian bureaucracy can be compared to the latter sort of bureaucracy.[5] The conditions under which it arose, however, are different. And this difference is due precisely to the fact that the Russia of 1917 was not simply a "backward" country, but a country that, besides its backwardness, exhibited certain well-developed features of capitalism (Russia was, in 1913, the fifth strongest industrial power in the world)—so well developed, as a matter of fact, that it was the theater of a proletarian revolution proclaiming itself socialist (long before this word had come to signify anything one wants and nothing at all).

The first bureaucracy to have become a ruling class in its society, the Russian bureaucracy appears precisely as the end product of a revolution that everyone thought had given power to the proletariat. It therefore represents a third, quite specific type (although in fact it was the first clearly to emerge within modern history): the bureaucracy born from the degeneration of a working-class

---

4. When we speak of a "historical function" in this context, we are not doing metaphysics, nor are we making a posteriori rationalizations. This is an abbreviation for saying: Either Russia would have developed a modern form of large-scale industry or the new State would have been crushed in some conflict or other (at the latest, in 1941).

5. It is in this sense that there is an element of truth in the connection Trotsky establishes between bureaucracy and backwardness (a theme ponderously repeated today by [Isaac] Deutscher, for example). What one obviously forgets to add is that in that case it really is a matter of an *exploitative regime* that carries out the process of primitive accumulation.

revolution. It *is* this degeneration—even if, from the outset, the Russian bureaucracy accomplishes such functions as "manager of centralized capital" and acts as the "stratum for developing a modern industrial economy by every means available."

[5. The Working Class in the Russian Revolution]

Keeping in mind precisely what came afterward, and recollecting too that the October 1917 "seizure of power" was organized and directed by the Bolshevik Party and that this Party in fact assumed this power as its own from day one, in what sense can one say that the October Revolution was proletarian (that is, if one refuses at least to identify a class simply with the party claiming power in that class's name)? Why not say—indeed, there has been no lack of people to say it—that there never was in Russia anything other than a coup d'état carried out by a party that, having somehow obtained the support of the working class, was merely trying to instaurate its own dictatorship and succeeded in doing so?

We have no intention of discussing this problem in scholastic terms. Our aim is not to ask whether the Russian Revolution fits into the category of "proletarian revolutions." The question that matters for us is this: Did the Russian working class play a historical role *of its own* during this period, or was it simply a sort of infantry, mobilized in the service of other, already established forces? In other words, did it appear as a relatively autonomous pole in the struggle and the whirlwind of actions, organizational forms, demands, and ideas of this period, or was it just a tool manipulated without great difficulty or risk, a relay station for impulses coming from elsewhere?

Anyone who has studied the history of the Russian Revolution even to the slightest degree could answer without hesitation. Petrograd in 1917, and even afterward, was neither Prague in 1948 nor Canton in 1949. The proletariat's independent role was clearly apparent—even, to begin with, by the very way workers flocked into the ranks of the Bolshevik Party, giving it majority support, which no one could have extorted from them or forced upon them at the time. This independent role was also shown by the rapport between the workers and this party and by the burden of the Civil War, which they spontaneously took upon themselves. Above all, however, it is shown by the autonomous actions they themselves undertook, already in February and July 1917 and even more so after October, when they expropriated the capitalists without waiting for, or even in acting against, the expressed will of the Party and when they organized production on their own. Finally, it is shown in the autonomous organs they set up: the Soviets and, in particular, the Factory Committees.

The Revolution's success was made possible only because a vast movement of total revolt on the part of the working masses, whose will was to change the conditions of their existence and rid themselves of bosses and Czar, converged with the activity of the Bolshevik Party. It is true that the Bolshevik Party alone, in late October 1917, was able to give articulate expression and a precise *intermediate objective* to the aspirations of the workers, the peasants, and the soldiers (the overthrow of the Provisional Government). This in no way means, however, that the workers were their passive infantry. Without these workers, both inside and outside its ranks, the Party was nothing, neither physically nor politically a force to be reckoned with. Without the pressure arising from their increasing radicalization, it would not even have adopted a revolutionary line. And at no moment, even long months after the seizure of power, could it be said that the Party "controlled" the movements of the working masses.

This convergence, however, which actually culminated in the overthrow of the Provisional Government and in the formation of a predominantly Bolshevik government, turned out to be temporary. Signs of a gap between the Party and the masses appeared rather early on, even though, by its very nature, such a gap could not be grasped in as a clear cut a way as one between organized political tendencies.

The workers certainly expected of the Revolution a total change in the conditions of their existence. They undoubtedly were expecting an improvement in their material conditions—knowing quite well that such an improvement would not come about immediately. Only the narrow-minded would tie the Revolution to this factor alone—or the workers' subsequent dissatisfaction to the new regime's incapacity to satisfy these hopes for material betterment. The Revolution began, in a certain sense, with a demand for bread. Long before October, however, it had already gone beyond the question of bread and had engaged people's total, passionate commitment.

For more than three years, the Russian workers put up with the most extreme material privations without flinching. At the same time, they supplied the bulk of the forces that were going to defeat the White armies. For them, it was a question of freeing themselves from the oppression of the capitalist class and of its State. Organized in the Soviets and in the Factory Committees, they found it inconceivable, even before but particularly after October, that the capitalists would be allowed to stay on. And in chasing them out of the factories, they were led to discover that they would have to organize and manage production themselves. The workers themselves expropriated the capitalists, doing so on their own authority and acting against the line of the Bolshevik Party (the nationalization decree of the summer of 1918 merely ratified what already had been done). And it was the workers who got the factories running once again.

[6. Bolshevik Policy]

As for the Bolshevik Party, this was not at all what they were after. Insofar as the Party developed any clear-cut line after October (and contrary to the mythology put out by Stalinists and Trotskyists alike, it can easily be shown, backed up by documentary records, that before and after October the Bolshevik Party was totally in the dark as to what it wanted to do after the seizure of power), it aimed at instaurating in Russia a "well-organized" economy along the lines of the capitalist model of the time,[6] a form of "state capitalism" (the expression unceasingly used by Lenin), upon which would be superimposed a "working-class" political power—in fact, this power would be exercised by the party of the "working class," the Bolshevik Party. "Socialism" (which effectively implies, Lenin writes without hesitation, the "collective management of production") will come afterward.

And this is not just a question of a "line," of something simply said or thought. In its deep-down mentality and in its real attitude, the Party was permeated from top to bottom with the unquestionable conviction that it ought to *lead, direct, manage [diriger]* in the full sense of the[se] term[s]. This conviction, which already existed long before the Revolution began (as Trotsky showed when he spoke of the "committee mentality" in his biography of Stalin), was indeed shared by all the socialists of the era (with a few exceptions, such as Rosa Luxemburg, the Gorter-Pannekoek tendency in Holland, and the "Left Communists" in Germany). This conviction was to be tremendously reinforced by the seizure of power, the Civil War, and the Party's consolidation of power. Trotsky himself clearly expressed this attitude at the time when he proclaimed the Party's "historical birthright."

This mentality was more than just a mentality: after the seizure of power, it almost immediately became a part of the *real social situation*. Individually, party members assumed leadership posts in all spheres of social life—in part, of course, because "one cannot do otherwise." This in turn, however, came to mean:

6. One quotation among a hundred: "And history . . . has taken such a peculiar course that it *has given birth* in 1918 to two unconnected halves of socialism existing side by side like two future chickens in the single shell of international imperialism. In 1918 Germany and Russia have become the most striking embodiment of the material realization of the economic, the productive and the socioeconomic conditions for socialism, on the one hand, and the political conditions, on the other" (V. I. Lenin, "'Left-Wing' Childishness and the Petty-Bourgeois Mentality," in *Selected Works: One-Volume Edition* [New York: International Publishers, 1971], p. 444). [T/E: As when Castoriadis cited this passage in "The Relations of Production in Russia," *PSW1*, p. 118, he omits Lenin's parenthetical swipe against "Menshevik blockheads." The careful reader might also note slight discrepancies between this English version of the quotation and that earlier one. My apologies. The above quotation is the one to be found in the volume cited. The version in *PSW*, vol. 1, came from another edition of Lenin's *Selected Writings*, which I failed to alter after I changed the page citation to correlate with the one-volume edition.]

because everything the Party did ensured that it could not be done otherwise.

Collectively, the only real instance of power was the Party, and very soon, only the summits of the Party. Immediately after the seizure of power the Soviets as institutions were reduced to the status of pure window-dressing (we need only look at the fact that, already at the beginning of 1918 in the discussions leading up to the Brest-Litovsk Peace Treaty, their role was absolutely nil).

If it is true that people's real social existence determines their consciousness, it is from that moment illusory to expect the Bolshevik Party to act in any other fashion than according to its real social situation. The real social situation of the Party is that of a directorial organ, and its point of view toward this society henceforth is not necessarily the same as the one this society has toward itself.

The workers offered no serious resistance to this evolution of events, or rather to this sudden revelation of the essence of the Bolshevik Party. At least we have no direct sign of such resistance. Between the eviction of the capitalists, followed by the restarting of the factories at the beginning of the revolutionary period, and the Petrograd strikes and the Kronstadt Revolt at its end (winter of 1920–21), we know of no articulate manifestation of autonomous activity on the part of the workers. The Civil War and the continuous mobilization of military forces during this period, the serious nature of immediate practical problems (production, food supplies, etc.), the very obscurity of the issues at stake, and, without doubt, above all the workers' confidence in the Party explain this lack of autonomous expression.

Two elements go to make up the workers' attitudes in this regard. On the one hand, the aspiration to rid themselves of all domination, to take the management of their affairs into their hands. On the other hand, the tendency to delegate power to this party that had just proven itself to be the sole irreconcilable opponent of the capitalist class and that was in fact conducting war against this class. The opposition, the contradiction, between these two elements was not and, one would be tempted to say, could not have been clearly perceived at this time.

It *was* seen, however, and with great insight, within the Party itself. From the beginning of 1918 until the banning of factions in March 1921, tendencies within the Bolshevik Party were formed that, with farsightedness and sometimes an astonishing clarity, expressed opposition to the Party's bureaucratic line and to its very rapid bureaucratization. These were the "Left Communists" (at the beginning of 1918), then the "Democratic Centralist" tendency (1919), and finally the "Workers' Opposition" (1920–21).

One will find in the *Historical Notes* we publish following Alexandra Kollontai's text details on the ideas and activities of these tendencies. In them were expressed the reactions of working-class members of the Party—and, no doubt, the attitudes of proletarian circles outside the Party—to the "state-capitalist" line of the leadership. They also expressed at the same time what can be called the "other component" of Marxism, the one that appeals to the masses' own activity and that proclaims that the emancipation of laboring people will be the work of these people themselves.

Nevertheless, these oppositional tendencies were defeated one by one, and finally eliminated in 1921, the same time that the Kronstadt revolt was crushed. The very feeble echoes of their critique of the bureaucracy that can be found later in the (Trotskyist) "Left Opposition" after 1923 do not have the same signification. Trotsky was opposed to the *bad policies* of the bureaucracy and to the excesses of its power. He never put into question its essential nature. Until practically the end of his life, he never brought up the questions raised by the various oppositions of the period from 1918 to 1921 (in essence: "Who manages production?" and "What is the proletariat supposed to do during the 'dictatorship of the proletariat,' other than work and follow the directions of 'its' party?").

We may therefore conclude that, contrary to the prevailing mythology, it was not in 1927, or in 1923, or even in 1921 that the game was played and lost, but much earlier, during the period from 1918 to 1920. Already in 1921, a revolution in the full sense of the term was needed in order to reestablish the situation. As events proved, a revolt such as the one at Kronstadt was not enough to bring about any essential changes. This warning shot did induce the Bolshevik Party to rectify certain aberrations relative to other problems (basically those concerning the peasantry and the relationship between the urban and agrarian economy). It thus led to a lessening of the tensions provoked by the country's economic collapse and to the beginning of the reconstruction of the productive apparatus. This reconstruction effort, however, was already firmly set in the groove of bureaucratic capitalism.

It was, indeed, between 1917 and 1920 that the Bolshevik Party established itself so firmly in power that it no longer could have been dislodged except by force of arms. And it was from the beginning of this period that the uncertainties of its line were ironed out, the ambiguities lifted, and the contradictions resolved. In the new State, the proletariat was to work, to be mobilized, and, should the need arise, to die in defense of the new power. It was to give its most "conscious" and most "capable" members to "its" party, where they would become the leaders of society. It was to be "active" and it had to "participate" whenever it was asked to do so, but it was to do so only and exactly to the extent that the Party demanded this of the proletariat. Finally, it was to bow completely to the Party's will on all essential matters. As Trotsky wrote during this period in a text that had an enormous circulation both inside and outside Russia, "The worker does not merely bargain with the Soviet State; no, he is subordinated to the Soviet State, under its orders in every direction—for it is *his* State."[7]

[7. The Management of Production]

The role of the proletariat in the new State was thus quite clear. It was that of enthusiastic and passive citizens. And the role of the proletariat in work and in production was no less clear. On the whole, it was the same as before—under capitalism—except that workers of

---

7. Leon Trotsky, *Terrorism and Communism* (Ann Arbor: University of Michigan Press, 1961), p. 168.

"character and capacity"[8] were to be chosen to replace factory managers who had fled. The main concern of the Bolshevik Party during
this period was not how one could facilitate the process of workers'
collectives taking over the management of production, but rather
was, What is the most rapid way of developing a stratum of managers and administrators for industry and for the economy as a whole?

One need only read the *official* texts of this period to eliminate
all doubts on this score. The formation and training of a bureaucracy as the managerial stratum in production (with the economic
privileges that inevitably go along with this status) were, practically from the beginning, *the conscious, straightforward, and sincere policy of the Bolshevik Party, headed by Lenin and Trotsky.* This was honestly
and sincerely thought to be a socialist policy—or, more precisely,
an "administrative technique" that could be put in the service of
socialism, since the class of administrators managing production
was to remain under the control of the working class, "personified
by its Communist party." The decision to place a manager at the
head of a factory instead of a workers' board [*bureau ouvrier*], wrote
Trotsky, had no political significance:

> It may be correct or incorrect from the point of view of the tech-
> nique of administration. . . . It would consequently be a most
> crying error to confuse the question as to the supremacy of the
> proletariat with the question of boards of workers at the heads
> of factories. The dictatorship of the proletariat is expressed in
> the abolition of private property in the means of production, in
> the supremacy over the whole Soviet mechanism of the collec-
> tive will of the workers, and not at all in the form in which indi-
> vidual economic enterprises are administered.[9]

Trotsky's phrase, "the collective will of the workers," is a metaphor-
ical expression used to designate the will of the Bolshevik Party.
The Bolshevik bosses stated this without any hypocrisy, unlike certain of their "defenders" today. Trotsky wrote at the time:

8. Ibid., p. 260.
9. Ibid., p. 162.

In this "substitution" of the power of the Party for the power of the working class there is nothing accidental, and in reality there is no substitution at all. The Communists express the fundamental interests of the working class. It is quite natural that in the period which brings up those interests, in all their magnitude, on to the order of the day, the Communists have become the recognized representatives of the working class as a whole.[10]

One can easily find dozens of quotations from Lenin expressing the same idea.

So we end up with the uncontested power of managers in the factories, under the Party's exclusive "control" (in reality, what kind of control was it, anyway?) And there was the uncontested power of the Party over society, without any control. From that point on, nobody could prevent these two powers from merging, nor could anyone stop the two strata embodying them from merging, nor could the consolidation of an irremovable bureaucracy ruling over all sectors of social life be halted. The process may have been accelerated or magnified by the entry of nonproletarian elements into the Party, as they rushed to jump on the bandwagon. But this was a *consequence,* and not a cause, of the Party's orientation.

It was during the discussion of the "trade-union question" (1920–21), which preceded the Tenth Party Congress, that opposition to this orientation of the Party was most forcefully expressed within the Party itself. Formally, the question was that of the role of the trade unions in the management of production and of the economy. The discussion inevitably focused once again on the problems of "one-man management [*commandement d'un seul*]" in the factories and on "the role of specialists," questions that had already been discussed bitterly and at great length during the previous two years. In Kollontai's text and in the appended *Historical Notes,* the reader will find a description of the various opposing stands on these issues.

---

10. Ibid., p. 109.

Briefly, the party leadership, with Lenin at its head, reaffirmed that the management of production should be in the hands of individual administrators (bourgeois "specialists" or workers selected for their "character and capacity") under the control of the Party. The trade unions were to have the tasks of educating the workers and of defending them against the production managers and the state managers. Trotsky demanded the trade unions' complete subordination to the State, their transformation into organs and appendages of the State (and of the Party). His argument always was the same: Since we are in a Workers' State, the State and the workers are one and the same thing, and therefore workers have no need for some separate organ to defend them from "their" State. The Workers' Opposition demanded that management of production and of the economy gradually be entrusted to "workers' collectives" in the factories, as these had been organized in the trade unions. They wanted "one-man management" to be replaced by a "collegial management" and the role of specialists and technicians to be reduced. The Workers' Opposition emphasized that the development of production under postrevolutionary conditions was an essentially social and political problem whose solution depended on the deployment of the creativity and initiative of the laboring masses, and that this problem was not merely administrative and technical. It denounced the increasing bureaucratization of the State and of the Party (already at this time, all posts involving responsibility of the least importance were filled by nomination from above and not by election), as well as the growing separation of the Party from the workers.

On certain points, it is true, the ideas of the Workers' Opposition were confused, and on the whole the discussion seems to have taken place on a formal level, just as the solutions proposed by both sides were also formal rather than substantive (the substance, in any case, had already been decided on elsewhere than in the Party Congresses). Thus, the Opposition (and Kollontai in her text) did not distinguish clearly between the (indispensable) role to be played by specialists and technicians qua specialists and technicians, under the control of workers, and the transformation of these specialists and technicians into unchecked [*incontrôlés*] managers of the production process. It developed a general critique of specialists and technicians without differentiating between the two categories, thus leaving its flanks exposed to the attacks of Lenin and Trotsky, who had an easy time showing that there could not be factories without engineers. From this position of advantage, Lenin and Trotsky came to the astonishing conclusion that this was a sufficient reason to entrust these engineers with dictatorial managerial powers over the whole operation of the factory. The Opposition fought ferociously for "collegial," as opposed to "one-man" management, a fairly formal aspect of the problem (a collegial form of management can be just as bureaucratic as one-man management), leaving in the shadows the real problem, that of the true source of authority. Thus was Trotsky free to say, "The independence of the workers is determined and measured, not by whether three workers or one are placed at the head of a factory, but by factors and phenomena of a much more profound character."[11] This absolved him from having to discuss the real problem, which is that of the relationship between the "one" or the "three" men and the collectivity of producers in the enterprise.

The Opposition also showed a relative amount of trade-union fetishism at a time when the unions had already fallen under the practically complete control of the party bureaucracy.

> The continuous "independence" of the trade-union movement, in the period of the proletarian revolution, is just as much an impossibility as the policy of coalition. The trade unions become the most important economic organs of the proletariat in power. Thereby they fall under the leadership of the Communist Party. Not only questions of principle in the trade-union movement, but serious conflicts of organization within it, are decided by the Central Committee of our Party.[12]

---

11. Ibid., p. 161 (reading "much" for "such").
12. Ibid., p. 110.

This being written by Trotsky in response to Kautsky's criticism of the antidemocratic character of Bolshevik power, Trotsky had no reason to exaggerate the extent of the Party's grip over the trade unions.

Nevertheless, despite these weaknesses and despite this relative confusion, the Workers' Opposition posed the real problem: Who is to manage production in the "Workers' State"? And it provided the correct answer: the collective organs of laboring people. What the party leadership wanted, what it had already imposed—and on this point there was no difference between Lenin and Trotsky—was a hierarchy directed from above. We know that this was the conception that triumphed. We know, too, where this "victory" led.

[8. On "Ends" and "Means"]

In the struggle between the Workers' Opposition and the leadership of the Bolshevik Party, we witness how the two contradictory elements of Marxism became dissociated. These two elements had coexisted in a paradoxical fashion in Marxism generally and in its incarnation in Russia in particular. For the last time in the history of the official Marxist movement, the Workers' Opposition made audible this appeal to the masses to act on their own, this confidence in the creative capacities of the proletariat, this conviction that with the socialist revolution commences a genuinely new period in human history, in which the ideas of the preceding period barely retain any of their value and in which the edifice of society is to be rebuilt from the bottom up. The Opposition's theses constitute an attempt to embody these ideas in a political program concerning the fundamentally important domain that is production.

The triumph of the Leninist outlook is the triumph of the other element of Marxism, which, to be sure, had long since—and even in Marx himself—become the dominant element in socialist thought and action. In all Lenin's speeches and writings of this period, what recurs again and again like an obsession is the idea that Russia ought to learn from the advanced capitalist countries; that there are not a hundred and one different ways of developing production and labor productivity if one wants to emerge from backwardness and chaos; that one must adopt capitalist methods of "rationalization" and management as well as capitalist forms of work "incentives." All these, for Lenin, are just "means" that apparently could freely be placed in the service of a radically different historical end, the building of socialism.

Thus Trotsky, when discussing the merits of militarism, came to separate the army itself, its structure and its methods, from the social system it serves. What is criticizable in bourgeois militarism and in the bourgeois army, Trotsky says in substance, is that they are in the service of the bourgeoisie. Except for that, there is nothing in them to be criticized. The sole difference, he says, lies in this: "*Who is in power?*"[13] Likewise, the dictatorship of the proletariat is not expressed by the "form in which individual economic enterprises are administered."[14]

The idea that like means cannot be placed indifferently into the service of different ends; that there is an intrinsic relationship between the instruments used and the result obtained; that, especially, neither the army nor the factory are simple "means" or "instruments," but social structures in which are organized two fundamental aspects of human relations (production and violence); that in them can be seen in condensed form the essential expression of the type of social relationships that characterize an era—this idea, though perfectly obvious and banal for Marxists, was totally "forgotten." It was just a matter of developing production, using proven methods and structures. That among these "proofs" the principal one was the development *of capitalism* as a social system and that a factory produces not so much cloth or steel but proletariat and capital were facts that were utterly ignored.

Obviously, behind this "forgetfulness" is hidden something else. At the time, of course, there was the desperate concern to revive

---

13. Ibid., p. 172 [T/E: We have retained the emphasis found in the French, but not in the English, translation].
14. Ibid., p. 162.

production as soon as possible and to put a collapsing economy back on its feet. This preoccupation, however, does not fatally dictate the choice of "means." If it seemed obvious to Bolshevik leaders that the sole effective means were capitalist ones, it was because they were imbued with the conviction that capitalism was the only effective and rational system of *production*. Faithful in this respect to Marx, they wanted to abolish private property and market anarchy, but not the type of organization capitalism had achieved at the point of production. They wanted to modify the *economy*, not the relations between people at work or the nature of labor itself.

At a deeper level still, their philosophy was to develop the forces of production. Here too, they were the faithful inheritors of Marx—or at least one side of Marx, which became the predominant one in his mature writings. The development of the forces of production was, if not the ultimate goal, at any rate the *essential means,* in the sense that everything else would follow as a by-product and that everything else had to be subordinated to it. Men, as well? Men, too, of course. "As a general rule, man strives to avoid labor . . . man is a fairly lazy animal."[15] To combat this indolence, all means of proven effectiveness must be put to work: compulsory labor—whose character changes completely when it is imposed by a "socialist dictatorship"[16]—and available technical and economic means:

> Under capitalism, the system of piecework and of grading, the application of the Taylor system, etc., have as their object to increase the exploitation of the workers by the squeezing out of surplus value. Under socialist production, piecework, bonuses, etc., have as their problem to increase the volume of social product, and consequently to raise the general well-being. Those workers who do more for the general interests than others receive the right to a greater quantity of the social product than the lazy, the careless, and the disorganizers.[17]

---

15. Ibid., p. 133.
16. Ibid., p. 149.
17. Ibid., p. 147.

This isn't Stalin speaking (in 1939); it is Trotsky (in 1919).

The socialist reorganization of production during the initial period is inconceivable without some "work obligation"—who does not work does not eat. That is certain. There probably also will be an attempt to standardize the amount of effort furnished by various shops and enterprises, which would require the establishment of certain norms and indices of work. All Trotsky's sophisms about the fact that "free labor" has never existed in history and will not exist until there is full communism should not make anyone forget, however, the crucial question: *Who* establishes these norms? *Who* controls people's work obligations, and *who* punishes those who do not fulfill these obligations? Will it be the organized collectives of laboring people? Or a specific social category, whose function therefore is to manage the work of others?

To manage the work of others—this is the beginning and the end of the whole cycle of exploitation. The "need" for a specific social category to manage the work of others in production (and the activity of others in politics and in society), the "need" for a separate business management and for a Party to rule the State— this is what Bolshevism proclaimed as soon as it seized power, and this is what it zealously labored to impose. We know that it achieved its ends. Insofar as ideas play a role in the development of history—and, *in the final analysis,* they play an enormous role—the Bolshevik ideology (and with it, the Marxist ideology lying behind it) was a decisive factor in the birth of the Russian bureaucracy.

Publishing Information

"ANARCHY AND 'SCIENTIFIC' COMMUNISM," by Luigi Fabbri, was first published in 1922 as *Anarchia e comunismo scientifico* by Libreria editrice tempi nuovi and translated by Paul Sharkey for the 1981 Cienfuegos Pamphlet *The Poverty of Statism*.

"THE SOVIET SYSTEM OR THE DICTATORSHIP OF THE PROLETARIAT?," by Rudolf Rocker, was first serialized in *Fraye Arbayter Shtime* as "Ratensistem oder diktatur?," May 15 through May 29, 1920. It was published in French in *Les Temps Nouveaux* as "Le système des soviets ou la dictature du prolétariat?" that same year. Numerous Spanish editions were based on the French. This English translation by Paul Sharkey is from the Spanish and was made for the 1981 Cienfuegos pamphlet *The Poverty of Statism*.

"THE IDEA OF EQUALITY AND THE BOLSHEVIKS," by Nestor Makhno, was first published in *Dyelo Truda*, no. 9, February 1926. It was translated by Paul Sharkey for the 1996 AK Press Makhno collection *The Struggle against the State and Other Essays*, edited by Alexandre Skirda.

"THE STATE AND REVOLUTION: THEORY AND PRACTICE," by Iain McKay, was written for this volume.

"A DECADE OF BOLSHEVISM," by Alexander Berkman, was first published in *Road to Freedom*, December 1927.

"PREFACE TO IDA METT'S 'THE KRONSTADT COMMUNE,'" by Maurice Brinton, was written for the pamphlet described below.

"THE KRONSTADT COMMUNE," by Ida Mett, was first published in 1938 as *La Commune de Cronstadt: Crépuscule sanglant des soviets* by

Editions Spartacus. It was translated by Solidarity in 1967 for Solidarity pamphlet no. 27 *The Kronstadt Commune*.

"THE STRUGGLE AGAINST FASCISM BEGINS WITH THE STRUGGLE AGAINST BOLSHEVISM," by Otto Rühle, was written in 1939 as part of a longer work and translated by Paul Mattick for *Living Marxism*, Vol. 4, no. 8, 1939.

"MY DISILLUSIONMENT IN RUSSIA—AFTERWORD," by Emma Goldman was first published by Doubleday in 1924 in *My Further Disillusionment in Russia*. A year earlier, the publisher had accidentally omitted twelve chapters, including the Afterword, from *My Disillusionment in Russia*, necessitating the follow-up book.

"CRIES IN THE WILDERNESS: ALEXANDER BERKMAN AND RUSSIAN PRISONER AID PRISONERS," by Barry Pateman, was written for this volume.

"BOLSHEVISM AND STALINISM," by Paul Mattick. This is an abridged version of a review that first appeared in *Politics*, Vol. 4, no. 2, March–April 1947.

"THE ROLE OF BOLSHEVIK IDEOLOGY IN THE BIRTH OF THE BUREAUCRACY," by Cornelius Castoriadis, was first published as "Le Rôle de l'idéologie bolchevique dans la naissance de la bureaucratie (Introduction à l'Opposition ouvrière d'Alexandra Kollontaï)" in *Socialisme ou Barbarie*, 35, January 1964. Translated by David Ames Curtis for Cornelius Castoriadis, *Social and Political Writings*, Volume 3 (Minneapolis: University of Minnesota Press, 1991). Ames made extensive use of Maurice Brinton's translation for Solidarity pamphlet no. 24 in 1967, *From Bolshevism to the Bureaucracy*.

Index

Z

AK Press is small, in terms of staff and resources, but we also manage to be one of the world's most productive anarchist publishing houses. We publish close to twenty books every year, and distribute thousands of other titles published by like-minded independent presses and projects from around the globe. We're entirely worker-run and democratically managed. We operate without a corporate structure—no boss, no managers, no bullshit.

The Friends of AK program is a way you can directly contribute to the continued existence of AK Press, and ensure that we're able to keep publishing books like this one! Friends pay $25 a month directly into our publishing account ($30 for Canada, $35 for international), and receive a copy of every book AK Press publishes for the duration of their membership! Friends also receive a discount on anything they order from our website or buy at a table: 50% on AK titles, and 20% on everything else. We have a Friends of AK ebook program as well: $15 a month gets you an electronic copy of every book we publish for the duration of your membership. You can even sponsor a very discounted membership for someone in prison.

Email friendsofak@akpress.org for more info, or visit the Friends of AK Press website: https://www.akpress.org/friends.html

There are always great book projects in the works—so sign up now to become a Friend of AK Press, and let the presses roll!